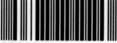

MYSTERIES AND SOLUTIONS
IN IRISH LEGAL HISTORY

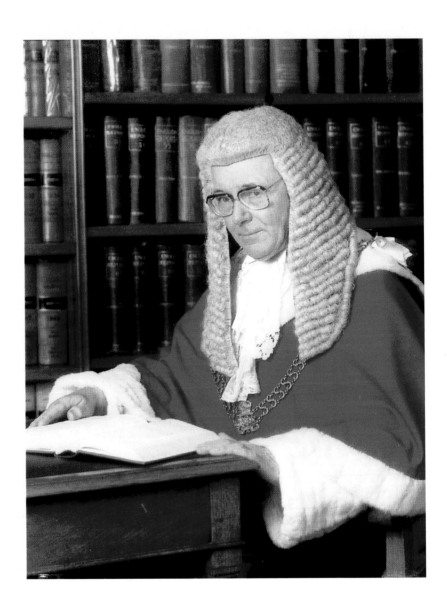

Mysteries and Solutions in Irish Legal History

Irish Legal History Society Discourses
and Other Papers, 1996–1999

D.S. GREER AND N.M. DAWSON

EDITORS

FOUR COURTS PRESS

in association with

THE IRISH LEGAL HISTORY SOCIETY

Typeset in 11 pt on 13 pt Plantin by
Carrigboy Typesetting Services, County Cork for
FOUR COURTS PRESS LTD
Fumbally Court, Fumbally Lane, Dublin 8, Ireland
e-mail: info@four-courts-press.ie
and in North America for
FOUR COURTS PRESS
c/o ISBS, 5824 N.E. Hassalo Street, Portland, OR 97213.

A catalogue record for this title is available
from the British Library.

ISBN 1–85182–576–2

Printed in Great Britain by
MPG Books, Bodmin, Cornwall

Contents

Editors' preface

FOLLOWING ITS inauguration in 1988, the Irish Legal History Society established the convention that each annual general meeting would conclude with a learned address or discourse on some aspect of legal history. The first such address, 'Legal history and the author: some practical problems of authorship', was delivered in Trinity College, Dublin by R.F.V. Heuston and published in *The Irish Legal History Society: inaugural addresses* (1989). A second volume containing the revised text of the next five contributions, together with a special lecture given under the part auspices of the Society in 1988 to mark the Dublin 'millennium', was published in 1995 under the title, *Explorations in law and history*.

The present volume contains the revised text of seven addresses delivered between 1996 and 1999 (including three which were given at the special meeting in Belfast in 1998 to mark the tenth anniversary of the Society), together with two papers which reflect the Society's involvement in the promotion of research – in the case of Dr Ohlmeyer, by means of a research grant and in the case of Mr McMahon, through a postgraduate studentship held jointly at University College, Dublin and the Queen's University of Belfast and made possible by the generosity of the Irish Department of Justice, Equality and Law Reform.

This collection takes its title from the survey of recent Irish legal history publications presented by Professor Nial Osborough in October 1998. Notwithstanding the considerable achievements of the Society and others working in the field, many challenges remain, as legal historians face 'an abundance of mysteries and a relative paucity of solutions'. Professor Osborough explains that many of the processes by which common law rules came to be recognised and applied in Ireland, the institutional framework within which those rules operated and the broader development of Irish constitutional law and practice remain wrapped in mystery. In some cases the solutions may be found by straightforward spade-work; but in others the task of the legal historian is more recondite and abstruse.

Who, for example, would have supposed that an attempt by a Scot to inherit land in England would shed valuable light on the constitutional relationship between England and Ireland in the seventeenth century? As Professor Baker explains, the case of *Craw v. Ramsay* has, to Irish eyes, been secreted 'in the obscurity of the English law reports'; but the extent to which Ireland was 'united and knit to the imperial crown' became relevant to the application of an Irish statute in England and required the English court of common pleas in 1670 to engage in a sophisticated legal analysis of the relationship between the two countries. The inter-relationship of the two jurisdictions in the seventeenth century also provides the theme for Dr McCafferty's examination of the Irish impeachment proceedings of 1641. Those proceedings must be seen as an attempt 'to follow the late precedents of England', and in particular the impeachment of Thomas Wentworth, earl of Strafford. The failure of the Irish house of commons to establish a power of judicature equivalent to that of the English house of commons also raised important questions concerning Ireland's constitutional relationship with England and the crown.

Another 'mystery' addressed in this collection is the role of individual lawyers, judges and jurists in shaping the law and the course of legal history. Professor Kelly characterises Giolla Na Naomh Mac Aodhagáin as 'a thirteenth-century legal innovator' whose treatise has survived to provide not only a comprehensive account of Old Irish law, but also to bear witness to its continuing vitality in post-Norman Ireland and to the occasional intermingling of brehon and common law concepts. Some five centuries later, Edmund Burke, one of Ireland's greatest intellectuals, abandoned a career at the bar in favour of writing and politics. As Professor McDowell explains, Burke's unsympathetic view of lawyers ('hunters after precedent' and 'scratchers of parchment'), of legal education ('a narrow and inglorious study') and of the law as a profession ('not calculated to develop the highest powers of the mind') was counterbalanced by his profound sense of the importance of law and of the principles of equity and public utility which under-pinned it. This perception of the law led Burke, for example, to oppose the penal laws in Ireland and coloured his approach to penal policy, whether in relation to capital offences or the non-payment of debts.

At a more practical level, R.R. Cherry played a notable part in the development of Irish law at the turn of twentieth century. Cherry's legal career was adversely affected by his opposition to the Boer war; but he ultimately attained high office as lord chief justice of Ireland – only to be subjected almost immediately to unusual pressure to resign. Daire Hogan reviews Cherry's career in law and politics and discusses some of the leading cases of his period on the bench; but he suggests that his most significant contribution to Irish law was the treatise on the Irish Land Law and Land Purchase Acts which is still affectionately known to Irish land lawyers simply as 'Cherry'. The contribution of individual judges is further explored by the late Lord Lowry, who has provided a series of graphic and acutely-observed pen portraits of the seven Irish Lords of Appeal in Ordinary who sat in the House of Lords between 1882 and 1951. Lord Lowry, who was himself a Lord of Appeal for six years, sheds light on their individual personalities and assesses their forensic achievements and judicial philosophies.

A third theme of this collection is the nature and significance of lay and legal participation in the legal process. As Dr Ohlmeyer seeks to demonstrate, the surviving seventeenth-century records of the Irish court of chancery contain information on the gender, religion and social standing of litigants – and on the religion of their lawyers – which not only illustrates the degree of participation in the legal process but also assists a wider understanding of early modern Ireland. Much the same can be said of Richard McMahon's study of manor courts in the west of Ireland before the Famine. Even in the first half of the nineteenth century, these courts, which were largely independent of central authority, appear to have fulfilled a significant role in local social and economic affairs, and may have been particularly important in the lives of the middle and lower orders of society.

Underlying all the contributions we find two more fundamental historical truths. First, the study of the law and its practice has much to add to a more general understanding of many aspects of Irish society and must be ignored by historians at their peril. Conversely, legal historians cannot afford to concentrate exclusively on doctrinal or conceptual analysis. The letter of the law must, of course, be determined – particularly if there is, or may be, a divergence between the English and Irish version of that law; but even if the law of the two jurisdictions appears to be identical, the 'solution' to the question of the significance of that law in Ireland, as in England, can only be fully resolved if we can untangle the 'mystery' of its wider impact on the society in which it operated.

It has been a great pleasure for us to act as editors of this fascinating and varied collection of learned papers and we wish to pay a warm tribute to the scholarship – and generous co-operation – of the contributors. We hope that their efforts will inspire further 'experiences' of Irish legal history to build on the welcome achievements of recent years. But we must also endorse Professor Osborough's warning that 'those of us who care, if not passionately, at least intelligently, about the past rightly dread the onset of an ignorance that must militate against our understanding it and – certainly no less important – militate against our ability to learn from it.'

It remains for us to express our thanks to Ms Helen Litton for compiling the index to this collection and to Four Courts Press for making its publication as simple and straightforward as possible. We should also wish to place on record the gratitude of the Irish Legal History Society to the various institutions which kindly provided a venue – and generous hospitality – for the Society's annual general meetings between 1996 and 1999, namely, the Public Record Office of Northern Ireland, the Royal Irish Academy, the Queen's University of Belfast, and the Faculty of Law, University College, Dublin.

DESMOND GREER &
NORMA DAWSON

Belfast, September 2000

List of contributors

J.H. BAKER is Downing Professor of the Laws of England in the University of Cambridge, a Fellow of St Catharine's College, and an Honorary Bencher of the Inner Temple. He is the author of *An introduction to English legal history* (3rd ed., 1990) and of numerous other publications and since 1980 he has been Literary Director of the Selden Society.

DAIRE HOGAN is a partner in McCann FitzGerald, solicitors of Dublin, and a former President of the Irish Legal History Society. He is the author of *The legal profession in Ireland, 1789–1922* (1986) and of a number of articles on the profession and biographical studies of lawyers and judges in the nineteenth and twentieth centuries.

FERGUS KELLY is a graduate of Trinity College Dublin in Early and Modern Irish, and is currently Director of the School of Celtic Studies at the Dublin Institute for Advanced Studies. He has concentrated on the edition and translation of Old Irish texts, mainly law-texts, hymns and proverbial material. In the Early Irish Law Series he has published *A guide to early Irish law* (1988) and *Early Irish farming: a study based mainly on the law-texts of the 7th and 8th centuries AD* (1997). At present he is working on the thirteenth-century legal treatise attributed to Giolla na Naomh Mac Aodhagáin.

LORD LOWRY was educated at the Royal Belfast Academical Institution and the University of Cambridge. He was called to the Bar of Northern Ireland in 1947, appointed QC in 1956 and elevated to the High Court bench in 1964. In 1971 he was appointed Lord Chief Justice of Northern Ireland, and served in that capacity until 1988, when he became a Lord of Appeal in Ordinary. He retired in 1994. As Lord Chief Justice at the time when the Irish Legal History Society was founded, Lord Lowry was (with Mr Justice Finlay) a founding Patron of the Society. He died in 1999.

JOHN MCCAFFERTY is a college lecturer in the Combined Departments of History in University College, Dublin. His main interests are in late medieval and early modern Irish ecclesiastical history and in the pursuit of a more integrated history of England and Ireland. Recent publications include: '"God bless your free Church of Ireland": Wentworth, Laud, Bramhall and the Irish convocation of 1634' in J.F. Merritt (ed.), *The political world of Thomas Wentworth* (Cambridge, 1996) and 'St Patrick for the Church of Ireland: James Ussher's Discourse' in *Bullán: An Irish Studies Journal*, 3 (1997–98), 87. He is currently conducting research on the High Commission court and preparing a monograph on the Church of Ireland.

R.B. MCDOWELL is a graduate of Trinity College Dublin, where he was a fellow and Professor of History for many years. His tenure of the office of

Junior Dean from 1956–1969 gave him 'practical experience of law and administration at a very modest level'. The author of works on British and Irish history in the eighteenth, nineteenth and twentieth centuries, he was one of the editors of Edmund Burke's *Correspondence* and his *Speeches and writings*. At the age of eighty-seven, he is 'understandably reluctant to refer confidently to work in progress', but is at present engaged as a co-editor of T. Wolfe Tone's *Works*, and hopes to produce a biography and a collection of essays.

RICHARD McMAHON is a graduate of the National University of Ireland, Galway, where he also completed a Master's thesis entitled 'The courts of petty sessions and the law in pre-Famine Galway'. In 1999 he was awarded the first Irish Legal History Society Postgraduate Studentship in University College, Dublin and the Queen's University of Belfast to pursue doctoral research on the administration of justice in Ireland during the first half of the nineteenth century.

JANE OHLMEYER is a Senior Lecturer in History and an associate member of the Research Institute of Irish and Scottish Studies at Aberdeen University. Her books include *Civil war and restoration in the three Stuart kingdoms: the career of Randal MacDonnell, marquis of Antrim, 1609–1683* (1993); *Ireland from independence to occupation, 1641–1660* (editor, 1995); and *Political thought in seventeenth-century Ireland: kingdom or colony?* (editor, 2000). She has also co-edited *The civil wars: a military history of England, Scotland and Ireland, 1638–1660* (with John Kenyon, 1998) and *The Irish statute staple books, 1596–1687* (with Eamonn Ó Ciardha, 1998). Dr Ohlmeyer is currently a Leverhulme Research Fellow and is working on a study of the Irish aristocracy in the seventeenth century.

W.N. OSBOROUGH is Professor of Jurisprudence and Legal History at University College, Dublin. Co-founder and joint secretary of the Irish Legal History Society, and a former editor of the *Irish jurist*, Professor Osborough is the author of numerous publications, including *Borstal in Ireland: law and the emergence of modern Dublin* and, most recently, *Studies in Irish legal history*.

List of illustrations

Portrait of Lord Macnaghten, by Hugh de Glazebrook.
Reproduced by kind permission of the Treasurer and Masters of the Bench of the Honourable Society of Lincoln's Inn, London.

Portrait of Lord Carson, by Sir John Lavery (1922).
Reproduced by courtesy of Felix Rosenstiel's Widow & Son Ltd, London (for the Lavery estate). Photograph reproduced by kind permission of the Trustees of the National Museums and Galleries of Northern Ireland.

Portrait of Lord Russell of Killowen (detail), by John Singer Sargent, 1900.
Reproduced by courtesy of the National Portrait Gallery, London.

Portrait of Lord MacDermott.
Reproduced by kind permission of the MacDermott family.

Earl Morley addressing the House of Lords, by Sir John Lavery, *c.*1923.
Reproduced by courtesy of Felix Rosenstiel's Widow & Son Ltd, London (for the Lavery estate). Photograph reproduced by kind permission of the Trustees of Glasgow Museums.

List of abbreviations

AC	Law Reports, Appeal Cases 1891–
AL	*Ancient Laws and Institutes of Ireland*, ed. W.N. Hancock, T. O'Mahony, A.G. Richey and R. Atkinson (Dublin, 1865–1901)
Am Hist Rev	*American Historical Review* (Washington, 1896–)
Anal Hib	*Analecta Hibernica* (Dublin, 1930–)
BL, Add MS	British Library, Additional Manuscripts
Butler Society J	*Journal of the Butler Society* (Kilkenny, 1968–)
Ch	Law Reports, Chancery Division 1891–
CIH	*Corpus Iuris Hibernici*, ed. D.A. Binchy (Dublin, 1978)
Cal Pat Rolls	*Calendar of Patent Rolls 1232–1247* (London, 1901–1913)
Cal. S.P. Ire.	*Calendar of the State Papers relating to Ireland, 1509–1573* (London, 1860–1911)
Cart	Carter's Common Pleas Reports 1664–1676
Co Inst	Sir Edward Coke, *Institutes of the Laws of England*
Co Litt	Sir Edward Coke, *The first part of the Institutes of the Laws of England; or, A commentary upon Littleton*
Commons' jn. Ire.	*Journals of the House of Commons of the Kingdom of Ireland*, 1613–1791 (Dublin, 1753–1791), reprinted and continued, 1613–1800 (Dublin, 1796–1800).
Co Rep	Coke's King's Bench Reports 1572–1616
Cork Hist Soc J	*Journal of the Cork Historical and Archaeological Society* (Cork, 1892–)
Correspondence	*The correspondence of Edmund Burke*, ed. T.W. Copeland (Cambridge, 1958–1978)
Cox CC	Cox's Criminal Cases 1843–1945
Cr & Dix CC	Reports of Cases argued and ruled on the circuits in Ireland during the years 1839–1846, ed. G. Crawford and E.S. Dix (Dublin, 1841–1847)
Dav	A report of cases and matters in law, resolved and adjudged in the King's courts in Ireland, collected and digested by Sir John Davies, Knight, the King's Attorney General in that kingdom (Dublin, 1762)
DNB	*Dictionary of National Biography*

EHR	*English Historical Review* (London, 1886–)
Eng Rep	English Reports 1210–1865
Hard	Hardres' Exchequer Reports 1655–1669
Hil	Hilary Term
HMC	Historical Manuscripts Commission
ICLR	Irish Common Law Reports (Dublin, 1849–1866)
IHS	*Irish Historical Studies* (Dublin, 1938–)
ILT & SJ	*Irish Law Times and Solicitors' Journal* (Dublin, 1867–)
IR	Irish Reports (Dublin, 1894–)
Ir Cir Rep	Reports of cases argued and determined on six circuits in Ireland ... in the years 1841–1843 (Dublin, 1843)
IRCL	Irish Reports, Common Law series (Dublin, 1867–1878)
Ir Econ Soc Hist	*Irish Economic and Social History* (Dublin, 1974–)
Ir Jur	*Irish Jurist* (new series) (Dublin, 1966–)
KB	Law Reports, King's Bench Division 1901–1952
Keb	Keble's King's Bench Reports 1661–1679
Latch	Latch's King's Bench Reports 1625–1628
Lev	Levinz's King's Bench and Common Pleas Reports 1660–1697
Lords' jn Ire	*Journal of the House of Lords of Ireland, 1634–1800* (Dublin, 1779–1800)
J Legal Hist	*Journal of Legal History* (London, 1980–)
Liber mun pub Hib	*Liber munerum publicorum Hiberniae* 1152–1827, ed. Rowley Lascelles (London, 1852)
Lofft	Lofft's King's Bench Reports 1772–1774
Mich	Michaelmas Term
Moo	Moore's King's Bench Reports 1512–1621
NAI	National Archives of Ireland
NI	Northern Ireland Law Reports (Belfast, 1925–)
NLI	National Library of Ireland
O Bridg	Orlando Bridgman's Common Pleas Reports 1660–1667
PD	Law Reports, Probate Division 1891–
PRO	Public Record Office, London
PRONI	Public Record Office of Northern Ireland
QB	Law Reports, Queen's Bench Division 1891–1901, 1952–

R	Rettie's Session Cases, 4th series (Scotland) 1873–1898
Rep Ch	Reports in Chancery 1615–1712
RSAI Jn	*Journal of the Royal Society of Antiquaries of Ireland* (Dublin, 1850–)
Rym Foed	Thomas Rymer, *Foedera: Conventiones, litterae, et cujuscunque generis acta publica* (London, 1704–1735)
SC	Cases decided in the Court of Session, 6th series (Edinburgh, 1906–)
Sid	Siderfin's King's Bench Reports 1657–1670
St Tr	T. B. Howell, *State Trials, 1163–1810* (London, 1816)
Statutes at large	The statutes at large passed in the parliaments held in Ireland ... 1310–1800 (Dublin, 1786–1801)
Stud Hib	*Studia Hibernica* (Dublin, 1961–)
T Jones	T Jones' King's Bench Reports 1667–1685
Trin	Trinity Term
Vaugh	Vaughan's Common Pleas Reports 1665–1673
Vent	Ventris' King's Bench Reports 1668–1688
Ves Jun	Vesey Junior's Chancery Reports 1789–1817
Writings and speeches	*The writings and speeches of Edmund Burke*, ed. P. Langford (Oxford, 1981)
YB	Year Book

Giolla na Naomh Mac Aodhagáin: a thirteenth-century legal innovator

FERGUS KELLY[*]

THE FAMILY OF MAC AODHAGÁIN (anglicised MacEgan, Keegan or Egan) dominated the field of Gaelic law in Ireland from the thirteenth to the sixteenth centuries.[1] Lawyers with this surname are often cited in English documents of the period, as well as being prominent in the Irish annals and frequently named as the scribes of legal manuscripts. The first member of the family to be mentioned in the Irish annals in a legal context is Giolla na Naomh son of Donn Sléibhe Mac Aodhagáin, who is undoubtedly one of the most interesting figures in the history of Gaelic law in Ireland. His death in battle in 1309 is recorded in the Annals of Connacht where he is described as 'chief legal expert of Connacht and a well-versed general master in every other art'.[2] There are similar words of praise in other annals: the Annals of Ulster describe him as 'the chief expert of Connacht and of Ireland'. He also features in the genealogies of the MacEgan family, where he is described as *ardollamh i mbreithemhnus Féinechuis*, 'high professor in Irish law'.[3]

Three texts are attributed to Giolla na Naomh. The only one of these which is so far available in an English translation is an 'Address

---

* The edited text of an address delivered in the Faculty of Law, Roebuck Castle, University College, Dublin, on 8 October 1999.

1 For brief accounts of the MacEgan family, see K. Simms, 'The brehons of later medieval Ireland' in D. Hogan and W.N. Osborough (ed.), *Brehons, serjeants and attorneys* (Dublin, 1990), 51 at pp. 57–59 and F. Kelly, *A guide to early Irish law* (Early Irish Law Series, vol. III, Dublin, 1988), pp. 252–55. For a more detailed survey, see J.J. Egan and M.J. Egan, *History of Clan Egan* (Irish American Cultural Institute, Ann Arbor, Michigan, 1979).

2 *The annals of Connacht*, ed. A. M. Freeman (Dublin, 1944), p. 218, s.a.1309, § 2.

3 'Geinealaigh Clainne Aodhagáin, AD 1400–1500', ed. C. Ní Maol-Chróin, in S. O'Brien (ed.), *Measgra i gcuimhne Mhichíl Uí Chléirigh* (Dublin, 1944), p. 139, § 18.

to a student of law', recently edited by Máirín Ní Dhonnchadha.[4] This is a poem of twenty-five stanzas, which summarises the educational needs of a thirteenth-century law-student. The attribution to Giolla na Naomh in the preamble is confirmed by a reference in the final quatrain where the author gives his own name and that of his father, and expresses the conviction that his reputation will live on after his death. He deals in particular with the type of reading necessary for a law-student, emphasising the importance of studying the abridgements (*na Bearradha Féine*), that is extracts from the Old Irish law-texts. The student is urged to learn every old legal precedent (*seanfhásach*) as the best judgment is given on such a basis. He must distinguish customary law (*urradhus*), promulgated law (*cáin*) and inter-territorial law (*cairde*). Giolla na Naomh warns against giving a biased judgment (*leithbhreath*) in return for a bribe. He recommends for particular study the law-text called the Heptads (*na Seachta*), a miscellany of legal facts arranged in sevens.[5] He further advises the student to become familiar with texts containing proverbial or gnomic material, such as the Teachings of Cormac[6] and the Testament of Morann.[7] These were obviously regarded as of general benefit for the intellectual and moral training of the future lawyer and judge.

Another poem attributed to Giolla na Naomh is of a much more technical nature.[8] It consists of seventy-six quatrains dealing solely with the law relating to distraint (*athgabál*). It has not yet been subjected to detailed study and is untranslated. It is clear, however, that it is a work based closely on the Old Irish law-text *Di Chetharshlicht Athgabálae*, 'on the four tracks of distraint'.[9] Giolla na Naomh's intention is to present in metrical form – no doubt to be committed to memory by the student – the essentials of the Old Irish text. He emphasises in the penultimate quatrain the fact

---

4 'An address to a student of law', ed. M. Ní Dhonnchadha, in D. Ó Corráin, L. Breatnach and K. McCone (ed.), *Sages, saints and storytellers: Celtic studies in honour of Professor James Carney* (Maynooth, 1989), p. 159.
5 *Corpus Iuris Hibernici*, ed. D.A. Binchy (Dublin, 1978) [hereafter abbreviated *CIH*], pp. 1.1–64.5 = *Ancient laws and institutes of Ireland*, ed. W. N. Hancock, T. O'Mahony, A.G. Richey and R. Atkinson (Dublin, 1865–1901)[hereafter *AL*], v, 118–351.
6 *Tecosca Cormaic: the instructions of King Cormac Mac Airt*, ed. K. Meyer (Todd Lecture Series XV, Dublin, 1909).
7 *Audacht Morainn*, ed. F. Kelly (Dublin, 1976).
8 *CIH*, iii, 871.1–874.34.
9 *CIH*, ii, 352.25–422.36 = *AL*, i, 64–305; ii, 2–119.8.

A sample page (p. 162) from the only surviving copy of the legal treatise attributed
to Giolla na Naomh Mac Aodhagáin, who died in 1309. It is found in the composite
fifteenth/sixteenth-century legal manuscript H 3. 18 (No. 1337) in the library of
Trinity College, Dublin. This page deals mainly with the law regarding killing and
injury, whether deliberate or accidental. For a transcript of this page, see *Corpus Iuris
Hibernici*, ed. D.A. Binchy (Dublin, 1978), ii, 695.4–33.

that in this composition he is adhering to legal tradition (*ar slicht na sen*, 'on the track of the ancients').

The longest surviving text attributed to Giolla na Naomh is a general Treatise on Irish law. Only one copy has come down to us: this is in an unidentified fifteenth- or sixteenth-century hand in the composite legal manuscript H 3. 18 (No. 1337) in the Library of Trinity College Dublin.[10] This text has not been edited, but I hope within a few years to provide an edition and translation in the Early Irish Law Series.

The purpose of the text is succinctly described in the preamble: 'A Treatise here which is taken from the hard text of Irish and put into clear Irish by Giolla na Naomh son of Donn Sléibhe Mac Aodhagáin, high professor of Irish law'. By 'hard text of Irish' he refers to the Old Irish law-texts, dating from the seventh to the ninth century, which would have been extremely intimidating documents to a thirteenth-century law-student, who would have spoken Early Modern Irish. Not only had many linguistic changes taken place between the Old and Early Modern periods of the language, but there was also the added difficulty of the arcane style of many of the law-texts, which were couched in terse alliterative verse with much specialised terminology. The author has thus set himself the task of clarifying – putting into 'clear Irish' – this material.

So far as is known, such a project had never been attempted before. The Old Irish law-texts deal mainly with a single subject – sometimes in great detail. For example, one text deals with the law pertaining to water-courses for mills,[11] another with bee-keeping,[12] another with the grades of poet,[13] another with sport-injuries,[14] and so on. There are also a few Old Irish collections of legal miscellanea, the longest of which is the Heptads (*na Seachta*) mentioned above. There seems to be no particular logic in the sequence in which legal topics are treated in this text. For example, the seven permissible grounds for divorce are followed by the seven legal and seven illegal drivings of cattle, which are in turn followed by the

---

10 D.A. Binchy has transcribed the text at *CIH*, ii, 691.1–699.4.

11 '*Coibnes Uisci Thairidne*', ed. D.A. Binchy, in *Ériu*, 17 (1955), 52.

12 *Bechbretha: an Old Irish law-tract on bee-keeping*, ed. T. Charles-Edwards and F. Kelly (Early Irish Law Series, vol. I, Dublin, 1983).

13 *Uraicecht na Ríar: the poetic grades in early Irish law*, ed. L. Breatnach (Early Irish Law Series, vol. II, Dublin, 1987).

14 '*Mellbretha*', ed. D.A. Binchy, in *Celtica*, 8 (1968), 144.

seven non-culpable blood-sheddings.[15] There is likewise no discernible order in the treatment of topics in *Gúbretha Caratniad*, 'the false judgments of Caratnia', a collection of exceptions to general legal rules.[16] To Giolla na Naomh belongs the credit, therefore, of being the first to organise material from the Old Irish law-texts into a single unit covering most of the major legal topics.

He starts off his Treatise with a discussion of the most serious crime which one person can inflict on another, namely *dunmharbhadh*, 'murder'. Although murder is frequently mentioned in the surviving Old Irish material, there does not seem ever to have been a law-text devoted specifically to this topic. Giolla na Naomh had therefore to organise the material in this section from scratch. He starts off by laying down the fines which are payable in the event of the murder of sons of dignitaries ranging from king (*rí*) to knight (*óglach*). It is not clear why he deals merely with the murder of the *sons* of such persons – all I can suggest is that this reflects the general statistic in criminology that young males are more likely to die a violent death than other categories of person. The fines are substantial and are given in terms of cattle. For example, the murderer of the son of a king, chieftain or chief poet must pay a fine (*éiric*) of 105 cows which are distributed among the victim's kin. If the killing is through accident or mistaken identity, the fine is halved; but if the murderer hides the body or does not admit his guilt, the fine is doubled.

Giolla na Naomh makes a distinction between the legitimate son (*ceartmhac*) of a dignitary and his illegitimate son (*sloinnteach*), for whose killing a lesser fine is due. The Old Irish law-texts make no such distinction. In general, these texts favour monogamy and give the main wife (*cétmuinter*) greater legal capacity than other wives or concubines. However, there is no evidence that a son by the main wife is of greater legal worth than sons by other unions. The only stipulation made in the Old Irish texts is that a son begotten on a slave-woman cannot inherit kin-land. It seems likely that the distinction between the rights of legitimate and illegitimate sons in the Treatise is an Anglo-Norman feature.[17]

15　*CIH*, i, 4.33–9.33 = *AL*, v, 132–151.
16　'Die falschen Urteilssprüche Caratnia's', ed. R. Thurneysen, in *Zeitschrift für celtische philologie*, 15 (1925), 302.
17　In English documents of the post-Norman period, there are many references to 'named', i.e. illegitimate sons affiliated to a known father: see K. Nicholls, *Gaelic and Gaelicised Ireland in the middle ages* (Dublin, 1972), pp. 77–79.

Another Anglo-Norman feature which is found in the section on murder is the use of a jury when a person denies a charge of murder. The term employed is *finné*, which is generally taken to be a borrowing of Anglo-Norman *visné* (*vyné*), 'jury'.[18] For example, if a person of low or criminal status is accused of murder with concealment of the body (the most reprehensible form of murder), the case is heard before a jury of sixty persons, of whom half represent the nobility (*grádh flatha*) and half represent the commoners (*grádh Féine*).

The second section of the Treatise deals with theft, with the emphasis on the theft of livestock. Because the main Old Irish law-text on theft, *Bretha im Gata*, survives only in part, it is difficult to say how much of Giolla na Naomh's material comes from this text and how much of it is from other sources. He makes a distinction between the procedure in the case of the theft of an animal of lesser value, such as a sheep, pig or goat and the theft of a cow. In the former case, the oath of four persons can exculpate the accused, whereas in the latter it is necessary for him to get twelve to swear on his behalf.[19]

Giolla na Naomh devotes much attention to the evidence provided by the physical reaction of a person when accused of theft.[20] This passage is based on an Old Irish list of the seventeen indirect signs of guilt, which may originally have been part of *Bretha im Gata*.[21] The treatment of this material in the Treatise is of particular interest as it illustrates the way in which Giolla na Naomh worked. Sometimes he simply quotes the Old Irish text verbatim. Thus one of the signs of guilt is given as 'similarity of clothing with the thief'. Giolla na Naomh obviously felt that this was self-explanatory. On other occasions, he provides an expansion or elucidation of the original text. For example, where the text refers to 'incomplete testimony' as a sign of guilt, he expresses the idea of there being a gap in the alibi in different words: 'getting testimony for part of the day or the night, and not for all of it'. He

18 In *Éigse*, 18 (1980–81), 107, R.A. Breatnach suggested this explanation of the word *finné*. It is more convincing than M.A. O'Brien's proposal in *Celtica*, 3 (1956), 169 that the word comes from *fir nDé*, 'iudicium Dei, ordeal'.
19 *CIH*, ii, 691.17–19.
20 Ibid., 692.6–19.
21 The complete text of the seventeen signs of guilt is found at *CIH*, iv, 1359.26–1367.3, and a partial version at *CIH*, iii, 822.6–823.10.

also expands on the circumstances in which the indirect evidence provided by a child can help to convict his or her relatives of theft. This is obviously a difficult legal area which is open to abuse. Hence the Old Irish text stresses that there must be no element of deception or trickery (*fogáethad*) in obtaining evidence from a child. Giolla na Naomh gives an example of the sort of questioning which was permitted. The victim of the theft of livestock could put to the child the question *cad dobí agud aréir*, 'what did you have [to eat] last night?'[22] The child's answer might help to establish the guilt of a parent or relative.

The next section of the Treatise deals with offences which do not directly affect a person, but are an affront to his honour. In general, these offences concern those of high status, and are described as *sárughudh*, 'insult, outrage'. Under this heading Giolla na Naomh includes offences such as insulting the king's steward or other official acting on the king's behalf, spilling blood in a royal house or in a place of public assembly, or harbouring a person who has been outlawed by the king.[23] For such offences the culprit must pay a fine of twenty-one cows to the king. Twice this amount is payable for more serious categories of insult, such as causing a king to go without food (*trosgadh ríogh*) – presumably by failing to provide the feast to which he is entitled. A similarly serious view is taken of the offence of violating the king's protection (*brisiudh a shlánaigheachta*) or dirtying his clothing.[24] Also included among offences deemed to be an insult to the king are rape and highway robbery. The culprit must therefore pay fines not only to the victims of his crime but also to the king. The Treatise also stresses the king's legal responsibilities. A payment is due for the offences of 'every idle person whom a king will allow to be in the land'.[25] He must likewise pay for any crimes committed by his foreign mercenaries or dependent aliens.

Giolla na Naomh then returns briefly to the subject of theft, and deals with the regulations concerning the tracking of stolen

---

22 *CIH*, ii, 692.16.
23 Ibid., 692.21–8.
24 The manuscript has *acur na edach*: *CIH*, ii, 692.29; Binchy suggests in a footnote that the first word is a scribal error for *salchur*, 'dirt'.
25 *CIH*, ii, 693.6, *cach dimain daleigfi rig beth a tir*. For the term *dim(h)ain*, 'idle person, etc.' see G. MacNiocaill, 'The origins of the betagh' in *Ir Jur*, i (1966), 292 at p. 295.

cattle (*lorg na gaide*).[26] The general principle is that if the owner of
stolen cattle traces them to somebody else's land, the latter must
pay the fine for theft unless he can show that the tracks continue
out of his land. This rule does not apply if a common road passes
through the land, or if the ground is hard and dry and therefore
not likely to show up cattle-tracks. The legal procedures described
here are not found elsewhere in the surviving legal material in the
Irish language. In a recent article,[27] Nial Osborough looks at the
topic of the tracking of stolen cattle in the wider legal context, and
quotes the very similar regulations set out in the Latin text of an
agreement entered into by Brian Mac Mathghamhna, king of
Airghialla, at the behest of Nicholas Mac Maol Íosa, archbishop of
Armagh. It is dated 1297, and thus belongs to roughly the same
period as Giolla na Naomh's Treatise. Osborough also describes
how some centuries later the same basic procedure was one of the
few features of Gaelic law recognised by the English judicial
system in Ireland. In the reign of Edward VI it was given the force
of law by the Irish Council (in 1552 or 1553). The custom was
approved by James I in 1612 and was likewise recognised in 'His
Majesties directions for ordering and settling the courts within his
kingdom of Ireland' in 1622. It remained on the statute-book until
it was abolished in 1640.

Giolla na Naomh proceeds then to summarise what Irish law
says with regard to the finding of lost property, whether within a
settlement (*baile*) or in a more remote place such as a wood, hill or
seashore.[28] The finder must publicise his find in the house of the
king, blacksmith, miller or judge or in a guest-house. If he does so,
he is entitled to receive a proportion of the value of the lost object
from the owner. If he fails to publicise his find, he is held to be
guilty of theft.

The Treatise then considers the special legal problems which
arise if a person from another territory commits an offence such
as theft when he is passing through on a journey or expedition or
military hosting. If his identity can be established, he may be sued
by the plaintiff within a specified period of time. This must be done

---

26 *CIH*, ii, 693.10–17. It is possible that at some stage in the transmission this
    material became detached from the main treatment of theft earlier in the
    Treatise.
27 W.N. Osborough, 'The Irish custom of tracts' in *Ir Jur*, xxxii (1997), 439
    (reprinted in W.N. Osborough, *Studies in Irish legal history* (Dublin, 1999), 64).
28 *CIH*, ii, 693.18–23.

within eight days if the suspect belongs to an adjacent territory or *tríocha céad*, and within fourteen days if he is from another territory in the same province. If he is from another province in Ireland, he must be sued within a month. The case must be heard in the territory of the accused.

Giolla na Naomh also deals with another thorny aspect of inter-territorial law – the ownership of cattle taken in a raid. Legislation was sometimes directed against the practice of cattle-raiding, as in the Law of Darí (*Cáin Darí*) which is summarised in a gloss 'not to steal cattle'.[29] It is clear from the annals, however, that cattle-raiding was a regular feature of early Irish life.[30] The Treatise deals with the legal situation which arises if cattle belonging to a farmer are taken by theft or force across the border of a hostile territory – there is therefore no legal mechanism through a peace-treaty (*cairde*) for recovering them. If the cattle are taken back into their own territory by another person, the original owner has no legal entitlement to reclaim them. This seems very unfair on him, but it was clearly felt that through having been driven across the border of the hostile territory the cattle lost their status as his property, and when recovered were regarded as war-booty.

Also in relation to the theft of livestock, Giolla na Naomh distinguishes three types of ownership.[31] The first is *sealbh machaigh*, 'ownership of the milking-enclosure', which applied to animals born on the farm and which have never been moved. The second is *reimhshealbh*, 'previous ownership', that is, cattle which have been acquired by purchase or other legal means before an accusation of theft has been made. The third category is *sealbh luinge*, 'ownership of boat', which is defined as 'cattle having been bought from a boat'. Giolla na Naomh is obviously conscious of the possibility that a thief might gain time by claiming that the cattle in his possession had been bought from some imaginary boatman. Hence the requirement that the accused swear that he is not merely seeking 'to extend the matter'.

In the next section dealing with the law relating to wounds and injury, Giolla na Naomh draws mainly on the Old Irish law-texts

---

29 F. Kelly, *Early Irish farming: a study based mainly on the law-texts of the seventh and eighth centuries AD* (Early Irish Law Series, vol. IV, Dublin, 1997), pp. 167–68.

30 A.T. Lucas, *Cattle in ancient Ireland* (Kilkenny, 1989), pp. 125–99.

31 *CIH*, ii, 693.34–40.

Bretha Crólige, 'judgments of blood-lying', and *Bretha Déin Chécht*, 'judgments of Dían Chécht' (a mythical physician), both of which have been edited and translated by Binchy.[32] One passage, however, is not found elsewhere in the surviving legal material and may be Giolla na Naomh's own composition. It deals with situations where killing or injury entails either no penalty or a reduced penalty.[33] The first situation is the obvious one of a person who is subjected to an unprovoked attack with the intention of killing or injuring him. He is at liberty to kill or injure his attacker, though Giolla na Naomh emphasises that he should make an effort to avoid the confrontation. The second case is of a person who physically attacks someone who has committed a serious offence against him, rather than going through the proper legal process of suing. If he kills the criminal he is only required to pay two-thirds of the normal fine for homicide. This sum is weighed against the fine which the criminal would have had to pay for his crime anyway. So, depending on the rank of the dead man and the nature of his offence, the final resolution of the matter may require a payment by the killer to the criminal's family, or vice versa. The third case is where the criminal kills the attacker. He must pay the fine for his original crime, and also two-thirds of the normal fine for manslaughter. The remaining third is waived because the aggrieved party attacked him physically and did not sue him for his crime in the proper manner.

The Treatise includes a long section on contracts and sureties.[34] Some of this discussion is based on earlier material. For example, the treatment of legal problems associated with the development of disease in recently purchased livestock goes back to Middle Irish commentary on this topic.[35] Similarly, the Treatise repeats the general regulation of the Old Irish texts that there is a twenty-four hour cooling-off period before a contract becomes binding. However, a further situation is envisaged in which a relative or other interested party may first hear of the existence of the contract *after* this period. Such persons include a brother, father, mother, wife or lord; a formal objection must be lodged as soon as

---

32 'Bretha Crólige' in *Ériu*, 12 (1938), 1 and 'Bretha Déin Chécht' in *Ériu*, 20 (1966), 1.
33 *CIH*, ii, 694.41–695.8.
34 Ibid., 695.32–697.10.
35 N. McLeod, *Early Irish contract law* (Sydney, 1992), pp. 288, 299 and 313–26; F. Kelly, *Early Irish farming*, pp. 192–216.

he or she hears of it – otherwise the contract stands. This section also devotes a great deal of attention to the duties of the paying surety (*cor*) who secures a contract.[36] If one of the parties to the contract defaults, his surety must make good what is owed. If the defaulter manages to escape from the jurisdiction, the surety may never be recompensed for what he has had to pay.

The Treatise proceeds next with a discussion of various legal consequences of harbouring persons who have committed some offence.[37] This section is of exceptional interest, because no special text on the subject of the harbouring of criminals has survived from the early period. There is a general ban on the harbouring of a proclaimed criminal. An exception is made in the case of the owner of a guest-house, who is free from liability if he harbours an outlaw for one night, provided he is unaware of his guest's criminality. Similarly, churches are free to harbour outlaws in a wartime situation – the text has *cealla bís edir da thír cogaidh*, 'churches which are between two territories at war' – unless the outlaw is using the church as a base for plunder. An unusual stipulation – mentioned earlier in the Treatise – is that a fine of six cows must be paid by one who provides food for a person who has been proclaimed by a king, even if he is an outlaw without guilt (*furfhuagarthach gan chinaidh*).[38]

The section on harbouring also contains a unique treatment of the various circumstances in which it is legal or illegal for a man to keep a woman other than his wife. If he takes away somebody else's wife – whether she be willing or not – he must pay a fine fixed by a judge and which depends on the rank of the husband or the woman's family.[39] If a man other than her husband impregnates a wife, the resultant child may be put to death by her husband, unless the actual father buys the child from him. Single women may evidently elope without legal consequences to them or to their seducers; according to the Treatise, 'the law does not order that anything be paid for them'.[40]

---

36 In the main Old Irish text on suretyship, *Berrad Airechta*, the paying surety is normally called the *ráth*, but in the Treatise he is the *cor*.
37 *CIH*, ii, 697.11–698.15.
38 Ibid., 692.36–37. See the discussion by G. Mac Niocaill, 'Aspects of Irish law in the late thirteenth century', in *Historical Studies*: X, ed. G.A. Hayes-McCoy (Indreabhán, Co. na Gaillimhe, 1976), 25 at p. 34.
39 *CIH*, ii, 697.34–37.
40 Ibid., 697.40, *ni ordaiginn dligi a beag d'ic inntib*.

The penultimate section of the Treatise is very brief, and discusses the topic of the pledge (*geall*), an object of value which a person gives into another's custody to indicate his readiness to carry out his legal obligations.[41] In this passage, Giolla na Naomh deals with the giving of pledges in the context of contracts involving livestock.

The final section is on the custom of the neighbour (*nós an chomhogais*),[42] and it broadly reflects the regulations on the rights and duties of neighbouring farmers as described in the eighth-century law-text *Bretha Comaithchesa*.[43] There are, however, many differences of detail. For example, Giolla na Naomh makes distinctions with regard to trespass by livestock which are not found in *Bretha Comaithchesa*. Thus, if a farmer's cattle break down his neighbour's firmly-constructed lawful fence (*fál daingean dlightheach*), he must pay him two cows. If the fence is badly made, he merely pays one and a half cows – that is, a cow and a heifer, and if there is no fence at all, the trespass-fine is only one cow.

At the end of this section, Giolla na Naomh abruptly brings his Treatise to a conclusion with the words *Finit air sin*, 'an end to that'. One might have expected some sort of summing-up or concluding statement. However, the lack of a structured ending is in keeping with the generally informal attitude to his material which Giolla na Naomh exhibits throughout the Treatise. For example, when dealing with the fines payable for illegal injury to persons of different ranks, he merely names those in the two highest grades and is content to refer to the rest as *lucht aile*, 'other people'.[44] Similarly, in his treatment of the circumstances in which it is legal to kill or injure another person, he states that there are fifteen such occasions. However, he lists only three, observing that there are 'many other matters comparable with them'.[45]

I hope that I have demonstrated in this necessarily brief survey something of the exceptional interest and importance of Giolla na Naomh's work. His Treatise testifies to the continuing vitality of Gaelic law in post-Norman Ireland. It is clear from this composition that thirteenth-century law was still firmly based on the Old Irish

41 *CIH*, ii, 698.16–24.
42 Ibid., 698.25–699.4.
43 *CIH*, i, 64.6–79.12; 191.1–205.21 = *AL*, iv, 68–159.
44 *CIH*, ii, 694.30–35. The grades are named in the Old Irish version (*CIH*, vi, 2286.31–6 = *Ériu*, 12 (1938), 6, § 2; *CIH*, i, 136.19–23, etc.).
45 *CIH*, ii, 695.17–20. A fuller version is to be found at *CIH*, iv, 1201.26–29.

law-texts of the seventh to ninth centuries. Specific mention is made of the medico-legal text *Bretha Crólige*,[46] and it is possible to identify quotations from other Old Irish law-texts such as *Bretha Déin Chécht*, *Bretha Étgid* and the Heptads.

While Giolla na Naomh's primary source was the Old Irish texts, he also sometimes quotes from the secondary material – glosses and commentary – which was added to these texts during the Middle Irish period, mainly in the eleventh and twelfth centuries. Thus his treatment of the punishment of children for their first, second and third offences[47] does not come from the brief reference to this subject in an Old Irish text,[48] but from the more detailed discussion in the associated Middle Irish commentary.[49] Similarly, his account of the receiving of stolen goods closely follows the wording of the commentary on this topic.[50]

Giolla na Naomh's practical treatment of topics such as contracts and injuries suggests that he had wide experience of legal practice, as well as being a learned academic lawyer. It seems likely that some passages in the Treatise are his own composition. I suspect, for example, that his discussion on the swapping of horses is original.[51] It must be stressed, however, that the existing legal corpus is so fragmentary – many law-texts surviving only in a few quotations – that it is impossible to be absolutely certain that a particular passage in the Treatise is original or not.

Another indication that Giolla na Naomh was not content merely to regurgitate his Old and Middle Irish sources is that he occasionally records that his opinion diverges from that of others. In relation to animal-disease, he contrasts his own opinion (*cétfaidh*) with the general usage (*gnáthughudh*).[52] In his discussion on personal injuries, he states that a man who is accused of injuring another in a fight which has not been witnessed needs to find seven persons to swear on his behalf. He notes that the Old Irish law-books (*leabhair*) only require three persons to swear in this situation.[53]

---

46 *CIH*, ii, 694.30.
47 Ibid., 695.13–17.
48 *CIH*, iv, 1339.21, 30.
49 Ibid., 1340.3–29.
50 *CIH*, ii, 694.11–16; *cf. CIH*, i, 172.1–32.
51 *CIH*, ii, 697.1–4.
52 Ibid., 696.8–10.
53 Ibid., 694.39–41.

Finally, the up-to-date approach to law adopted by Giolla na Naomh in his Treatise is exemplified by his quite frequent use of legal terminology of Anglo-Norman origin.[54] Sometimes, such terms are used beside a corresponding Irish word with no apparent difference in meaning. Thus he uses *baránta*, 'guarantor, surety' (a borrowing from Anglo-Norman *warantie*) beside *urradh*, a native term with the same meaning.[55] He likewise may call the royal steward *seiniscal* (from Anglo-Norman *seneschal*) or use the older terms *maor* or *rechtaire*.[56] Giolla na Naomh's terminology also reflects the influence of Anglo-Norman inheritance customs. On two occasions he employs the term *sínfhogas*, an otherwise unattested compound of the Anglo-Norman loan, *sín*, 'assign, appointed heir' and the Irish word *fogas*, 'kinsman'.[57]

As well as vocabulary, there are also legal concepts which are likely to be of Anglo-Norman origin. Gearóid Mac Niocaill has drawn attention to Giolla na Naomh's use of the phrase *tír do chur fair*, 'to put the country on him (a suspected thief)'.[58] Neither the expression nor the concept seems to belong to early Irish legal tradition. Mac Niocaill suggests a connection with the practice in later medieval English law of *ponere se super patriam*, 'to put oneself on the country'.[59] The case would thus be resolved by the general consensus of the locality as to the guilt or innocence of the accused.

---

54 By contrast, in his poem on distraint (*CIH*, iii, 871.1–874.34), which is a much more traditional composition, he uses no Anglo-Norman loanwords.

55 *CIH*, ii, 693.30, 33, 34 and 694.6, 8.

56 *CIH*, ii, 691.29, 32; *cf.* ibid., 692.21, 22 and 699.4. Gearóid Mac Niocaill notes ('A propos du vocabulaire social irlandais du bas moyen âge' in *Études Celtiques*, 12 (1968–71), 512 at p. 537) that the term *seiniscal* is associated in the Treatise with a high-ranking king (*ardrí*).

57 *CIH*, ii, 692.2, 39. In the spelling *sighin*, the word occurs in the phrase *oighridhe agus sighinoighridhe*, 'heirs and assigns', in later legal documents: see G. Mac Niocaill, 'The interaction of the laws' in J. Lydon (ed.), *The English in medieval Ireland* (Dublin, 1984), 105 at p. 115.

58 *CIH*, ii, 691.22–23; *cf.* ibid., 693.13, 14.

59 G. Mac Niocaill, 'Aspects of Irish law', p. 37.

Records of the Irish Court of Chancery: a preliminary report for 1627–1634

JANE OHLMEYER[*]

GIVEN THE IMPORTANCE of the court of chancery as one of the four central courts that operated in seventeenth-century Ireland, it is remarkable that it has attracted so little attention from historians. There are, of course, exceptions. Genealogists and local scholars have long recognised the significance of chancery material for the study of family and local history.[1] Kenneth Nicholls, who calendared many of the extant pre-1641 pleadings in the National Archives, has demonstrated the importance of the chancery records as sources for social, economic, legal and cultural history, especially for Gaelic Ireland,[2] while Mary O'Dowd's fascinating recent

* I would like to thank the Society for funding this pilot project, which enabled a research assistant, Dr Éamonn Ó Ciardha, to enter into an access database two of the six surviving recognizance books in the British Library (Add. MS 19,841–42) and to locate material, housed in the National Archives, relating to these cases. I am also grateful to the archivists at the National Archives, especially David Craig, Phil Connolly and Gregory O'Connor, for their co-operation, to Robert Marshall, James McGuire and Mary O'Dowd for their support for this project, and to Aidan Clarke, Norma Dawson, Brian Donovan, Raymond Gillespie, Desmond Greer, Henry Horwitz, Patrick Little, Bríd McGrath, Éamonn Ó Ciardha and particularly Kenneth Nicholls for answering numerous queries and for their incisive comments on this report. Finally, I would like to thank the University of Aberdeen, especially Allan Macinnes, my head of department, Duncan Davidson and Janet Hendry, for their practical support.

1 R. Refaussé and H. Smith, 'W.H. Welpy's abstracts of Irish chancery bills, 1601–1801', in *Irish Genealogist*, 7 (1986–89), 166 provides a crude guide to some of the extant pleadings. See also T. Blake-Butler, 'Chancery bills, 1610–1634' in *Butler Society J*, 3 (1991), 380 and J. Chinnery, 'A chancery bill of 1692–3' in *Cork Hist and Archaeological Soc J*, 25:121 (1919), 25.

2 See for instance 'Some documents on Irish law and custom in the sixteenth century' in *Anal Hib*, no. 26 (1970), 105, where the court procedures are explained and a selection of salved chancery pleadings are printed in full; 'A calendar of salved chancery pleadings concerning County Louth' in *Co. Louth Archaeological J*, 17:4 (1972), 250 and 18:4 (1974), 112, where the salved pleadings are calendared; 'Irishwomen and property in the sixteenth century'

article on female litigants in chancery indicates that between circa 1570 and 1635 they constituted thirteen per cent of all litigants.[3]

The general scholarly neglect of chancery records stems in large part from the destruction of so much material in the fire of 1922 (hence the importance of the nineteenth-century transcripts prepared by the Record Commissioners), while fire, smoke and water damage left many of the records that did survive in very poor condition. This misfortune, combined with the fact that the bulk of the chancery records have never been systematically catalogued and are organised according to the stage of a particular case, perhaps explains the reluctance of all but the most persistent researchers to use them.[4] However, much more material, albeit incomplete and difficult to interrogate, appears to have survived the disaster of 1922 than was once thought.[5] A rigorous analysis of these records, especially the pleadings, proofs, bill books, and decree rolls (currently housed in the National Archives), together with the entry books of recognizances entered in the court of chancery (housed in the British Library) remains to be undertaken.[6]

in M. MacCurtain and M. O'Dowd (ed.), *Women in early modern Ireland* (Dublin, 1991), 17, and *Land, law and society in sixteenth-century Ireland* (O'Donnell Lecture, NUI, 1976).

3   'Women and the Irish chancery court in the late sixteenth and early seventeenth centuries' in *IHS*, xxxi (1999), 470 at p. 475: 'The typical female litigant ... was recently married or widowed, came from a merchant or landed family, and lived in an English-speaking part of Ireland'. Other scholars are increasingly using the chancery records, especially the pleadings, as sources for the social and economic history of early seventeenth-century Ireland. See particularly D. Edwards, 'The Ormond lordship in County Kilkenny, 1515–1642' (unpublished Ph.D. thesis, Trinity College, Dublin, 1998) and B. Donovan's forthcoming Ph.D. thesis (also Trinity College, Dublin) entitled, 'Lordship and liberty to colony: County Wexford 1536–1625'.

4   H. Wood, 'The public records of Ireland before and after 1922' in *Transactions of the Royal Historical Society, 4th series,* 13 (1930), 17. For a detailed listing of the extensive amount of chancery material that survived until 1922, see H. Wood, *A guide to the records deposited in the Public Record Office of Ireland* (Dublin, 1919), pp. 1–44. For a rough guide to the original records and later transcripts that survived the fire and chancery material donated, usually by solicitors, to the National Archives after 1922 see *The fifty-fifth report of the deputy keeper of the public records and keeper of the state papers in Ireland* (Dublin, 1928), pp. 114 and 125–27 and *The fifty-sixth report of the deputy keeper of the public records and keeper of the state papers in Ireland* (Dublin, 1931), pp. 34–36, 203–04 and 213–308.

5   For a general listing, see Appendix I to this report.

6   Material associated with chancery cases was documentary; witness statements, for example, were recorded by designated local officials for future use. The evidence generated in the course of a chancery suit was, therefore,

Yet with effort the extant seventeenth-century records of the Irish court of chancery can be reconstituted.[7] From this it will be possible to estimate, however crudely, the number of cases heard in a given year and the nature and scale of the litigation.[8] For example, in 1627 6,000 bills were filed in the English court of chancery – where the records are remarkably complete – and between 1600 and 1800 that court handled 750,000 cases.[9] Were

more likely to survive than in a common law action where oral testimony was given before a jury and rarely recorded. The legal material generated by a given suit was organised according to the type of document (recognizances, pleadings, decrees, etc). The pleadings and proofs in particular provide a wealth of detail about the nature of the dispute and often include supporting documentation – witness statements, wills, marriage settlements, household inventories, leases and bonds. Given the paucity of personal estate archives, especially for the gentry, professional and merchant classes, these supporting documents are particularly interesting.

7 I am currently applying for a grant to facilitate the compilation of a relational database of all extant pre-1690 chancery records. This database, to be published on the web, would provide the following information: names of plaintiffs and defendants, together with their addresses and details of their status/occupation; the date a pleading was lodged or a decree issued; the names of the presiding judges, masters, clerks, and barristers; a summary of the case; the fate of the case (if known); the various stages of a given case (if known); and the length of time that the case was pursued in the court. When this material has been entered into a user-friendly web-based database, scholars will enjoy unprecedented access to the chancery records and will be able to interrogate them in a variety of ways.

8 H. Horwitz, *Chancery equity records and proceedings, 1600-1800* (PRO Handbook No. 27, 2nd ed., London, 1998), p. xi.

9 Ibid., p. 24. English chancery records clearly contain Irish material that requires further examination. For example, a deposition dating from 1619 relates how the second earl of Castlehaven had mortgaged a considerable portion of his Irish patrimony in order to finance £3,000 worth of 'building': J. Ainsworth, 'Some abstracts of chancery suits relating to Ireland' in *RSAI Jn.*, 9 (1939), 39. A preliminary examination of these records (PRO C2/CHASI) by Dr Patrick Little has yielded some tantalising results. Irishmen, including O'Cahans, O'Neills, MacCarthys, Carrolls, FitzGeralds, FitzWilliams, Roches, Barrys and Butlers, together with leading peers – Cork, Ranelagh, Baltinglass and Thomond – appear, predominantly as plaintiffs. Many of these cases refer to land transactions in England – see e.g. *Cork v. Castlehaven* (PRO C2/CHASI/C66/24), which concerns the former's purchase of Castlehaven's house in Stalbridge, Devon. Equally interesting are the exclusively Irish cases that appear in English chancery. For instance, PRO C2/CHASI/C26/41: 24 Oct. 1629 deals with Sir James Carroll's complaint against the earl of Londonderry about bonds sealed in Ireland, while PRO C2/CHASI/C64/60: 11 Feb. 1631 relates to the earl of Cork's complaint against Sir William Power for slander. In 1636 Strafford complained that Irish litigants were by-passing the Irish courts (especially chancery) by taking their suits directly to the English chancery: *The earl of Strafforde's letters and despatches, with an essay towards his life ...*, ed. W. Knowler (London, 1739), i, 526. I am extremely grateful to Patrick Little for bringing these references to my attention.

Irish people as litigious as their English neighbours? How did the nature of the litigation change over time in Ireland? How did this relate to broader social and economic developments, especially the impact of colonisation and of the revolution in landholding associated with the 1650s? What proportion of the extant cases were settled after a bill of complaint was lodged? How many cases were pursued until a final decree was issued and what proportion of decrees were appealed? As for the litigants, where did they reside? What was their status or occupation? How many were women or minors? Although surnames remain only a crude guide to ethnicity and religious belief, this information will nevertheless shed light on the ethnic origins of individual litigants and indicate whether, over the course of the century, certain social and religious groups used chancery more than others. This data will also illuminate the operation of the law of equity in Ireland and the personnel who served in chancery as judges, masters and clerks, together with individual barristers and solicitors.[10] How successful were the 'career' lawyers in pursuing their cases and enriching themselves? Did catholic barristers represent protestant clients and vice-versa? Did the number of catholic lawyers increase over time? What role did the legal profession play in early modern Irish society?[11] How did the suits pursued in chancery relate to the other courts, especially exchequer which was also an important equity court?

In short these records, when fully available, should enrich our understanding of a wide variety of subjects ranging from the complex processes inherent in the colonisation of seventeenth-century Ireland to the political, social, economic, legal, cultural, ecclesiastical and even environmental history of the period, together with literacy and gender studies. Serious scholarly study of the

---

10 For some fascinating insights into predominately protestant lawyers in the later seventeenth century see T.C. Barnard, 'Lawyers and the law in later seventeenth-century Ireland' in *IHS*, xxviii (1993), 256.

11 Historians of early modern Europe and America are only beginning to address these issues. See, for example, W. Prest (ed.), *Lawyers in early modern Europe and America* (London, 1981), pp. 13–14, where Prest points to 'our general ignorance about the interaction between lawyers and their clients' in early modern times: 'Were lawyers in fact retained largely by an elite clientele, or did they also serve peasants and urban artisans to any significant extent? Were they mere instruments of class rule, or also in some sense mediators between disparate social ranks and worlds? How well did they serve their clients? How and how much were they paid in return?'

Irish court of chancery would also pave the way for comparative work, particularly with England, where the chancery records (housed in the Public Record Office in London) have received more attention from historians than their Irish counterparts.[12]

THE JURISDICTION AND PROCEDURES OF THE IRISH COURT OF CHANCERY

The jurisdiction of the court of chancery in the first part of the seventeenth century is difficult to define precisely. In England, the clash with Coke and the common law courts had ended in 1616 with apparent victory for Ellesmere in the form of James VI and I's decree confirming the chancellor's jurisdiction to hear a case after judgment had been given by a common law court.[13] But after Ellesmere's death in 1617, the new chancellor, Bacon, showed restraint 'in using the power of injunction to suspend proceedings at common law',[14] and the practice of the common law judges to assist the chancellor in various ways continued. The increase in business, at least in England, led to chancery dismissing bills for land worth less than £10 per annum and for other matters less than

---

12 The Public Record Office has recently completed a trail database of PRO C6 (approximately 25,000 chancery pleadings from the reign of Charles I) which could easily be linked to the projected database in an attempt to trace any Irish cases referred to the English court or the names of Irish litigants. I am grateful to Roger Powell for bringing this work to my attention. For an excellent introduction to the English chancery records, see Horwitz, *Chancery equity records.* See also H. Horwitz and C. Moreton, *Samples of chancery pleadings and suits: 1627, 1685, 1735, and 1785* (List and Index Society, vol. 257, London, 1995); W. P. W. Phillimore and E. A. Fry (ed.), *A calendar of chancery proceedings: Bills and answers filed in the reign of Charles I* (London, 1889); 'A genealogist's kalendar of chancery suits at the time of Charles I' in *The Ancestor,* 1 (1902), 265; 2 (1902), 208; 3 (1902), 49; 5 (1903), 81; 7 (1903), 75; 9 (1904), 36: 11 (1904), 161; 12 (1905), 56, which covers 441 suits from the early bundles of PRO C2. For a general introduction to the English court see W.J. Jones, *The Elizabethan court of chancery* (Oxford, 1967) and J.H. Baker, *An introduction to English legal history* (3rd ed., London, 1990), ch. 6. For more recent examples of how this material has been used by scholars see H. Horwitz, 'Recordkeepers in the court of chancery and their "record" of accomplishment' in *Historical Research,* 70 (1997), 34; H. Horwitz and P. Holden, 'Continuity or change in the court of chancery in the 17th and 18th centuries?' in *Journal of British Studies,* 35 (1996), 24 and M. Beresford, 'The decree rolls of chancery as a source for economic history' in *EHR, 2nd series,* 32 (1979), 1.
13 Baker, *Introduction to English legal history,* pp. 124–26.
14 Horwitz, *Chancery equity record*s, p. 4.

forty shillings per annum,[15] and as a court of equity it refused to 'intermeddle with matters merely determinable at common law'.[16] 'The office of the Chancellor', according to Lord Ellesmere in 1615, 'is to correct men's consciences for frauds, breaches of trust, wrongs and oppressions of what nature soever they be, and to soften and mollify the extremity of the law'.[17] In disputes over land chancery was not entitled to determine the legal title; but it could regulate the conduct of the legal owner in cases of fraud, penalties, forfeitures and the taking of undue advantage, 'quiet' the possession of tenants or owners, and determine traditional equitable interests which arose by way of use or mortgage. The court also exercised jurisdiction in respect of wills and the administration of estates, charitable bequests and donations, the specific performance of contracts and other equitable remedies such as injunctions and the discovery and production of evidence.[18]

The law administered by the court of chancery in Ireland in the early seventeenth century differed from that in England in a number of respects. In particular, the Statute of Uses passed in 1535[19] in an

---

15 Jones, *Elizabethan court of chancery*, p. 197. This does not appear to have been the case in Ireland, particularly prior to 1603.

16 *His Majesty's Directions for ordering and settling the courts within his kingdom of Ireland* (Dublin, 1622, reprinted, 1638), as presented by G.J. Hand and V.W. Treadwell in *Anal Hib*, no. 26 (1970), 179 at p. 199. These Directions laid down guidelines for the reform of the courts and marked an attempt to make justice more readily available. Of the 47 Directions, six (XVII–XXII) related specifically to chancery. See also Horwitz, *Chancery equity records*, p. 30. There are examples of cases being transferred to chancery from other courts and vice versa. For example, in June 1627 a case brought by John Suple, a gentleman from Limerick, was removed from the jurisdiction of the court of Munster to that of chancery: BL, Add. MS 19,841, f. 19v. In October 1628 the lord chancellor mandated that Donell O Murrey and Edmund Kellie of Roscommon settle their dispute over land 'by course of common law': BL, Add. MS 19,841, f. 122.

17 *Earl of Oxford's case* (1615) 1 Rep. Ch. 1, at p. 6.

18 Jones, *Elizabethan court of chancery*, ch. XII. Cf J.R. O'Flanagan, *Lives of the lord chancellors and keepers of the great seal of Ireland, from the earliest time to the reign of Queen Victoria* (London, 1870), i, 13 gives the following illustrations of Irish chancery proceedings in the 16th century: 'For an injunction to stay proceedings at law. To compel the defendant as feoffee in trust to make an estate to the plaintiff and his heirs in certain lands and tenements. To be relieved from an unjust demand made by the defendant, who is the keeper of a tavern which the plaintiff had visited, and praying a writ of certiorari. For discovery of deeds alleged to be in the defendant's possession. To set aside a deed obtained by fraud, and to obtain an injunction to stay proceedings.'

19 27 Hen. VIII, c. 10.

attempt to revive royal revenues reduced by the efficacy of uses in England, did not apply to Ireland, and similar legislation was not enacted until 1634.[20] This may, however, have had little practical effect, since it now appears to be accepted that the restrictions of the 1535 Act had been largely circumvented by conveyancers, aided and abetted by the chancery judges, before the end of the sixteenth century.[21] It would seem, rather, that the reason for enacting the Irish statute was to bring Irish law into line with that in England, and it is probably for that reason also that a number of other statutes dealing with the making of wills with respect to land, fraudulent conveyances, reversions, arrears of rent, limitation of actions, fines and recoveries and the administration of estates were also enacted in 1634.[22] In its Irish context, chancery has also been perceived as 'a mediator between English common law and Gaelic customary law' and appears to have been more inclusive than the common law courts.[23]

While the Irish court of chancery was closely modelled on its English counterpart, it developed distinct procedures.[24] Even though Sir Richard Bolton's *Directions to be observed in proceedings in the Court of Chancery* (published in 1639) presumably outlined reforms of existing chancery procedures, it nonetheless provides a fascinating insight into how the court may have operated during the early decades of the seventeenth century.[25] Though poorly organised, Bolton's *Directions* outlined sixty rules that determined procedures from the lodging of bills of complaint to the appeal of a decree.

---

20 10 Chas. I, sess. 2, c. 1 (Ir.).
21 Baker, *Introduction to English legal history*, pp. 328–30.
22 J.C.W. Wylie, *Irish land law* (London, 1975), pp. 20–21 and 75. From Strafford's perspective the Statutes of Wills and Uses consolidated the government position and allowed the king even greater 'power in the education of the heirs of all the great families in the kingdome' and provided 'a meanes to breede them up in our religion': T. Carte, *History of the life of James, first duke of Ormond* (2nd ed., Oxford, 1851), vi, 214. See also Knowler, *Earl of Strafforde's letters and despatches*, i, 355.
23 O'Dowd, 'Women and the Irish chancery court', p. 470.
24 Compare Sir Richard Bolton, *Directions to be observed in proceedings in the court of chancery* (Dublin, 1639), reprinted in *A collection of such of the rules and orders of the court of chancery in Ireland, as apply to the practice of the court*, ed. C. O'Keeffe (Dublin, 1815) with the proceedings outlined in Horwitz, *Chancery equity records*.
25 Bolton, *Directions to be observed*. Procedures, certainly pre-1603, were probably looser still. I am grateful to Kenneth Nicholls for bringing this to my attention. These rules were later expanded and revised – see M. Boyle, *A*

Stage I: The pleadings

The formal process began with the submission by the plaintiff(s) of a 'bill of complaint', in English (hence 'English bill'), stating the grievance and asking for redress.[26] The bill, which included the name, address and status/occupation of the plaintiff, outlined the wrong supposedly done by the defendant and gave all the relevant details.[27] It was not valid unless signed by counsel or an attorney, and on receipt was filed in one of the offices of the six clerks and dated on the day of filing. Many suits appear never to have moved formally beyond this stage. No doubt in many cases the parties reached an out-of-court settlement of the matter in dispute. In others, it seems likely that the plaintiff's purpose in issuing a bill was limited to bringing facts to light or securing the appointment of a commission to settle problems of account or to survey disputed land.[28]

If the case did proceed, the court issued a subpoena requiring the defendant(s) to submit, under oath, a formal 'answer' to the bill of complaint.[29] The answer usually complained of the insufficiency and inaccuracy of the plaintiff's bill and set out the defendant's version of the matter in controversy.[30] Provided he or she did so

---

collection of rules and orders appointed to be used and observed in the high court of chancery of Ireland (Dublin?, 1685), reprinted in *A collection of such of the rules and orders*. The later rules are more coherent and clearly aimed to keep unnecessary litigation out of chancery by introducing punitive fines and a much tighter schedule for the lodging of documentation.

26 Proceedings could also begin by information, if the plaintiff was the attorney general, or by petition: Wood, *Guide to the records*, p. 4.

27 If any necessary fact was omitted, the bill might have to be amended. In such a case, 'Where an Answer shall be certified insufficient, the defendant is to pay costs' on an increasing scale until he or she submitted 'a perfect answer': Bolton, *Directions to be observed*, p. 17.

28 Jones, *Elizabethan court of chancery*, pp. 214 and 286. The English chancery also had an informal mechanism for scrutinising bills with a view to summary dismissal of those considered to be frivolous or vexatious, and no doubt in other cases proceedings were simply allowed to lapse. Moreover, it was open to the defendant to attempt to bring the proceedings to a halt by means of a demurrer, plea or disclaimer: ibid., pp. 196–97 and 206–11.

29 Enforcement was occasionally a problem. For example, a recognizance of March 1629 noted the 'remoteness of the defendants' dwellings', the fact that Thomas Kirkpatrick was gone 'suddenly' into Scotland and that when William Perry was served with a subpoena he was unfit and unable to travel 'without endangering his life': BL, Add. MS 19,841, f. 186.

30 During this stage of the proceedings, the plaintiff could also secure an injunction against the defendant which barred him or her from proceeding

within three months, the plaintiff could respond by means of a 'replication' which could either be a general denial of the defendant's answer or deal more specifically with the defendant's allegations and introduce new matters in support of the plaintiff's case. In response to the replication, the defendant could lodge a 'rejoinder'. These formal documents were collectively known as the 'pleadings'.[31] Once the pleadings had been filed, the court could be asked to determine the case and issue a decree after the 'bill and answer [were] read in court'.[32] Many cases were dealt with in this way, without a formal hearing.[33]

Stage II: The proofs, hearing and decree

Under the full chancery process, however, the exchange of pleadings was accompanied or followed by obtaining proofs of evidence, normally in the form of sworn witness statements, together with any other documentary evidence relevant to the case (such as wills, deeds, bonds, or account books). For this purpose, both parties nominated 'such commissioners as shall be indifferent, and not allied unto, nor any ways dependent' upon the litigant and

in another court – providing it was 'upon matter of equity' – until the matter was settled in chancery, or from taking any action that might damage the plaintiff's suit. A defendant could also lodge a 'cross bill', a form of counterclaim in respect of the same matter which allowed him or her to highlight certain features of the case: Bolton, *Directions to be observed*, pp. 6 and 15. An example is to be found in BL, Add. MS 19,841, f .174. According to Jones, *Elizabethan court of chancery*, p. 200, 'many cross bills went no further than an attempt to ferret out evidence or documents which, it was surmised, the ... plaintiff was keeping up his sleeve'.

31 In English chancery practice, the progress of the case could be interrupted at almost any stage by interlocutory motions or applications brought by either party – for example, to challenge an adversary's pleadings or to seek an injunction. As Jones explains, 'these interlocutory applications could involve delay and expense, but the orders reached upon them were often effective in ending the suit': *Elizabethan court of chancery*, p. 15.

32 Bolton, *Directions to be observed*, p. 18. This was noted in the hearings book, and any direction of the court entered in the order book: Wood, *Guide to the records*, p. 4.

33 In 1627 a random sample of 285 cases appearing in the English court of chancery indicates that 77.5% (221 cases) were 'pleadings only' suits and only a very small proportion proceeded to the hearings stage: Horwitz, *Chancery equity records*, p. 26. Jones, *Elizabethan court of chancery*, p. 15 says that 'it was common for commissions of various kinds to be given the responsibility of hearing and ending a case' and adds that 'a Chancery case did not have to involve the appearance of the defendant in court, and it did not have to terminate with a formal hearing and decree'.

these commissioners examined the witnesses.[34] The court required the commissioners to 'set down the examination of every witness at large, without referring to the testimony of one to another'.[35] If either party refused to do this, the court nominated examiners who took evidence from witnesses (or deponents) in the form of written questions (known as interrogatories) and these depositions were returned directly to the court.[36]

On completion of this stage, a day could be set for the hearing of the case. In theory – but not necessarily in practice – the case now came before the judge (the lord chancellor), who often referred it to a master of chancery. The master reviewed the evidence and prepared a report for the court.[37] Finally the chancellor or the master of the rolls (who could hear cases when the chancellor was not sitting), after assessing the evidence and hearing the arguments of counsel, issued a decree which was usually enrolled at the insistence of the successful party. If either party failed to attend the hearing in person the case could be determined in favour of his opponent and 'dismissed with costs'.[38] A decree issued by the court was enforced by imprisonment of the defaulting party or by sequestration of his or her property.[39]

Stage III: Appeal

A decree could only be challenged if the defendant submitted a 'bill of review' or appealed directly to the house of lords. In theory no bill of review would be accepted 'except it contain error in law'.[40] Before proceeding, the party submitting the bill of review had to 'enter into recognizance with sureties, for the satisfying of the costs and damages for the delay, if it fall out against him'.[41]

---

34 Bolton, *Directions to be observed*, p. 8.
35 Ibid., p. 9. See also pp. 19 and 20.
36 Certainly in England the depositions could then be published, with the result that 'both sides could take advantage of examinations conducted for their adversary': Jones, *Elizabethan court of chancery*, p. 15.
37 No master's report appears to have survived the 1922 fire: Wood, *Guide to the records*, p. 4.
38 Bolton, *Directions to be observed*, p. 9.
39 Ibid., p. 13. Thus in September 1633 James Walshe was imprisoned 'in the Marshalsea of the Four Courts' for not performing a chancery decree on behalf of Richard and Ellinor Butler against James Walshe and Robert, his father: BL, Add. MS 19,842, f. 69.
40 Bolton, *Directions to be observed*, p. 12.
41 Ibid., p. 13. The regulations issued in 1685 governing appeals were even more specific: 'That no bill of review is to be admitted, except it be for Error

THE CHANCERY PILOT PROJECT: THE ENTRY
BOOKS OF RECOGNIZANCES, 1627–34[42]

An examination of the recognizances entered between 1627 and 1634 formed the basis of a pilot project undertaken between December 1999 and March 2000.[43] The recognizances taken by one of the masters of chancery[44] were a form of registered bond which a litigant(s) entered into for a fixed sum and the court could apparently require a recognizance at any stage of the proceedings. Virtually every recognizance lists the name, address, status or occupation of the litigant(s) or the office that they held, together with the date on which the recognizance was entered and the name of the presiding chancery official(s).

in Law, apparent in the body of the decree ... or except it be upon new matter risen in time since the decree, whereof the party could not before have had advantage ... and in case of a bill of review, the party is to enter into recognizance with sureties, with a fit penalty, to answer all costs and damages if the bill of review be dismissed, and perform the decree made against him, except the performance of it extinguisheth the party's right at common law, as in making assurances or releases ... and in that case the Court will dispense with the performance of that part of the decree': Boyle, *A collection of rules and orders*, p. 22.

42 Accessibility of the recognizance entry books and funding constraints determined why these records were selected for the pilot project. However, using the data provided in the recognizances, Dr Ó Ciardha was able to track the progress of a significant number of cases through the court and to identify the barristers linked to these suits from the extant Chancery pleadings book (NAI, SR 2/3/20), Chancery bill book (NAI, SR 2/3/21), and the Repertories to chancery decree rolls prepared by the Record Commissioners (NAI, RC 6/2). Ideally all of the surviving chancery records – and not just the recognizance books – should be entered into a relational database.

43 In all, six volumes of entry books of chancery recognizances survive, covering the years 1570–1634 (BL, Add. MS 19,837–19,842). The volumes were purchased by the British Library on 1 June 1854 at Sir William Betham's sale, see P.B. Phair, 'Sir William Betham's Manuscripts' in *Anal Hib*, no. 27 (1972), pp. 13, 14–15. I am grateful to Kenneth Nicholls for bringing this reference to my attention. Prior to 1922 there were some additional chancery recognizance books for 1614–15 and 1618–19 in the Irish Public Record Office: Wood, *Guide to the records*, p. 24. Unfortunately the volumes covering the years 1635–1690 do not appear to have survived. The British Library volumes are in good condition and are easily accessible to scholars. The recognizance, a common law document, was recorded in formulaic Latin. The seventeenth-century entry books of recognizances in the English chancery do not appear to have survived. I am grateful to Professor Horwitz for his insights on these records.

44 The masters of chancery between 1627 and 1634 were Thomas Cary, Patrick Hanna, Henry Mainwaring, Sa[muel] Mayart and Jo[hn] Philpot.

This information, relating to 415 individual recognizances dating between 1627 and 1634, was extracted and entered into a relational database. As Table 1 shows, the records even for this short period are far from complete, with no recognizances being entered at all between November 1629 and early May 1633 and nothing after 19 March 1634. There is no obvious explanation for this other than that a different clerk kept the recognizances for these years in a separate volume that has not survived. However, a close examination of the extant recognizances indicates that they were entered at regular intervals over the course of a given year. Given the apparently complete figures for the years 1627–29, it is possible to estimate the total number of recognizances entered between 1627 and 1634 at 960 (or ten per month for 96 months).

Table 1: List of extant recognizances, 1627–34

Date of recognizances	Number of months	Number (and % of total)
29.3.1627 – 20.12.1627	9 months	77 (18.5%)
8.1.1628 – 24.12.1628	12 months	142 (34%)
20.1.1629 – 2.11.1629	10 months	82 (20%)
3.11.1629 – 7.5.1633	Missing	Missing
8.5.1633 – 28.12.1633	8 months	85 (20.5%)
2.1.1634 – 19.3.1634	3 months	20 (5%)
Not stated	Not stated	9 (2%)
TOTAL	42 months	415 (100%)

The bonds required by the recognizance ranged from £10 to £5,000 and they usually represented double the value of a given suit. For example, in a dispute over a debt of £30, the court required a bond of £60.[45] In 1627 Jane Lambert, spinster, entered into a recognizance for a bond of £100 as security for £50 the court might require her to pay Hester Lambert, baroness of Cavan, 'upon full hearing of the cause in controversie'.[46] The vast majority of bonds (80 per cent) were for under £500 (i.e. the value of the

45 BL, Add. MS 19,841, f. 2v.
46 BL, Add. MS 19,841, f.15. The case was also pursued in English chancery – see PRO, C2/CHASI/L37/71 and C2/CHASI/L46/43. I owe these references to Simon Healey.

land(s), debt(s), settlement(s), etc in dispute was under £250); while only nine percent of bonds were for over £1,000 (see Table 2).

Table 2: Size of the bond required by the recognizance

Bond (£ sterling)	Number (% of total)
£10–199	187 (45%)
£200–499	142 (35%)
£500–999	47 (11%)
Over £1,000	38 (9%)
Not stated	1
TOTAL	415

In the vast majority of cases (245 or 59 per cent of the total number of records) it is not specifically indicated why a recognizance was required.[47] Typical of these entries is this one entered before Henry Mainwaring on 21 April 1627 for a bond of £60:

The condition [of this recognizance] is such that if the above bounden John Wawe doe and shall in all points well and duelye perform and fullfill such judgement and decree as the Right Honourable the Lord Chancellor and Court of Chancerie shall pronounce and soe decree in the cause nowe depending in the said court between the said John Wawe pl[ain]t[iff] and the said Bridgett Worth and Baldwin Harris def[endan]ts. If upon hearing of the cause it be adjudged or decreed against the s[ai]d compl[ainan]t. That then the recogn[izance] to be void otherwise to stand and remayne in full force strength and virtue in same.

> Capr et recognit coram mr
> Hen. Maynwaring
> Signed: John Wawe[48]

However, for 170 entries some explanation was offered as to why the court insisted upon a recognizance and what the dispute was

---

47 In 40 instances it was specifically stated that a recognizance had been cancelled at the request of one of the litigants (for example BL, Add. MS 19,841, f. 8), by order of the court (for example BL, Add. MS 19,841, f. 167v), or after a full hearing of the court (for example BL, Add. MS 19,841, f. 127). In one instance cancellation was due to the death of the litigants: BL, Add. MS 19,841, f. 82v. Most recognizances were cancelled 6–24 months after they had been entered. There was, however, no obligation on the part of the litigants to record the cancellation of a recognizance.
48 BL, Add. MS 19,841, f. 2.

about (see Table 3). A significant proportion (47 per cent) of these 'identified' recognizances concerned suits over land – contested mortgages, landlord-tenant disputes, remedies for defective transfer, and performance of leases (failure to pay rents, to improve or build property or deforestation). The amount of detail that some of these recognizances contain is remarkable. One condition dating from April 1627 provided townland names for 452 acres of arable and pasture and 100 acres of waste-land 'in the territorie of Elie O'Carroll assigned and past by ... patent under the great seal ... by the permission of the said John O'Carroll unto the said Owen Oge McGillefoyle'.[49] Another, dated June 1629, related how Patrick Barnewall and Thomas Hamble of Smithstowne mortgaged (for £80) to Nicholas Dowdall of Drogheda, alderman, 'one house and garden ... one shopp in the street called Boothstreet in Drogheda', together with two orchards (one just outside the Duleek Street gate and the other 'without St. Lawrence's gate'), lands and a mill in Counties Meath and Louth for 81 years.[50] Other recognizances detailed lands that the king handed out to planters. In July 1628, for example, the court took action against Sir John Seyton of Lothian in Scotland when he failed to meet the 'conditions of plantation' for lands he held in Co. Longford, especially those regarding 'buildings'.[51] Another recognizance recited letters patent of 18 January 1607 granted to Thomas Maule, esquire, and John Fowler, gentleman, 'as natives' for 2,133 acres of mountain, pasture, woods, and moorland 'in the territorie of Elie Carroll in the Kings Countie' and required them to 'perform all the conditions for plantation'.[52] When these records are combined with other extant documentation relating to land, especially the surveys of the mid-seventeenth century, it may be possible to disentangle many of the complex transfers of property that accompanied the colonisation of Ireland during the early seventeenth century.[53]

49 Ibid., f. 5.
50 Ibid., f. 163v.
51 Ibid., f. 101v.
52 Ibid., f. 128v.
53 See particularly the database of the various mid-seventeenth century surveys prepared by Mary O'Dowd and Kevin McKenny (Irish Manuscripts Commission, forthcoming) and J. Ohlmeyer and E. Ó Ciardha (ed.), *The Irish statute staple books, 1596–1687* (Dublin, 1998).

Table 3: Nature of a recognizance (approximate figures)

Nature	Number	% of total recognizances (415)	% of identified recognizances (170)
Not stated	245	59%	n/a
Land	80	19%	47%
Debt	50	12%	29.5%
Business	7	2%	4%
Estate matters (wills, minors)	6	1%	3.5%
Marriage/maintenance	8	2%	5%
Court/procedures	19	5%	11%

Fifty-seven recognizances related to debt and business affairs, especially trade. For example, one condition dating from September 1627 referred to licences issued to Garret Johnson, 'merchant stranger', to transport forty packs of linen per year into the Low Countries.[54] Other people turned to chancery for the recovery of outstanding debts. For instance, a recognizance of November 1633 recited a decree awarding Thomas Leake of Nottingham the sum of £65 he had loaned twenty-four years previously, together with £156 in damages. Charles Hargill of Cork challenged this and the court then required Leake to 'bringe in the said originall bond' before the original decree could be enforced.[55] Fourteen of the 'identified' recognizances dealt with disputes over estate matters (issues arising out of wills such as the payment of legacies, the administration of a trust, and provision for minors) or with marriage settlements and maintenance for wives or widows. Thus in 1627 the court, taking a bond for £1,000, required Sir John Vaughan of Londonderry and Thomas Perkins of Lifford to build within three years 'a church and a schoolhouse for a free school' in the town of Lifford in accordance with the instructions outlined in Sir Richard Hansard's will of 29 September 1619.[56] Similarly the court ensured that £200 be paid to Sir James Ware 'for the use of the children' of Christopher Conway of Dublin, esquire, and his

54 BL, Add. MS 19,841, f. 23.
55 BL, Add. MS 19,842, f. 92.
56 BL, Add. MS 19,841, f. 9v.

wife, Marie als Ware.[57] In 1634 three recognizances (each with a bond for £1,000) required Patrick, Lord Kerry and Lixnaw, to pay his three sisters – Eleanor, Maria (or Margaret) and Mary Fitzmaurice – their marriage portions of £500, together with '20 markes sterling on the feast of Easter and Michaelmas by equal portions'.[58]

A further 19 recognizances concerned court appearances and the fact that a litigant failed to comply with a given procedure. Thus John Bee, a Dublin goldsmith, in 1628 entered into a bond for £100 to secure his appearance in chancery 'at the first sitting daie of the next Hillary tearme and answer a Bill of Complaint exhibited against him' by Michael Bee, a Dublin tanner.[59] A recognizance (with a bond for £1,000) forbade Sir Charles Coote to leave Ireland 'without permission' and required him to make a personal appearance in chancery on 6 November 1633.[60]

While it is not specifically stated, it would appear that a significant number of these identified recognizances related to decrees from which a litigant was appealing and to suits referred by the chancellor for arbitration. For example, in November 1628 Sir James Barrett accepted on behalf of his mother and nephews 'the judgement, arbitration, sentence ... of Dermot McCartie, of the Loughert, esq, James Barry of Lislee, esq, and Teige McCartie of Downnemanin, gent ... [to] arbitrate and finally to determine' the possession of ploughlands in Killingglorie, in Barret's Country, Co. Cork. However, if the parties failed to agree with the verdict of the arbitrators, which was to be 'published in writing', they had to accept 'the final judgement of Morrice Roch', otherwise 'the former order of the court of Chancery will stand'.[61]

Of the 1,135 litigants identified in the pilot project, 748 appeared as plaintiffs and 387 as defendants.[62] With the exception

---

57 Ibid., f. 139.
58 BL, Add. MS 19,842, ff. 138, 140 and 141. At this point only Maria was married, to Walter Bermingham, esquire.
59 BL, Add. MS 19,841, f. 48.
60 BL, Add. MS 19,842, f. 27.
61 BL, Add. MS 19,841, f. 106. See also ibid., f. 181 which also appears relevant.
62 An alphabetical listing is available on request from the author, Department of History, University of Aberdeen, Aberdeen AB24 3FX or via e-mail (*j.ohlmeyer@abdn.ac.uk*). Occasionally a litigant's name was recorded in more than one recognizance; but it has only been counted here once, unless she or he appeared as both a plaintiff and a defendant. In addition to the names of

of thirty-six women (twelve plaintiffs and twenty-four defendants who, apart from widows and spinsters, appeared alongside their husbands), the bulk were men: yeomen, husbandmen, merchants, tradesmen,[63] clerics,[64] municipal and government officials, and aristocrats.[65] By far the most important litigants, particularly as plaintiffs, were members of the landed gentry (individuals who described themselves as 'knights', 'baronets', 'esquires' and 'gentlemen').[66] The majority of litigants gave their place of residence as Dublin, but the names of towns and townlands from all thirty-two counties – together with France, Scotland (Glasgow, Edinburgh and St Andrews) and England (especially London, Exeter, Chester and Nottingham) – appear.[67] In addition to originating from every county in Ireland, it appears that the litigants embraced every ethnic and religious group living in early modern Ireland and that all sections of the community enjoyed access to chancery. A disproportionately large number of catholic Gaels appear which, given the relative dearth of sources relating to Gaelic society and culture, is particularly significant.

the litigants, other parties involved in a dispute were listed in the conditions of the recognizance. For example, William O Flannegan of Drishaghan, Roscommon, gent, Tirlogh O'Flanegan of Lugboye, William O Harrington of Cloncallin, Brien O Kerrie, Owen O Croghor, Donogh Duffe O Mulledie, Dermot O Cullenan, Teige O Kerrine, Teige O Garine, Dermot McQuillenan, John O Harregan, Brian O Kerrine, Dermot O Gallame, Brian O Hartegan and Shane Mc Knaylan were required to 'perform such judgements and decrees as laid down by the Lord Chancellor, being all undertenants of the lands in dispute': BL, Add. MS 19,841, f. 1v.

63 They included apothecaries, bakers, barber-surgeons, brewers, butchers, carpenters, cloth-workers, coopers, drapers, fish-mongers, glovers, goldsmiths, haberdashers, innkeepers, joiners, mariners, metal-workers, painters, saddlers, shoemakers, smiths, tailors, tallow chandlers, tanners, upholsterers and vintners.

64 They included bishops, deacons, deans and vicars.

65 The peers included the earls of Ormond, Barrymore, and Thomond; Viscounts Baltinglass, Corren, Fermoy, Ikerrin and Ranelagh, and Lords Athenry, Kerry, Kinsale, Lambert, Longford and Mountnorris.

66 This was also true of the statute staple records, see Ohlmeyer and Ó Ciardha (ed.), *Irish statute staple*, pp. 8–13. Horwitz' detailed analysis of the English chancery records indicates that the largest category in 1627 was 'gentlemen and above' (31.4%), but this pattern changed over time as the number of gentry litigants decreased while the numbers of commercial and female litigants increased: Horwitz, *Chancery equity records*, p. 42.

67 The place of residence of plaintiffs embraced every Irish county, but no defendants apparently came from Carlow, Fermanagh, Leitrim or Monaghan.

The lord chancellor, the master of the rolls, and the masters of chancery were assisted by the six clerks, who in turn employed under-clerks. In theory the judges and masters had trained in civil law; but the majority had also been exposed – thanks to time spent at the inns of court in London – to the common law.[68] The lord chancellor, as judge, played a critical role as the arbiter who provided the redress that the common law courts may have denied litigants. Between 1619 and 1638 Sir Adam Loftus, Viscount Loftus of Ely (1568–1643), who had served as a master of chancery from 1598 to 1619, held this office.[69] The son and heir of Sir Dudley of Rathfarnham, he was admitted to the Middle Temple on 10 November 1604 and as an honorary fellow to Lincoln's Inn on 7 August 1628.[70] During the chancellor's absences, the master of the rolls sat as judge in his place.[71] Francis Aungier, baron of Longford (1558–1632), was appointed master of the rolls in 1609 and held the office until his death in 1632. He was a distinguished lawyer, first attending Trinity College, Cambridge, before being admitted to Gray's Inn in 1577 (he was called to bar in 1583 and became a bencher in 1602).[72] Christopher Wandesford succeeded

68 For a useful introduction to the differences between common and civil lawyers in early modern England, see B.P. Levack, 'The English civilians, 1500–1750' in Prest (ed.), *Lawyers in early modern Europe*, pp. 108–25.

69 See *DNB* entry on 'Loftus'. In April 1638 he was imprisoned for sixteen months for refusing to obey a decree ordering him to settle certain properties on his son, Robert. As a result of this feud with Wentworth, his tenure as lord chancellor came under close scrutiny, generating a remarkable amount of documentation. See for examples HMC, *Report on manuscripts in various collections*, vol. III (London, 1904), pp. 156–212 and HMC, *Ninth Report. Part II Appendix* (London, 1884), pp. 292–316.

70 *Register of admissions to the Honourable Society of Middle Temple from the fifteenth century to the year 1944: vol. 1 1501–1781*, ed. H.A.C. Sturgess (London, 1949) and *The records of the Honourable Society of Lincoln's Inn: vol. 1: Admissions from AD 1420 to AD 1799* (London, 1896), p. 206. See also C. Kenny, *King's Inns and the Kingdom of Ireland: The Irish 'Inn of Court' 1541–1800* (Dublin, 1992), pp. 87–88, 102, 108, 142, 276 and 282.

71 For instance, the chancellor also sat as speaker of the house of lords. Thus, in 1640, when the commons impeached both the chancellor and the master of the rolls, the court of chancery was unable to sit, and matters of law in the court of wards could not be heard: *Cal. S. P. Ire., 1633–47*, p. 288.

72 Wood, *Guide to the records*, p. x and *The register of admissions to Gray's Inn, 1521–1889*, ed. J. Foster (London, 1889), p. 137. Aungier married Douglas FitzGerald, sister of Gerald, 14th earl of Kildare and had estates in

Aungier in May 1633 and held this office until his death in 1640.[73]

Four masters of chancery assisted the chancellor and the master of the rolls. With the exception of Edward Dowdall (who became a master in the early 1630s), all appear to have been protestants and a number had recently arrived in Dublin.[74] For example, Henry Mainwaring, who was admitted to Inner Temple in 1604, originated from Shropshire; while Samuel Mayart, the son and heir of Gilbert of Ipswich, Suffolk, had attended the Middle Temple from February 1607, being called to the bar in 1614 (he was admitted to King's Inns in 1616).[75] Their responsibilities included providing detailed reports on those cases which progressed beyond the pleadings stage; they evaluated all matters that the chancellor or master of the rolls referred to them, took affidavits, and executed deeds of conveyance to purchasers under decrees.[76] If a case involved disputed property or land belonging to minors it passed to the care of a master, who was responsible for managing it. As Table 4 shows, recognizances were always entered before the chancellor, master of the rolls or one of the masters of chancery.[77]

Cambridgeshire and Surrey, a house in London and one in Aungier St., Dublin, where he died in 1632. See also Kenny, *King's Inns*, pp. 221, 276, 283 and 288.

73 Of Yorkshire provenance, he had been educated at Clare College, Cambridge, was admitted to Gray's Inn in 1612 and became one of Strafford's closest supporters: see *DNB* entry on 'Wandesford'; B. McGrath, 'A biographical dictionary of the membership of the Irish House of Commons 1640–1641' (unpublished, Ph.D. thesis, Trinity College Dublin, 1997), pp. 297–98 and Kenny, *King's Inns*, pp. 109, 110, 112, 118 and 289.

74 Dowdall was admitted to King's Inns in 1608: Kenny, *King's Inns*, p. 276.

75 *Students admitted to the Inner Temple, 1547–1660* (London, 1878), p. 166; Sturgess (ed.), *Middle Temple*, i, 88, and Kenny, *King's Inns*, pp. 277 and 284.

76 Wood, *Guide to the records*, p. 24.

77 These were usually entered in Dublin, though Aungier and Mainwaring took recognizances in Drogheda and Kilkenny.

Table 4: *Chancery officials and the taking of*
recognizances, 1627–1634

Name of the judge/master	Number of recognizances (% of total)	
Adam Loftus, chancellor	25	(6%)
Francis Aungier, master of the rolls	29	(7%)
Henry Mainwaring	194	(47%)
Thomas Cary	112	(27%)
Samuel Mayart	23	(6%)
Patrick Hanna	10	(2%)
John Hay, Edward Dowdall, John Philpot[78]	3	(1%)
Not stated[79]	19	(4%)
TOTAL	415	

The six clerks conducted all formal proceedings and court business and barristers and solicitors, hired by litigants, had to proceed through them. Since the records rarely divulge their Christian name, it is difficult to identify the clerks who worked in chancery between 1627 and 1634 with any certainty.[80] 'Johnson' was probably Thomas Johnson, a Welshman who enjoyed Aungier's patronage and in 1640 became MP for Carrick-on-Shannon; while 'Moore' could have been John Moore, MP in 1640 for Philipstown and a relation of Loftus.[81] 'E. Dowdal' – probably Edward of Athboy, Co. Meath, who was admitted to Gray's Inn on 2 November 1599 – appears to have been the only catholic clerk – though he may well have conformed.[82]

Litigants employed their own counsel to present their case: he prepared the pleadings (many include the signature of counsel)

78 These date from 1633.
79 Two of these recognizances were taken before Piers Creagh, mayor of Limerick, presumably at the request of the chancellor or one of the masters.
80 Their names are recorded as [James] Browne, [Peter] Clayton, E[dward] Dowdal, [John] Harrison, [Thomas] Johnson and [John] Moore.
81 McGrath, 'Biographical dictionary', pp. 185–86 and 222–23. Johnson married a granddaughter of Richard Long, who had also sat as a clerk in chancery: NLI, Genealogical Office, 72, p. 227.
82 D. Cregan, 'Irish catholic admissions to the English inns of court, 1558–1625' in *Ir Jur*, v (1970), 108.

and made oral presentations on behalf of a client.[83] Once a decree had been given the barrister for the winning side drew up a copy 'without any material variance' that the chancellor then signed.[84] The court provided strict guidelines within which barristers and their clients worked. For instance, 'If any Bill, Answer, Replication, or Rejoinder shall be found of an immoderate length, the parties and the counsel under whose hand it passeth, shall be fined'.[85] Others received punishment for not providing adequate documentation. For instance, in 1633 John Worsley, a gentleman from Co. Down, petitioned the master of the rolls, complaining that he had been in prison for four months 'for not putting in a more full Answer' to a bill of complaint entered by Sir Henry Hart, from Kent. Once he agreed to submit a full answer and make a personal appearance in court, Christopher Wandesford ordered his release.[86] If any of the court documentation contained 'any matter libellous or slanderous' the case would be dismissed and the parties and their lawyers punished 'for the abuse of the Court'.[87]

The personnel of the court, the patronage links that permeated it, and the extent to which barristers used chancery as a means of enriching themselves and furthering their political careers remain to be studied.[88] However it appears that the legal community was a close-knit one in which chancery officials and barristers became closely inter-linked. The participants in the funeral procession of Francis Aungier, baron of Longford, provide an interesting snapshot of how his clientage networks permeated the profession. Among the chief mourners were five of the six clerks – James Browne, Peter Clayton, John Harrison, Thomas Johnson and Edward Dowdal (one of the four coffin bearers) – and the clerk of

83 Their names are not given in the recognizance entry books, but are listed in extant records in the National Archives: see Appendix II to this report for details. The court required that 'in the entry of every order conceived upon motion [oral representation to the bench], the name of counsel or attorney that made the motion ... shall be expressed': Bolton, *Directions to be observed*, p. 7.

84 Ibid., pp. 10–11.

85 Ibid., p. 16.

86 BL, Add. MS 19,842, ff. 116–17.

87 Bolton, *Directions to be observed*, pp. 17 and 21.

88 In 1640 it was alleged that that the fees levied in the civil and church courts were 'immoderately high' and posed 'an unspeakable burthen' on those people who wished to use the courts: *Lords' jn. Ire*, i, 152–53. The '1641 Depositions' (TCD, MS 809 and 810) provide some insights into the wealth accumulated by lawyers. For example, in 1642 Gerald Lowther estimated that as a result of the rising he had lost fees and entertainments worth £500: TCD, MS 809, f. 290. .

decrees and recognizances, Gilbert Domville.[89] Given that their offices were in the gift of the master of the rolls, or subject to his approval, their presence at his funeral is not surprising.[90] In addition, at least three barristers who regularly pleaded in chancery – Jerome Alexander, Edward Ascough and John Pollexon – formed part of the cortege.[91] The career of Maurice Eustace, a member of the Kildare gentry and a protestant despite his Old English provenance, also provides an interesting example of the importance of patronage and illustrates the mobility within the Irish legal world. Eustace's funeral sermon, preached in July 1665 by his personal chaplain, provides a wealth of detail on his rise to prominence. Between 1610 and 1619 he studied divinity at Trinity, before becoming a lecturer in Hebrew 'and by his accurate knowledge in that Language (a thing rare in men of his Country) and his great care in instructing his pupils, he made early discoveries of his future preferment'. After nine years 'he was (by the perswasion of his friends) remov'd to Lincoln's Inn; where he made it his business not to learn the modes and vices of the place, but to qualifie himself for the service of his King and Country'. Upon his return to Ireland he did 'engage in the publique practise of the laws'. He quickly attracted the attention of Lord Chancellor Loftus, who 'took him into his particular favour, and not only committed all his private concerns unto his management, but very much relied on his advice and opinion in the most intricate matters of Chancery'. This 'profound lawyer' went on to become serjeant at law, master of the rolls, speaker of the house of commons and, after the Restoration, lord chancellor, a privy councillor and a lord justice.[92]

Eustace was simply one of the many barristers pleading in chancery between 1627 and 1634. Appendix II provides the

---

89 *Some funeral entries of Ireland,* ed. W. FitzGerald (London, 1909), pp. 159–60.

90 Wood, *Guide to the records,* p. 42. In 1605 an officer was appointed, who was styled 'clerk of the decrees and recognizances': ibid., p. 28. Domville held this post between 1627 and 1634. He died in Oct. 1637 – see NLI, Genealogical Office, 70, p. 239.

91 FitzGerald (ed.), *Funeral entries,* pp. 159–60. See also Appendix II to this report.

92 *A sermon preach'd at the funeral of Sir Maurice Eustace ... at St. Patrick's, Dublin, the fifth day of July 1665* (Dublin, 1665), pp. 30–31. Eustace was admitted into Lincoln's Inn in 1619 and King's Inns in 1627: McGrath, 'Biographical dictionary', pp. 150–52. See also A. R. Hart, *A history of the king's serjeants at law in Ireland: Honour rather than advantage?* (Dublin, 2000), pp. 50–51 and 57–60.,

names of counsel who acted for litigants involved in suits where
the court required recognizances (and should, therefore, be regarded
as a random sample and not a complete listing). Of forty-eight
lawyers at least nineteen have been tentatively identified as
protestants and twenty-one as catholics: the vast majority had
attended one of the four inns of court in London.[93] The protestants
comprised numerous recent arrivals, including members of the
English bar. For example, Jerome Alexander, who hailed originally
from Norfolk, attended Furnival's Inn before being admitted to
Lincoln's Inn in 1606 and called to the bar in 1616. After being
convicted in star chamber of falsifying documents, he was
disbarred and moved, in disgrace, to Ireland where he established
a lucrative legal practice and involved himself in Irish politics,
sitting in the 1634 parliament as MP for Lifford.[94] A significant
proportion of these protestant lawyers – including Ascough,
Bolton, Bysse, Catelyn, Donnellan, Eustace, Hilton, and Lowther
– went on to hold prominent legal positions (attorney general,
solicitor general, serjeant at law, justice of the king's bench or
common pleas, baron of the exchequer and lord chancellor) or
administrative posts (lord justice and privy councillor). Denied
office because of their recusancy, a number of catholics – Allen,
Aylmer and Plunkett – nevertheless appear to have pleaded in
chancery prior to the passage of the Graces in 1628 and it is
possible that they conformed and took the oath of supremacy.[95]
Once prohibitions against them were formally lifted, catholic
barristers appeared in chancery in increasing numbers. They
included men like Darcy, Dillon and Martin, who all had well-
established practices and an enviable array of clients (including
the earls of Antrim, Clanricard and Cork) and went on to play a
prominent role in frustrating Strafford's attempts to plant
Connacht. Whatever their religion, many of these lawyers sat, as
Bríd McGrath's research has shown, as MPs particularly in the

---

93 As Cregan made clear in 'Irish catholic admissions', pp. 96–97, determining
    the religion of individual entrants is problematic. Occasionally a person's
    religion was noted in the records of the Inns; conduct during the 1640s and
    whether an individual was listed as a 'papist' in the books of survey and
    distribution can also determine religious belief. Yet confusion and occasional
    errors are sometimes inevitable.
94 See Appendix II to this report.
95 D. Cregan, 'Irish recusant lawyers in politics in the reign of James I' in *Ir Jur*,
    v (1980), 306. See also Kenny, *King's Inns*.

parliaments of 1634 and 1640, with Catelyn serving as speaker in the commons in 1634 and Rives replacing Bolton as speaker in the lords in 1641.[96] Moreover during the 1640s catholic lawyers – Berford, Blake, Clinton, Darcy, Dillon, Martin, and Plunkett – became leading confederates.[97]

Given that these recognizances for 1627–1634 represent only a very small percentage of the total number of suits pursued in chancery during these years it seems clear that Ireland, like seventeenth-century England, was a highly litigious society and one in which the legal profession flourished. Thus these chancery records provide the raw data for a much-needed study of the extent and nature of litigation and of the legal profession in Stuart Ireland, together with the procedures and officials of the court of chancery. The fascinating material unearthed in the course of the pilot project clearly only represents the tip of the iceberg. The full potential of these rather dull, dry, and repetitive legal records remains to be unlocked; but if this can be done they will serve as a vital key to enriching our understanding of the social, economic, and legal history of early modern Ireland.

APPENDIX I

Extant Chancery records in the British Library and the National Archives relating to early modern Ireland[98]

Prior to the fire in 1922, the Public Record Office, Ireland (now the National Archives), housed many of the records relating to each of the stages outlined above. A list of what survived the fire is given below.[99]

---

96 M. Perceval-Maxwell, *The outbreak of the Irish rebellion* (Dublin, 1994), pp. 137–39 and McGrath, 'Biographical dictionary'.
97 J. Ohlmeyer, 'Irish recusant lawyers during the reign of Charles I' in M. Ó Siochrú (ed.), *A kingdom in crisis: the confederates and the Irish civil wars* (Dublin, 2000) and M. Ó Siochrú, *Confederate Ireland 1642–1649* (Dublin, 1999).
98 Brian Donovan compiled the listings of the National Archives and I am grateful to him for permitting me to reproduce them here.
99 See also footnote 4 above.

British Library, London[100]

BL, Additional MS	Description
MS 19,837	Entry Books of recognizances in Court of Chancery, 1570–90
MS 19,838	Entry Books of recognizances in Court of Chancery, 1605–1610
MS 19,839	Entry Books of recognizances in Court of Chancery, 1619–23
MS 19,840	Entry Books of recognizances in Court of Chancery, 1623–25
*MS 19,841	Entry Books of recognizances in Court of Chancery, 1627–1628
*MS 19,842	Entry Books of recognizances in Court of Chancery, 1633–1634

(* Entered into a Microsoft Access database as part of the Chancery Pilot Project)

National Archives, Dublin

Salved Chancery pleadings (material salvaged from the 1922 fire): Series 1

Series	Bundle labels	Description	Condition
1C.2.144–171	A-Z, AA- BB etc.	Series of Chancery pleadings, answers, etc. mostly pre-1640 calendared by Kenneth Nicholls	Fair to Good
1C.2.172–186	none	Additional 15 bundles of Chancery records, mostly post-1640	ditto
1C.2.173	none	Mainly late 17th century and 18th century Chancery pleadings with supplementary items	Damaged but readable
1C.2.174	none	ditto	ditto
1C.2.175	none	ditto with some 19th century.	Damaged

---

100 The chancery records relating to the Irish statute staple housed in the British Library have been published in J. Ohlmeyer and E. Ó Ciardha (ed.), *The Irish statute staple books, 1596–1687* (Dublin, 1998).

(continued from page 39)

Series	Bundle labels	Description	Condition
1C.2.176	none	Chancery pleadings and answers c.1680–1760	Good
1C.2.177	none	ditto	ditto
1C.2.178	none	ditto	Damaged
1C.2.179–86	none	ditto	ditto

Series 1		No. of Bundles	No. of records (approx.)
Salved Pleadings (A-Z, AA-BB)		28	6,000
Additional salved (1C.2.173–186)		15	3,000
Total		43 bundles	9,000 records

Salved Chancery pleadings (material salvaged from the 1922 fire): Series 2

Series	Bundle labels	Description	Condition
1C.3.83	Parcel 16	Bundle of documents shown in Chancery cases dating c.1670–1750. They include full rentals, household accounts, cash receipts, several schedules and various deeds.	Good, mostly vellum
1C.3.84	Parcel 17	A bundle of 19th century deeds, indentures, and lots of transcripts of deeds made by the Registrary Office. Dates cover 1661–19th century. Large number relate to Co. Sligo.	Good, paper

(continued from page 40)

Series	Bundle labels	Description	Condition
1C.3.85	Parcel 18	Bundle of late 17th to early 18th century answers in Chancery (and possibly other courts). Very large documents enclosing deeds, schedules, etc.	Fair, vellum
1C.3.86	Parcel 19	Bundle of 17th century answers and replications in Chancery, mostly late 17th century although a few may pre-date 1650. They include schedules of debts, rents, etc.	Poor but readable, vellum
1C.3.87	Parcel 20	Ditto, but more badly damaged.	ditto
1C.3.89	Parcel 22	1690–1764 answers, pleadings, etc. in Chancery.	Good, vellum
1C.3.90	Parcel 23	Late 17th and early 18th century pleadings, etc. in Chancery.	Good, vellum
1C.3.91–104		miscellaneous	

Series 2	No. of bundles (approx.)	No. of records
1C.3.68–82	15	3,000
1C.3.83–104	22	4,400
Total	37	7,400

Chancery material that survived the 1922 fire

Strong Room List	Shelf Reference
Chancery Pleadings Book 1627–1630	SR, Press 2, Shelf 3, No. 20
Chancery Bill Books 1633–1640	SR, Press 2, Shelf 3, No. 21
Chancery Bill Books 1633–1639	SR, Press 2, Shelf 3, No. 22
Chancery Bill Books 1640–1648	SR, Press 2, Shelf 3, No. 23
Index to Pleadings	SR, Press 2, Shelf 3, No. 44

(continued from page 41)

Strong Room List	Shelf Reference
Index to Ancient Pleadings 1561–1617	SR, Press 5, Shelf 4, No. 1
Index to Ancient Pleadings 1617–1624	SR, Press 5, Shelf 4, No. 2
Index to Ancient Pleadings 1624–1629	SR, Press 5, Shelf 4, No. 3
Index to Ancient Pleadings 1629–1634	SR, Press 5, Shelf 4, No. 4
Index to Ancient Answers 1569–1618	SR, Press 5, Shelf 4, No. 5
Index to Ancient Answers 1618–1622	SR, Press 5, Shelf 4, No. 5
Catalogue of Deeds in Chancery Edward III to George II	1A.52.129
Calendar of Chancery Pleadings 1633–4	1A.49.128
'Chancery' records	1C.25.15–28; 1A.26.36–39
Chancery: Answers Salved 1618–1827	2B.80.7–8
Chancery & Exchequer (Miscellaneous Carton Salved)	2B.81.6
Repertories to Chancery Decree Rolls prepared by the Record Commissioners 1536–1624	RC 6/1
Repertories to Chancery Decree Rolls prepared by the Record Commissioners 1624–1685	RC 6/2
Repertories to Chancery Decree Rolls prepared by the Record Commissioners 1685–1732	RC 6/3

APPENDIX II

Provisional list of barristers pleading in the court of chancery,
1627–1634[101]

The names of the barristers pleading in the court of chancery have been
extracted from NAI SR 2/3/20, 2/3/21 and RC 6/2. Only the names of
counsel who acted for litigants named in the British Library recognizances are given here and so this list must be regarded as a random
sample rather than a complete listing. Unfortunately the Christian name

101 Dr. Bríd McGrath has provided invaluable assistance in identifying many of
     these men, particularly those who sat as MPs in the 1613, 1634 or 1640
     parliaments. Much of her research on many of these MPs remains unpublished.

of the barrister is rarely divulged which makes it difficult to identify many of them with any precision.

The date given in square brackets after the name indicates when they first appeared in the records examined for the pilot project. A number, especially those pleading in 1627 and 1628, may well have been practising prior to this date.

Catholic barristers are indicated in bold. Since a number were pleading in chancery prior to the passage of the Graces in 1628, it is possible that they conformed and took the Oath of Supremacy.

Aglionby [1627] – possibly Ambrose, of Harrenge in Middlesex, who was admitted to the Inner Temple in 1597 and called to the bar on 8 August 1606.[102]

Alexander [1628] – probably Jerome, son and heir of Jerome of Thorplands, Norfolk, who attended Furnival's Inn before being admitted to Lincoln's Inn in 1606 (he was called to the bar in 1616) and King's Inns in 1628.[103] After being convicted in star chamber of falsifying documents, he was disbarred and moved, in disgrace, to Ireland where he established a lucrative legal practice. He sat as the MP for Lifford in the 1634 Parliament.

Allen [1627] – there are a number of possibilities: Stephen, admitted to King's Inns in 1612 and attorney general for Ulster in 1617;[104] Robert, admitted to King's Inns in 1623;[105] and finally John, son and heir of John Allen of Rathumney, Co. Wexford, admitted to Lincoln's Inn on 19 August 1620.[106]

Ascough [1629] – probably Edward, son and heir of Sir Edward of Lincolnshire, admitted to Lincoln's Inn in 1608 (to the bar in 1615) and King's Inns in 1629. He became the attorney general for Ulster in 1638 and sat as the MP for Clogher in the 1634 parliament.[107]

---

102 *Students admitted to the Inner Temple, 1547–1660* (London, 1878), p. 149 [hereafter *Inner Temple admissions*]; *A calendar of the Inner Temple records, vol. 2: James I (1603) – Restoration (1660)* (London, 1898), pp. 21, 125 and 129 [hereafter *Inner Temple records*]. In 1621 he was involved in a dispute with Langthorne, and Aglionby was ordered to comply or 'his chamber shall be seized'. This may well have precipitated his departure for Dublin.
103 *The records of the Honourable Society of Lincoln's Inn, vol. 1: Admissions from AD 1420 to AD 1799* (London, 1896), p. 176 [hereafter *Lincoln's Inn records*].
104 C. Kenny, *King's Inns and the Kingdom of Ireland: the Irish 'Inn of Court', 1541–1800* (Dublin, 1992), pp. 276 and 283.
105 Ibid., p. 278.
106 D. Cregan, 'Irish catholic admissions to the English inns of court, 1558–1625' in *Ir Jur*, v (1970), 108 at p. 110.
107 Cregan, 'Irish catholic admissions', p. 108; Kenny, *King's Inns*, p. 278.

Aylmer [1627] – possibly Gerald of Dubberstown, Co. Meath, who was admitted to Gray's Inn on 24 October 1604 and King's Inns in 1628.[108]

Berford [1633] – possibly Richard, son of John of Kilrow, Co. Meath, admitted to Gray's Inns on 26 June 1604 and King's Inns in 1628.[109]

Bermingham [1627]

Bisse [1633] – probably John, son and heir of Christopher of Dublin, who first attended Trinity College, Dublin before being admitted to Lincoln's Inn on 6 October 1624 and King's Inn in 1632. In 1634 he became Recorder of Dublin. He sat as MP for Charlemont in the 1634 parliament and for Dublin in 1640. After the Restoration he became chief baron of the exchequer and a privy councillor.[110]

Blake [1633] – possibly Richard, from a rich Galway merchant family, who was admitted to the Middle Inn in 1612. He sat as the MP for Galway in the 1634 parliament and for Galway Co. in 1640 and played a prominent role in the confederate association.[111] This may also have been Richard's Galway cousin, Valentine Blake, who was admitted to the Middle Temple in 1628. He sat as the MP for Tuam in the 1634 parliament and for Galway in 1640 and was also a leading confederate, especially in provincial affairs.[112]

Bolton [1627] – probably Richard of Fenton, Stafford, admitted to the Inner Temple in 1601; he allegedly left London after being censured in star chamber. In 1605 he became Recorder for Dublin and in 1610 was admitted to King's Inns. He sat as MP for Dublin City in the 1613 parliament and later served as solicitor general, chief baron of the exchequer, and lord chancellor in 1639 (he was impeached in 1641).[113]

Brereton [1627] – possibly John, who was admitted to the Inner Temple in 1609 and King's Inns in 1613. He later became prime serjeant.[114]

---

108 Kenny, *King's Inns*, p. 279.
109 Cregan, 'Irish catholic admissions', p. 108; Kenny, *King's Inns*, p. 278.
110 B. McGrath, 'A biographical dictionary of the membership of the Irish House of Commons 1640–1641' (unpublished, Ph.D. thesis, Trinity College Dublin, 1997), pp. 96–77; *Lincoln's Inn records*, i, 196; Kenny, *King's Inns*, pp. 279 and 285.
111 McGrath, 'Biographical dictionary', pp. 68–69.
112 Ibid., pp. 70–71; J. Ohlmeyer, 'Irish recusant lawyers during the reign of Charles I' in M. Ó Siochrú (ed.), *A kingdom in crisis: the confederates and the Irish civil wars* (Dublin, 2000).
113 *Inner Temple admissions*, p. 160; *DNB* entry on 'Bolton'; C. Lennon, *The lords of Dublin in the age of reformation* (Dublin, 1989), p. 233; Kenny, *King's Inns*, pp. 108–109, 118, 275, 289 and 296. [See also J. McCafferty, 'The Irish impeachment proceedings of 1641', the next paper in this collection – ed.]
114 Kenny, *King's Inns*, pp. 210n, 276 and 283; A.R. Hart, *A history of the King's serjeants at law in Ireland* (Dublin, 2000), p. 164.

Brooke [1627]

Browne, W [1629] – possibly William, son and heir of Richard of Athboy, Co. Meath. After attending Barnard's Inn he was admitted to Gray's Inn on 21 May 1617. This may also have been William Browne of Mulrankin, Co. Wexford, MP in the 1640 parliament, but this is less likely since he does not appear to have attended the inns of court.[115]

Catelyn, N [1627] – probably Nathaniel, originally from Suffolk, he was educated at Cambridge and admitted to Lincoln's Inns in 1605 and King's Inns in 1622. He served as Recorder of Dublin, second serjeant at law and speaker of the House of Commons in 1634.[116]

Cheevers [1628] – possibly Mark, son and heir of Christopher, admitted to Lincoln's Inn on 1 August 1618 and King's Inns in 1628;[117] or John, admitted to Lincoln's Inn in 1608 and King's Inns in 1613.[118]

Clinton [1629] – probably Peter, son and heir of Thomas Clinton of Dowdestown, who was admitted to Lincoln's Inn on 20 January 1614 and King's Inns in 1628. As a member of an established Old English family from Louth he sat as MP for Louth in the 1634 parliament and later joined the confederate association.[119]

Comerford [1629] – possibly Fulke from Kilkenny, admitted to the Inner Temple in 1603 and to King's Inns in 1608.[120]

Comyns [1634]

Cooke? [1628] – possibly Allan, who apparently held a DCL from Trinity. He became a master of chancery in 1636 and later vicar general of Dublin. He also sat as the MP for Cavan in the 1634 and 1640 parliaments.[121] It could also have been Richard, admitted to King's Inns in 1623.[122]

Cowley [1633] – possibly Michael from Kilkenny, who was admitted to the Inner Temple in 1595 and King's Inns in 1607; or James, his son, who was admitted to Gray's Inn on 11 August 1619 and King's Inns in 1628.[123]

---

115 McGrath, 'Biographical dictionary', pp. 84–85; Cregan, 'Irish catholic admissions', p. 109.

116 Kenny, *King's Inns*, p. 278; Hart, *History of the King's serjeants*, pp. 50, 52–57 and 166.

117 Cregan, 'Irish catholic admissions', p. 110; Kenny, *King's Inns*, pp. 205 and 278.

118 Kenny, *King's Inns*, pp. 209, 276, 283 and 285.

119 Cregan, 'Irish catholic admissions', p. 110.

120 Ibid., p. 111; Kenny, *King's Inns*, p. 276.

121 McGrath, 'Biographical dictionary', pp. 110–11.

122 Kenny, *King's Inns*, p. 278.

123 Cregan, 'Irish catholic admissions', pp. 111 and 109; Kenny, *King's Inns*, pp. 275 and 278.

Darcy [1628] – presumably Patrick, seventh son of Patrick of Galway, who was admitted to the Middle Temple on 21 July 1617 and to King's Inns in 1628. As one of the most respected and able lawyers of the day he played a prominent role in opposing Strafford's plans to plant Connacht. He sat as the MP for Navan in the 1634 parliament and possibly for Tyrone in 1640 and later became a leading confederate.[124]

Davis [1628]

Deane [1627] – possibly Edward, who was admitted to King's Inns in 1629.[125]

Dillon, John [1628] – probably John, son and heir of Hubert of Killeyenen, Co. Westmeath. He first attended Furnivall's Inn before being admitted to Lincoln's Inn on 9 March 1617 and King's Inns in 1628. A respected lawyer, he later became an active member of the confederate assembly.[126]

Dongan [1633] – possibly Thomas, fourth son of John of Castleton, Co. Kildare. He first attended Thaives Inn before being admitted to Lincoln's Inn on 12 August 1615.[127] This might also be John, presumably a relative since he also hailed from Castleton, Co. Kildare, who was admitted to Gray's Inn on 23 May 1623.[128] It might even have been Thomas Dongan, second son of Sir Walter, admitted to Lincoln's Inn on 9 August 1627.[129]

Donnellan, Ja. [1627] – probably James, third son of Nehemiah, late archbishop of Tuam. After attending Trinity he was admitted to Lincoln's Inn on 11 June 1616 at the 'request of Sir James Ley, Atty. Courts of Wards and Liveries, late Ch. Justice of K. Bench, Ireland', in 1623 he was called to the bar and admitted to King's Inns.[130] He sat as the MP for Trinity College in the 1634 parliament, became chief justice for Connacht and later served as a justice of the common pleas.

Dormer [1629] – possibly Nicholas of New Ross, who as admitted to the Inner Temple in 1595 and King's Inns in 1607.[131] He sat as MP for New Ross in the 1634 and 1640 parliaments.[132]

---

124 McGrath, 'Biographical dictionary', pp. 125–27; Cregan, 'Irish catholic admissions', p. 112.
125 Kenny, *King's Inns*, p. 279.
126 Cregan, 'Irish catholic admissions', p. 110.
127 Ibid., p. 110.
128 McGrath, 'Biographical dictionary', pp. 144–45; Cregan, 'Irish catholic admissions', p. 109.
129 *Lincoln's Inn records*, i, 204; Ohlmeyer, 'Irish recusant lawyers'.
130 *Lincoln's Inn records*, i, 173.
131 *Inner Temple admissions*, p. 144.
132 Cregan, 'Irish catholic admissions', p. 111; McGrath, 'Biographical dictionary', p. 146.

Eustace [1628] – probably Maurice, who attended Trinity before being admitted into Lincoln's Inn in 1619 and King's Inns in 1627. He sat in the 1634 parliament as MP for Athy and in 1640 for Kildare county. As a protégé of Loftus he quickly rose to prominence and became serjeant at law, speaker of the 1640 parliament and, after the Restoration, lord chancellor, a privy councillor and lord justice.[133]

Farrer [1629]

Goodman [1628] – possibly John, son and heir of John of Blakesware, Hertfordshire, entered the Middle Temple on 22 May 1618;[134] or James Goodman, who was admitted to King's Inns in 1628.[135]

Hilton [1629] – possibly William of Dublin, who was admitted into the King's Inns in 1608 as 'an attorney of the common bench' and given permission to plead at the bar in 1614. On 13 August 1616 he was admitted to Gray's Inn and by 1628 had become one of the benchers at King's Inns and attorney general for Connacht.[136] He later became a baron of the exchequer and a justice of the common pleas. He sat in the 1634 parliament as MP for Armagh.

Leyns [1628]

Lowther [1627] – probably Gerald, son and heir of Gerrard of Penrith, Cumberland, who was admitted to Gray's Inn on 16 February 1608 and to King's Inns in 1618 (becoming a bencher in 1624). He served as attorney general for Munster and then as chief justice of the common pleas.[137]

Lynch [1629] – there are two possibilities: Stephen, son and heir of Nicholas of Galway, was admitted to the Middle Temple on 29 July 1612 and to King's Inns in 1628; while Thomas, son and heir of Mark of Galway, was admitted to the Middle Temple, 28 July 1618 and to King's Inns in 1628.[138]

---

133 McGrath, 'Biographical dictionary', pp. 150–52; *A sermon preach'd at the funeral of Sir Maurice Eustace* ... (Dublin, 1665), pp. 150–52. See also Hart, *History of the King's serjeants*, pp. 50–51, 57–60 and 169.
134 *Register of admission to the Honourable Society of Middle Temple from the fifteenth century to the year 1844, vol. 1: 1501–1781*, ed. H.A.C. Sturgess (London, 1949), p. 108 [hereafter cited as *Middle Temple register*].
135 Kenny, *King's Inns*, p. 279.
136 *The register of admissions to Gray's Inn, 1521–1889*, ed. J. Foster (London, 1889), p. 144 [hereafter *Gray's Inn admissions*]; Kenny, *King's Inns*, pp. 160n, 207, 209, 210 and 276.
137 *Gray's Inn admissions*, p. 116; Kenny, *King's Inns*, pp. 109, 126, 128, 208, 277 and 289, and TCD, MS 809, f.209–v.
138 Cregan, 'Irish catholic admissions', p. 112; Kenny, *King's Inns*, p. 279.

Man [1627] – possibly John, son and heir of Bartholomew late reader of Middle Temple, who was admitted to the Middle Temple on 20 February 1592 and called to the bar on 7 June 1605.[139]

Martin [1629] – possibly Richard, son and heir of Oliver of Galway who attended the Middle Temple between 1622 and 1629 (he was admitted to King's Inns in 1630). A prominent lawyer, he actively promoted the Graces and opposed Strafford's attempts to plant Connacht. He sat as the MP for Athenry in the 1634 parliament and for Augher in 1640 and later became an active confederate.[140]

Petre [1627] – possibly Thomas of London, admitted to the Inner Temple in 1601 and called to the bar in 1610.[141]

Plunkett [1627] – probably Nicholas, son of Christopher, Lord Killen, of Co. Meath, who was admitted to Gray's Inn on 15 May 1622 and to King's Inns in 1628. A prominent member of one of the most influential Old English families of the Pale, he became one of the foremost lawyers of the day. He sat as MP for Meath in the 1634 and 1640 parliaments and a leading confederate, sitting as speaker in the General Assembly.[142] Though less likely this may also have been Sir Christopher Plunkett of Dunsoughly, Co. Dublin, who was admitted to Gray's Inn on 10 August 1610;[143] or Walter, second son of Thomas, a Dublin alderman, who was admitted to Lincoln's Inn on 14 March 1620;[144] or Walter Plunkett of Louth, who was admitted to Gray's Inn on 10 August 1602.[145]

Pollexon [1628] – probably John, who was admitted to the Inner Temple in 1603 and to King's Inns in 1613.[146]

Rives/Ryves, W. [1627] – probably William, originally from Dorset, who was admitted to the Middle Temple in 1592 and called to the bar in 1600 (becoming a bencher in 1618). He entered King's Inns in 1620 and became attorney general and later justice of the king's bench. He sat as the MP for Belturbet in the 1634 parliament and in 1641 replaced Sir Richard Bolton as speaker of the House of Lords after Bolton's impeachment.[147]

---

139 *Middle Temple register*, i, 63.
140 McGrath, 'Biographical dictionary', pp. 208–10; Cregan, 'Irish catholic admissions', p. 112.
141 *Inner Temple admissions*, p. 158.
142 Cregan, 'Irish catholic admissions', p. 109; McGrath, 'Biographical dictionary', pp. 244–46.
143 *Gray's Inn admissions*, p. 124.
144 Cregan, 'Irish catholic admissions', p. 110.
145 *Gray's Inn admissions*, p. 104. His name does not appear on Cregan's list; presumably he was protestant.
146 Kenny, *King's Inns*, pp. 209, 276 and 283.
147 Ibid., pp. 277 and 289.

Sall [1633]

Sarsfield [1628] – possibly Patrick, son and heir of John, esquire, of Limerick. He first attended Barnard's Inn before being admitted to Gray's Inn on 21 February 1616 and King's Inns in 1628.[148]

Sexten/Sexton [1628] – possibly Stephen, son and heir of Edmund of Limerick, admitted to Lincoln's Inn on 25 June 1618 and King's Inns in 1625.[149]

Tyrrell [1628] – possibly Mathew, son and heir of Sir John of Dublin, admitted to Lincoln's Inn on 10 June 1612.[150]

Veldon/Virdon [1629] – possibly Christopher of Clanmore, Co. Louth, admitted to Gray's Inn on 22 October 1601 and King's Inns in 1607.[151]

Waddinge [1629] – there are a number of possibilities: Paul, son of Thomas, esquire, of Waterford was admitted to Gray's Inn on 14 August 1612;[152] Richard, son and heir of Thomas of Callyoogly, admitted to Lincoln's Inn on 4 September 1619;[153] or Thomas, son and heir of Richard, esquire, of Waterford, admitted to Middle Temple on 31 May 1613.[154]

Weldon [1629] – possibly Walter, originally from Staffordshire, who sat as MP for Athy in the 1613 parliament. Though less likely, it may also have been his son and heir, Thomas, admitted to Lincoln's Inn on 15 July 1625.[155]

White [1628] – there are two possibilities: Thomas, son and heir of Patrick of Clonmel, who attended Clifford's Inn before being admitted to the Middle Temple on 5 August 1606;[156] or Henry of Clonmel, who was admitted to the Inner Temple in 1615 and sat as MP for Clonmel in the 1634 parliament.[157]

---

148 Cregan, 'Irish catholic admissions', p. 108; Kenny, *King's Inns*, p. 279.
149 Cregan, 'Irish catholic admissions', p. 110; Kenny, *King's Inns*, p. 278.
150 Cregan, 'Irish catholic admissions', p. 110; Kenny, *King's Inns*, p. 275. For his father, who was apparently protestant, see Lennon, *The lords of Dublin*, pp. 272–73.
151 Cregan, 'Irish catholic admissions', p. 108.
152 Ibid.
153 Ibid., p. 110.
154 *Middle Temple register*, i, 100. Since Cregan did not include him in his list of recusant admissions, he was presumably protestant.
155 *Lincoln's Inn records*, i, 198.
156 Cregan, 'Irish catholic admissions', p. 112.
157 *Inner Temple admissions*, p. 213; Cregan, 'Irish catholic admissions', p. 111.

'To follow the late precedents of England': the Irish impeachment proceedings of 1641

JOHN McCAFFERTY[*]

ON 12 MAY 1641 Thomas Wentworth, earl of Strafford and lord lieutenant of Ireland, was executed in front of a London crowd estimated to be 200,000 strong. Having been impeached and tried for, as John Pym put it, 'the honour of His Majesty's government ... the safety of his person ... [and] the stability of his crown', Wentworth was then convicted by act of attainder. The following day, Richard Bolton, the lord chancellor of Ireland, Gerard Lowther, the chief justice of the common pleas and John Bramhall, the bishop of Derry made formal written answers in the Irish house of lords to articles of impeachment against them. They all died in their beds. A recent writer, reflecting on the law of treason in England in the 1640s, argues that it is pointless trying to establish the 'legality' of Wentworth's trial.[1] The prosecution, he maintains, made use above all 'of political vocabularies ... [and] commonplaces of political language ... in order to legitimate an extreme course of action – the execution of a leading minister of state'.[2] The Irish impeachments were umbilically attached to this 'late precedent of England'.[3] While they lagged behind events across

[*] This is the amended text of an address given to the Society in the Faculty of Law, Roebuck Castle, University College Dublin on 8 October 1999. For assistance in preparing this paper I would like to thank Ms Elisabeth Stuart, the archivist of the Duchy of Cornwall office, Buckingham Gate, London and also Mr James McGuire, Professor John Morrill, Mr Richard Nolan, Professor Nial Osborough and Mr Brian Sommers.
1 D.A. Orr, 'Sovereignty, state and the law of treason in England 1641–1649' (unpublished Ph.D. thesis, University of Cambridge, 1998), p. 56. In the discussion of treason which follows below my debt to Alan Orr's yet unpublished dissertation is immense. See also W.R. Stacy, 'Impeachment, attainder and the "revival" of parliamentary judicature under the early Stuarts' in *Parliamentary History*, xi (1992), 40.
2 Orr, 'Sovereignty, state and the law of treason', p. 59.
3 *Lords' jn. Ire.*, i, p. 166 (27 Feb. 1641).

the sea, they deprived Wentworth of key witnesses and promoted the sense of crisis in the three kingdoms. Roughly parallel impeachment proceedings in Dublin and London had a domestic application in the Irish capital – to rid the country of a viceroy, his ministers and his many works and reset the relationship of the political nation (especially the Old English) to the crown. In essence, as the ever-purple Audley Mervyn had it, this entailed the removal of those 'persons impeached who resemble the opaqous body of the earth interposed to eclipse that light and vigour which the solar aspect of His Majesty would communicate unto his subjects'.[4]

High claims were made in the 1620s for impeachment, a procedure which had lain dormant since the fifteenth century. In 1621 John Pym boasted that parliament was the 'great eye of the kingdom to find out offences and punish them' and exulted a little later in having 'done great works [so] … judgement … which hath slept this 300 years and is the greatest benefit that may be is now revived'.[5] Pym's arithmetic was incorrect; but his confidence in the revival of parliamentary judicature was not misplaced. Nurtured on medieval precedent and trained in the rebarbative politics of the 1620s, it was to prove lasting. Indeed, impeachment proceedings were part midwives of personal rule in England. In the Long Parliament, impeachment was a stormy petrel – a sign of things to come. Always dramatic, often an occasion for histrionic debates and great declarations of principle, impeachment was nonetheless just one part of an extension of judicature by both lords and commons in England. When the Irish house of commons began their proceedings in February 1641, they were striking not only at Wentworth and his government but also making the assertion that they were of the 'high court of Parliament in Ireland', the triers and receivers of petitions of the whole nation.

One of the chief difficulties facing the Irish parliament in 1640–1641 was that they attempted to do, all at once, what it had taken the English parliaments of James I and Charles I over a decade and a half to achieve. Even the very use of the term 'impeachment' in a particular legal sense was something which had come about tentatively and unsteadily under James. But from the outset the

---

4   *A speech made before the lords in the upper house of parliament in Ireland, March 4th, 1640 [1641]* (London, 1641), p. 8. For Mervyn's career, see A.R. Hart, 'Audley Mervyn: lawyer or politician?' in W.N. Osborough (ed.), *Explorations in law and history* (Dublin, 1995), p. 83.

5   C.G.C. Tite, *Impeachment and parliamentary judicature in early Stuart England* (London, 1974), p. 51.

Irish commons were most consciously engaged in an 'impeachment'. What did they mean by this?

Virtually all those proceedings in England between 1376 and 1459 and between 1610 and 1641 which are held to be impeachments were initiated in the house of commons.[6] The suit belonged to the commons and, even if aimed at the closest associates of the king, was always deemed to be *ex parte regis*. While impeachments were invited in the lower house, its seventeenth-century members rapidly discovered that there were no precedents to support any right of judgment beyond matters pertaining to their own privileges. They could not even administer oaths to witnesses. On the occasions they attempted to do so, glacial rebukes were sent down from the upper house to the knights, citizens and burgesses. Indeed, some proceedings even failed because of the dislike taken by the peers to the very tone of the commons' action. Very gradually a system (which proved to be of remarkable durability) emerged. Conferences between members of both houses, while always vulnerable to cries of 'privilege', became the mainstay of impeachment and the means by which the commons acquired an interest and involvement in the trial in the house of lords. In the course of the parliaments of 1621 and 1626, a custom of regular conferences sprang up. Commons' committees collected most of the evidence and presented the charges to the lords. On completion of proceedings in the upper house, the commons were invited in to demand a judgment.[7] Thus, although the house of commons failed in their spasmodic attempts to establish judicature over those beyond their own membership, the involvement of the peers and their determination to defend their role as judges put real backbone into impeachment.

As the 1620s progressed, parliament as the 'great eye' of the kingdom of England, moved from close scrutiny of the particular to broad observation of the general. Emphasis shifted away from punishment of specific crimes or offences committed by office-holders to an attack on the overall conduct of ministers. Whatever the source of the accusation, impeachment came to be seen as a response to grievances and, accordingly, the term 'complaint' is often used alongside or even instead of 'impeachment', as Sir Audley Mervyn did in his 1641 pamphlet, *Ireland's complaint against Sir George Radcliffe*. These ideas of grievance and complaint,

6   Ibid., pp. 16–18.
7   Ibid., pp. 38, 74–82 and 113.

coupled with a sense of parliament as the grand jury of the whole kingdom, had two important consequences. The first, for which there were reassuring medieval precedents, was that an impeachment could begin on the basis of 'notoriety' or 'common fame'. As Thomas Wentworth himself argued in 1626, it was only upon common fame that men might safely accuse the great.[8] The second consequence was closely related to the first – that particular crimes could be encompassed within a general charge. In 1621, for example, Sir Francis Michell was impeached for abuse of his alehouse licence – a specific charge, but characterised as an 'offence to the country'.[9] When Buckingham was impeached in 1626, there were specific charges regarding his conduct as lord high admiral; the house of commons used them only for illustrative purposes in their presentation to the lords of 'ten causes of the two evils afflicting this kingdom'. The cause of all the causes was, of course, Buckingham. A similar deployment of a general charge was vital for initiating the Wentworth impeachment and in his attainder on grounds of 'constructive' treason.[10] Indeed, in Ireland there was to be nothing but a general charge; no specific crimes or treasons were contained in the impeachment proper.

Impeachment was *ex parte regis*; but by the start of Charles I's reign, while no-one dropped the vital fiction of the ill-advised monarch, the intention was to reform, even purge, royal government and correct the errors of the king. James VI and I had appreciated this change of emphasis and, in consequence, fired several warning shots cautioning parliament, for example, against 'challenging an omnipotency or ... erecting a judicature which is not known how far it may reach'.[11] In the end, though, James alienated his ministers and servants, with the result that as early as 1621 the king-in-parliament had been excluded from what was to become an established process. In contrast to his father, Charles I opted for the exclusion of his parliaments rather than his familiars; the young king prorogued and threatened and dissolved – yet still fell short of challenging the right of his English parliament to judicature.

---

8 Ibid., p. 191.
9 Ibid., pp. 92, 183 and 193.
10 Ibid., p. 193.
11 Ibid., p. 125.

Strafford, Bolton, Lowther, Bramhall and Radcliffe were all accused of treason. Impeachment was not, of course, the only route to a conviction for treason. Like impeachment, the concept of treason had not stood still. An English statute of 1534[12] had characterised treason as a crime of usurpation or deprivation; under the Tudors it came to be conflated with *praemunire*.[13] This last offence, much beloved of sixteenth and seventeenth-century English protestant apologists, made legal action in alien courts (the Roman *curia* being the chief target) an offence. Here was a crime conceived of as an encroachment on the powers of the king, against his sovereign authority and a transgression which was destructive of the law of the land – the very common law itself. These notions of usurpation of regal power and subversion of fundamental law were central to the impeachments of Wentworth, the Irish office holders and Archbishop Laud of Canterbury. In each of these cases, treason and *praemunire* were blended.

In 1608, after the English parliament's thwarting of his plans for 'more perfect union', James as would-be emperor of Great Britain sponsored a test case on the rights of the *postnati* to hold land in two kingdoms.[14] The reports on *Calvin's case* (as it is known) contain much discussion of the king's two bodies – his natural body and his body politic – in order to determine matters of ligeance. Both Coke and Bacon were of the view that it was 'by policy of law' that the king was rendered a political body; any attempt to destroy the king's kingdom, his 'state' or political body, was a 'constructive compassing of his death' and therefore treason.[15] Unlawful appropriation of sovereign jurisdiction, especially the power to give law, through maladministration, corruption or other

---

12 26 Henry VIII, c. 13 (Eng.), extended to Ireland in 1537 by 28 Henry VIII, c. 7 (Ire.).

13 Orr, 'Sovereignty, state and the law of treason', pp. 16–20.

14 See B. Galloway, *The union of England and Scotland, 1603–1608* (Edinburgh, 1986), pp. 137–60; L.A. Knafla, *Law and politics in Jacobean England* (Cambridge, 1977), pp. 184–85 and 202–53; H. Wheeler, '*Calvin's case* (1608) and the McIlwain-Schulyer debate' in *Am Hist Rev*, lxi (1956), 587; J. Wormald, 'The creation of Britain: multiple kingdoms or core and colonies?', in *Transactions of the Royal Historical Society, 6th series* (1992), 175. [See also the references to this case in Professor Baker's contribution to this collection – ed.]

15 T.B. Howell, *A complete collection of state trials and proceedings for high treason and other crimes and misdemeanors from the earliest period to the present time* (London, 1809–1826), ii, cols. 559–691; Orr, 'Sovereignty, state and the law of treason', pp. 45, 48, 100 and 104–05.

means, was no less than endeavouring to destroy the king's political body (and his natural body along with it). It was a constructive compassing of the king's death. In Ireland, it could be argued, where the king was present only in the form of his political body, anyone who usurped the sovereign authority to give law was as manifest a traitor as any madman wielding a dagger at the court.

These concepts of treason and impeachment and the relevant actions were available to both English and Irish lords and commons in 1640–1641. Together with the petition of right, the great parliamentary swansong of 1628, they offered a set of interlocking ideas about relations between crown and parliament and between subject and crown. They made up, in short, a shared political vocabulary for Englishmen. Wentworth himself, Lord Deputy Wandesforde and Lord Lambart (who led the attack in the Irish upper house) had, amongst others in Dublin, sat in impeaching English parliaments.[16] In 1641 the Strafford trial gave the lead; but each step taken in Ireland showed every mark of familiarity with the doings of the English parliaments of 1621, 1624, 1626 and 1628.[17] Even if no Strafford trial had been running concurrently, there were sufficient members and peers in Dublin in the winter of 1640 with a mastery of impeachment proceedings to carry it all forward. More vitally there were orators whose command of the language of treason was more than sufficient for them to declare urgently: 'the realm is in danger, the king is usurped, the fundamental law is subverted'.

The Irish parliament of 1640–1642 brought forth a great wave of paper. The commons churned out grievances, remonstrances, queries to the judges, instruments and declarations. It waded knee-deep in petitions, replications and answers – and also managed

16 Patrick Darcy was naturally steeped in Sir Edward Coke's *Institutes* and had probably heard that veteran of many impeachments with his own ears in his days in the inns of court. The fourth part of the *Institutes* has a chapter on parliament as a court.

17 There is one other remote but tantalising connection between Dublin and Westminster. In 1613 the clerk of the Irish parliament had been sent across the water to take instruction on procedure from his English counterpart. If this connection was maintained in 1634 there is the possibility that contact might have been established with Henry Elsynge. Elsynge had become clerk in 1621, and so witnessed the major trials and was the author of a manuscript work, *The moderne form of the parliaments of England*, which had a section on parliamentary judicature.

impeachment along the way.[18] The urge of the Irish commons to complain, to query, to define and to declare was intimately connected with the impeachment proceedings. Lord Lieutenant Strafford's fall in England, along with other events, allowed the political nation in Ireland room to move. Wentworth had pursued his own particular interpretation of Poynings' act and, with fair success, he cut the Old English off from the oxygen of royalty – so depriving them of their accustomed means of redress against Dublin Castle. He carried off, in the end, the relatively unparalleled feat of uniting Old English catholics and New English protestants against him.

After a first obsequious summer session, the Irish commons sniffed the change in the wind blowing across the three kingdoms and promptly declared their sole right to determine subsidy rates. In this way they made their first encroachment into Dublin's stationery stocks, by voting forty-four grievances against the 'vexatious proceedings' of the established clergy.[19] Nestling within denunciations of *mescán* (dishes of butter) and Mary gallons (a tithe on ale) were complaints about abuse of process in the ecclesiastical courts, and it was on the heels of this exotic litany that members of the ecclesiastical court of high commission were to consider whether they had exceeded their jurisdiction.[20] Foreshadowed in this shot at the Church of Ireland, the softest of targets, were the key themes of the impeachment – alleged maladministration of justice and abuse of prerogative courts and powers – all of which tended to destruction of the commonwealth.

Many immensely important things happened during the winter of 1640 and in the following spring and summer. The intention of this paper is to concentrate on the impeachments and thus offer only a broad description of other affairs.[21]

18 Three set-piece speeches became pamphlets; two were by Mervyn, *A speech made before the lords in the upper house of parliament in Ireland, March 4th, 1640 [1641]* (London, 1641) and *Captain Audley Mervyn's speech, delivered in the upper house to the lords in parliament, May 24, 1641 concerning the judicature of the high court of parliament in Ireland* (London, 1641) and one by Patrick Darcy, *An argument delivered by Patrick Darcy, esquire by the express order of the house of commons in Ireland, 9 June, 1641* (Waterford, 1643; Dublin, 1764).
19 *Commons' jn. Ire.*, i, p. 150 (17 June 1640).
20 Ibid., p. 148.
21 For a full account see A. Clarke, 'The breakdown of authority, 1640–41', in T.W. Moody, F.X. Martin and F.J. Byrne (ed.), *A new history of Ireland III: Early modern Ireland, 1534–1691* (Oxford, 1976), p. 270 and A. Clarke, 'The

Following the remonstrance against the clergy, Lord Deputy
Wandesforde prorogued parliament until 1 October 1640. In the
second session the opposition grew further in confidence and
produced another remonstrance attacking Strafford's government
of the past eight years. It was this latter document which provided
the English house of commons with the raw material for articles
of impeachment against Strafford. Wandesforde prorogued again –
but died on 3 December. Two days later, Bishop Atherton of
Waterford was hanged for sodomy. This was a grave embarrassment
for the government, as Atherton had been one of the bright young
men of Wentworth's drive to restore church temporalities. In any
case the viceroy had more pressing concerns following his own
arrest on 11 November.

From this point onwards it is clear that there was a degree of
coordination between the Irish and English parliaments.[22]
Throughout the spring and early summer of 1641 the Irish commons asserted their vaunted right to investigate and to complain.
In the middle of July, Charles went so far in meeting their desire
to dismantle the works of the now late earl of Strafford that the
united opposition was nonplussed. New English and Old English
had begun, once more, to go their separate ways, when the rebellion
of October 1641 transformed the Irish political landscape for
good.

Impeachment came in February 1641, having been on the cards
since the previous November's remonstrance. The fourteenth article
read: 'that by the powerfulness of some ministers of state in this
kingdom the parliament in its members and actions hath not its
natural freedom'.[23] On 16 February 1641, the commons drew up
a list of twenty-one queries for the Irish judges to answer which
not only provided fodder for the managers of Strafford's trial, but
were also a most appropriate trailer for the coming impeachments
in Ireland.[24] Starting with the large question 'whether the subjects

policies of the Old English in parliament, 1640–41' in *Historical Studies*: V, ed.
J.L. McCracken (London, 1965), p. 85.

22 This is undocumented and accordingly difficult to demonstrate – see Clarke,
'Policies of the old English', pp. 89–90.

23 *Commons' jn. Ire.*, i, p. 162 (7 Nov. 1640). A copy of this declaration arrived
in London on 21 November in the hands of Sir Audley Mervyn and was
presented to the English house of commons' committee for Irish affairs. Sir
John Clotworthy introduced two Old English MPs into the house of
commons: Clarke, 'Breakdown of authority', p. 280.

24 *Commons' jn. Ire.*, i, p. 174.

of this kingdom be a free people and to be governed only by the common laws of England and statutes of force in this kingdom', the commons moved on to question the legality of most key elements of the governance of the kingdom in the 1630s. What jurisdiction did the council board really have? Could acts of state or proclamations alter the common law?[25] Could a viceroy censure those who travelled to England to appeal to the king? If the judges deemed even a fraction of the practices mentioned in the queries illegal then the earl of Strafford and his ministers had certainly compassed the destruction of the king's political body. The judges, feeling cornered, begged not to have to answer, then played for time, and when making answer in May were as cautious as only a profoundly nervous bench could be.

On 17 February 1641, the lower house, sitting as a grand committee, penned a 'protestation concerning the Earl of Strafford and his manner of government'. This went straight to the heart of the matter: 'Since the said Earl of Strafford's time, he ... his advisers, councillors, and ministers have altered the face of the government of the said kingdom by the introducing of a new, unlawful, arbitrary and tyrannical government by the determination of all or most causes upon paper petitions, and other unjust and unwarrantable proceedings and actions to the particular profit of himself and his ministers.'[26] Ten days later a select committee of thirty-one was appointed to draw up charges for the impeachment of Bolton, Bramhall, Lowther and Radcliffe.[27] Captain Audley Mervyn was promptly sent up to the lords to ask for their arrest and their sequestration from the upper house and all other places of judicature.[28] The indirect reference to parliamentary judicature contained in the message to the lords at the very outset of proceedings was not just *pro forma*, but rather the first demonstration of a plaintive insistence on the right to it. In their bid to reset relations between parliament and the executive throughout these months the opposition's very stridency betrays a mixture of brittle exhilaration and pure nerve.

25 On this, see in particular W. N. Osborough, 'The Irish custom of tracts' in *Ir Jur*, xxxii (1997), 439.
26 *Commons'jn. Ire.*, i, p. 176.
27 Ibid., p. 185 (27 Feb. 1641). M. Perceval Maxwell, *The outbreak of the Irish rebellion of 1641* (Dublin, 1994), p. 167 counts 17 protestant and 14 catholic members. Radcliffe featured in name only as he was under arrest in England during this time.
28 *Commons'jn. Ire.*, i, p. 186; *Lords'jn. Ire.*, i, pp. 165–66 (27 Feb. 1641).

Although the Irish lords' journals from 5 March 1641 to 1 August 1642 are not extant, there is a reasonable record of the debate held there on that February Saturday when Mervyn approached with his message of impeachment.[29] Much of the sparring was between Ormond (displaying even at this tender age his characteristic skills) and Charles, Lord Lambart.[30] Most attention was paid to the technical problems arising from the impeachment of Sir Richard Bolton, the speaker of the upper house and keeper of the great seal.[31] Ormond's contention was that as the king was not present to choose a new speaker, a dissolution must follow. Lambart was strongly opposed to bail as a compromise. After some stiff exchanges, they eventually agreed to inform the commons that they would gladly order the arrest of Bishop Bramhall. In their response Mervyn and the impeachment committee pressed the point that this was no less than high treason of the most deliberate kind: 'not abortive or of half an hour's birth but the collection of many years' proceedings'. They also threw in a reference to Lord Keeper Finch, to which Ormond took huge exception. Bolton stayed on the woolsack and was, moreover, in the odd position of reassuring the commons that the lords 'would proceed as was fit in the matters moved by them'.[32]

In his opening remarks, Lord Lambart had urged his peers to 'follow the late precedents of England'.[33] He reminded them that Strafford had been committed prior to charges being laid and touched again on Finch's flight and doubted that the accused could be bailed.[34] When Mervyn came back up, probably about an hour later, he repeated Lambart's speech almost *verbatim*, putting all his emphasis on recent precedents across the sea and on the idea of a general charge. Crouching behind this obviously-prepared script was a procedural point of some importance. Some English impeachments had miscarried at the point of transmission

---

29 *Lords' jn. Ire.*, i, pp. 165–68.
30 Lambart had sat for Bossiney in Cornwall in 1626 and 1628–29. In 1641 the member for Bossiney was Sir John Clotworthy who, of course, made a searing speech against Strafford.
31 For some of these see Lords Justices to Secretary Vane, 8 Mar. 1641 (PRO, S.P. Ire., 63/258/70).
32 *Lords' jn. Ire.*, i, p. 168. Following his impeachment in England, Finch had fled the country.
33 Ibid., p. 165.
34 Two of the three judges who spoke on 27 February 1641 deemed it permissible.

from one house to the other. 'The late[st] precedents of England' were not simply a *vade mecum* for Mervyn and Lambart; they also constituted a valuable defence. In 1621 the Westminster parliament had debated a precedent of 1450 when the commons attacked the earl of Suffolk; but the lords had refused to sanction imprisonment until a specific accusation was laid before them.[35] Overlaying 1450 with 1640 by way of 1621 was convenient on 27 February 1641; but the Irish impeachments would go on to deviate from the Strafford trial sufficiently to give the prosecution a number of headaches. There would undoubtedly have been problems with this particular way of proceeding even if the very judicature of the Irish parliament had not been challenged. As it was, that right would be challenged within the week by one of the accused.

On 1 March Lowther and Bolton entered their recognizances.[36] Lowther, who had been ill on 27 February, also made a short speech declaring his conscience to be clear. Interestingly, he referred to the house as 'this supreme court' without hesitation or qualification; but he then went on to speak of human fallibility in breezy terms which betray his estimate of the proceedings as being lacking in any real weight beyond the immediately political.[37] Three weeks later Bishop Bramhall struck a very similar note, in a letter to his wife enclosing a copy of the charges, by remarking that 'my Lord Chancellor and the Chief Justice believe [them] not to be of any great moment'.[38] Although this might have been a necessary bravado in a letter to an anxious spouse, it seems reasonable to assume that all three impeached men saw the entire business as a ploy to ensure that they were unable to appear as defence witnesses in Strafford's trial which began on 22 March.

On 4 March 1641 articles of impeachment were written into the record of the lower house:[39]

First that they, the said Sir Richard Bolton, Knight, Lord Chancellor of Ireland, John Lord Bishop Of Derry, Sir Gerard Lowther, Knight, Lord Chief Justice of the Common Place and Sir George Radcliffe, Knight, intending the destruction of the Commonwealth of this realm have traitorously

---

35 Tite, *Impeachment and parliamentary judicature*, p. 50.
36 *Lords' jn. Ire.*, i, pp. 170–71 (1 Mar. 1641).
37 Ibid., p. 170.
38 John Bramhall to Eleanor Bramhall, 23 Mar. 1641, in *The Rawdon papers*, ed. E. Berwick (London, 1819), pp. 74–76.
39 *Commons' jn. Ire.*, i, pp. 198–99.

contrived, introduced and exercised an arbitrary and tyrannical government against law throughout this Kingdom, by the countenance and assistance of Thomas Earl of Strafford, then Chief Governor of this Kingdom.

Secondly that they and every of them ... have traitorously assumed to themselves and every of them regal power over the goods, persons, lands and liberties of His Majesty's subjects of this Realm; and likewise maliciously, perfidiously, and traiterously given, declared, pronounced and published many false, unjust, and erroneous opinions, judgements, sentences and decrees in extrajudicial manner against law; and have perpetrated, practised and done many other traiterous and unlawful acts and things; whereby, as well divers mutinies, seditions and rebellions have been raised, as also many thousands of His Majesty's liege people of this Kingdom have been ruined in their goods, lands, liberties and lives; many of them being of good quality and reputation, have been utterly defamed by pillory, mutilation of members and other infamous punishments; by means whereof His Majesty and the Kingdom have been deprived of their service in juries and other publick employments, and the general trade and traffic of this Island for the most part destroyed, and His Majesty highly damnified in his customs and other revenues.

Thirdly, that they ... the better to preserve themselves and the said Earl of Strafford in these and other traiterous courses have laboured to subvert the rights of Parliament and the antient courses of Parliamentary proceedings: and all which offences were contrived, committed, perpetrated and done at such times, as the said Sir Richard Bolton, Sir Gerard Lowther, Sir George Radcliffe, Knights, were Privy Councillors of State within this Kingdom, and Sir Gerard Lowther, Knight, was Lord Chief Justice of the Common Place, and against their oaths of the same: and at such time, as the said John Lord Bishop of Derry was actually Bishop of Derry within this Kingdom; and were done and perpetrated contrary to their, and every of their Allegiance, and several and respective oaths taken in that behalf.

Fourthly, for which, the said Knights, Citizens and Burgesses, do impeach the said Sir Richard Bolton, Knight, Lord Chancellor of Ireland, John Lord Bishop of Derry, Sir Gerard Lowther, Knight, Lord Chief Justice of the Common Place and Sir George Radcliffe, Knight and every of them, of High Treason against Our Sovereign Lord the King, His Crown and Dignity.

Here were three articles which reproduced in a condensed form the line of attack taken in the June 1640 grievances, the remonstrance, the queries and the protestation. The accused were connected to Strafford through traitorous confederation and conspiracy. Allegedly, the goal of the confederates was 'destruction of the commonwealth' through 'arbitrary and tyrannical government' achieved by usurpation of regal power 'over the goods, persons, lands and liberties of His Majesty's subjects'. The fruits of such a subversion of fundamental law were mutiny, rebellion, ruin, mutilation and the pillory. As Audley Mervyn put it: 'Magna Carta ... lies prostrated besmeared and grovelling in her own gore'.[40] Put more plainly, the accused were held to have obliterated the fundamental rights of Englishmen.

The great problem with these shocking articles was, as Richard Bolton crisply reminded the lords, that the charges were far too general.[41] This compiler of the first printed collection of Irish statutes blew a great hole in the enemy stockade: 'there is no precedent here of any such proceedings since Poynings' Act ... and the explanation [of it] in 3 & 4 Phillip and Mary, and therefore ... it trenches much upon His Majesty's prerogative'. In short his argument was that the Irish parliament did not, by mere force of analogy, have the same powers as the English parliament; it did not possess the right of judicature, and to claim it was a genuine usurpation of regal power. Bolton's reply set the parameters within which the remainder of the impeachment proceedings took place. His skilful mortaring undoubtedly provoked the Irish commons into keeping proceedings going well after Strafford's execution on 12 May 1641. Now the Dublin assembly required more than a viceroy's head; it was clear that it needed a new deal. By asking for a new explanation of Poynings' act, it shifted from a political to a constitutional programme. It got almost nowhere. On the day, Lambart's spluttering reply showed just how destructive Bolton had been: 'if Poynings' Act be so understood as that parliament can do nothing but pass bills [then] ... it is scarce a parliament'.[42]

Despite Bolton's objections, the proceedings continued. Indeed, in Bramhall's case they were still going on in the spring of 1645. However, as far as the procedure itself went, there is little to add after 4 March 1641. But there are some points of considerable interest worth commenting on before coming back to some of the issues raised by the articles and the defence put in by the accused and, of course, the vindications of judicature offered by Darcy and Mervyn.

The lords now had to vote to receive or reject the general articles and on whether the lord chancellor and lord chief justice were to be committed. After consulting the lords justices, bail was set for both Bolton and Bramhall and the upper house received the articles, thus preparing the way for a trial. The behaviour of the Irish bishops is worth commenting on in this regard. As in

40 *A speech made before the lords*, p. 4.
41 *Lords' jn. Ire.*, i, pp. 176–77 (4 Mar. 1641).
42 Ibid., p. 177.

Strafford's trial, an attempt was made to exclude them on the grounds that here was a matter of blood. However, unlike their English counterparts, the Irish prelates did not withdraw; they insisted on voting and the judges upheld their right to do so on the grounds that this was not an act of attainder.[43] On both sides of the Irish Sea parliamentary fire was concentrated on Wentworth's use of conciliar jurisdiction and proceedings by paper petitions.[44] As those decisions 'at the board' were overturned and nullified first by the commons and then, in July, by royal assent, the bishops (of whatever theological hue) saw that they risked losing all the many temporal recoveries and gains of the past eight years.[45] In consequence, convocation petitioned the lords justices in mid-June defending the legality of 'paper petitions' on the basis of the *Directions for the ordering and settling of the courts ... of Ireland* issued by James I in 1622.[46] Sustained attacks on Strafford's administration in general and the impeachments in particular left the Irish episcopate high and dry. The highly-aggressive temporalities resumption campaign of the 1630s had cut most of the cords binding churchmen and Protestant gentry. Strafford and Bramhall, along with associates such as the executed Atherton, had torn up the social contract of Irish protestantism.[47] Restoration bishops would turn out to be a chastened lot.

On 13 May 1641 the three accused made formal written answers.[48] Charles, who when Prince of Wales had heard numerous

---

43 Ibid., p. 178. Donnellan took the view that the bishops were only barred by canon law and had the right to vote if they pleased.

44 See Clarke, 'Breakdown of authority' and 'Policies of the Old English', passim and M. Perceval Maxwell, *The outbreak of the Irish rebellion of 1641* (Dublin, 1994), chs. 4 and 7.

45 J. McCafferty, 'John Bramhall and the reconstruction of the Church of Ireland, 1633–1641' (unpublished Ph.D. thesis, University of Cambridge, 1996), passim.

46 See G.J. Hand and V.W. Treadwell (ed.), 'His majesty's directions for ordering and settling the courts within his kingdom of Ireland, 1622' in *Anal Hib*, no. 26 (1970), p. 179. The convocation's petition is to be found in PRO, S.P. Ire., 63/274/44 and 45.

47 In letters to Secretary Vane the Lords Justices remarked on the particular venom against Bramhall, who had to put up a bond for £20,000 not for bail, but for the 'privilege' of house arrest: Lords Justices to Vane, 18 May 1641 (PRO, S.P. Ire., 63/259/15) and *Commons' jn. Ire.*, i, p. 210. The bail bond is to be found in Henry E. Huntington Library, University of California, Hastings papers (Irish), HA 14065 (hereafter *Hastings papers*).

48 Date of reply given in Lords Justices to Vane, 18 May 1641 (PRO, S.P. Ire. 63/259/15). Bramhall's answer (both draft and fair copy) are in *Hastings*

precedents cited by Coke and others in 1621, asked the Irish commons to produce theirs.[49] The English privy council also pressed the committee of the Irish commons in England to produce precedents.[50] On 24 May the commons adopted a declaration (reminiscent in places of the 1541 act for kingly title[51]) to the effect that 'this court of parliament of this kingdom hath always and ought to have full power and authority to hear and determine all treasons'.[52] However, on 11 June Speaker Eustace wrote to the committee in England reporting that the lack of response to the declaration was causing anxiety at home.[53] Despite this, the commons pressed on by setting up a committee to draw up particular charges, conferring with the lords about procedure, asking permission from the lords justices for sight of all privy council records from 1633 onwards and making the necessary arrangements for keeping all interrogatories and depositions secret.[54] Outwardly, at least, the lower house remained defiant and when on 10 July the lords justices requested they forebear from further proceedings against Bolton and Lowther, they reacted by formally sending evidence concerning use of threats at the council board to the charges committee.[55]

Even when they knew of the king's formal response to the Irish grievances after 16 July the commons persisted in going through the motions and insisting that there should be no bail for the

---

papers HA 14072–3. The written replies of Bolton, Bramhall and Lowther are to be found in the Duchy of Cornwall office, Buckingham Gate, London, Bound MS: *Political tracts and treatises: subsidies and the Irish grievances 1640–41*, pp. 12–20 (hereafter Duchy of Cornwall office, *Political tracts*).

49 See Tite, *Impeachment and parliamentary judicature*, pp. 104–05, 125 and 222, and PRO S.P. Ire., 63/258/70.

50 Committee to Speaker Eustace, 25 June 1641: Duchy of Cornwall office, *Political tracts*, p. 34.

51 33 Henry VIII, c. 1 (Ire.).

52 *Commons' jn. Ire.*, i, pp. 212–14. They went on to state that a dearth of records caused by centuries of war and troubles in Ireland made it difficult to produce necessary precedents and that, moreover, 'the few ancient records which are left here were, and are as yet, at the command of the said Lord Chancellor and Lord Justice who even since their impeachment had the custody of the parliament rolls in their private studies': ibid., p. 213.

53 Speaker Eustace to the Committee, 11 June 1641: Duchy of Cornwall office, *Political tracts*, pp. 30–31.

54 *Commons' jn. Ire.*, i, pp. 236 (19 June 1641), 238 (22 June 1641) and 249 (7 July 1641).

55 Ibid., p. 254.

bishop of Derry.[56] A year later in very altered political conditions, Bolton and Lowther were restored to their places due to the absence of particular charges. However, the commons' committee insisted that they had such charges in preparation for John Bramhall and George Radcliffe.[57] Even when the bishop made further petitions in April 1644 and February 1645 the house was unmoved.[58] The lords finally discharged him in April 1644, and effectively ended the impeachment process.[59]

In its head, through the charge of conspiracy, and in all its members – accusation, type of charge and timing – the Irish impeachment was utterly wedded to Strafford's in England. As we have seen, the accused certainly thought so. There is a major overlap between the articles and act of attainder against Strafford and the Irish articles and various remonstrances and grievances of the Irish parliament. These similarities were of legal as well as political significance, for it was central to the managers of Strafford's trial that the same fundamental law was current in England as well as Ireland – that there was commonality of legal heritage. Accordingly, the arguments advanced by Darcy and Mervyn and found in the parliamentary declarations had an English, as well as an Irish, application. There were, of course, points of difference, some of which gave rise to considerable technical difficulties. Attacking the speaker and the keeper of the great seal was just one headache. The allegations of conspiracy and confederation were tricky and would have been immensely difficult to prove. Indeed, impeaching a group rather than an individual was itself an innovation.

When Bolton stated that there was no treason in the charges but the word itself, he was drawing on very precise knowledge, because in his *A justice of the peace for Ireland* (1638) all the relevant statutes were cited, including Irish particulars such as the burning of houses or ricks of corn or the cessing of horsemen or footmen without royal authority.[60] In his written reply of 13 May,[61] he also

---

56 The King's answer is in PRO, S.P. Ire., 63/260/1.
57 *Commons' jn. Ire.*, i, p. 297 (21 June 1642).
58 Ibid., pp. 321 (10 Apr. 1644) and 337 (3 Feb. 1645).
59 Lords' *jn. Ire.*, i, pp. 203–04 and 217.
60 Ibid., pp. 176–77 (4 Mar. 1641). See also Richard Bolton, *A justice of the peace for Ireland* (Dublin, 1638), i, 263–66.
61 Duchy of Cornwall office, *Political tracts*, p. 14.

argued that none of the charges came within the compass of the key treason statutes of 1351[62] and 1399.[63] Lowther made a similar response and that was all the precise legal argument possible in face of such general articles.[64] While Bolton cited Poynings' act and the act explaining it (as Bramhall had also done in June 1640, when the house of commons had claimed the sole right to determine subsidy assessments), none of the defendants made an explicit attempt to deny judicature to the Irish parliament in May 1641.[65] This was a tactical response on two levels. First, refusal to recognise the court is rarely wise. Secondly, it is likely that they were aware that the king was going to make a request for precedents. Just after Strafford's execution, Archbishop Ussher informed Bramhall that the king would be looking for post-1495 precedents and expressed his belief that proceedings would collapse directly.[66] Bramhall also did not develop an argument which he had sketched out in his request of 6 March for bail – if it was treason to act upon paper petitions then not only he himself, but every judge and sheriff in the kingdom, was guilty.[67] Unlike the others, the bishop of Derry had not been a privy councillor and so was simply obeying orders.

On 13 May the trio put on a united front. Their written answers are virtually identical in dismissing the general charges clause by clause and each pointing out that his entire fortune and those of his family lay in Ireland – making any plot to destroy the commonwealth on their part a crazy suicidal act. They all reserved the right to answer any future charges.

Like their English counterparts in 1626 the Irish commons based their accusation upon 'common fame' and 'notoriety'; but they were simultaneously accepting and examining bundles of particular petitions. In England the rise of impeachment had prompted a widening of judicature over those who were not MPs or peers.[68] The

62 25 Edw. III, stat. 5, c. 2 (Eng.).
63 1 Henry IV, c. 10 (Eng.).
64 Duchy of Cornwall office, *Political tracts*, pp. 19–20.
65 *Lords' jn. Ire.*, i, pp. 176–77. Bramhall's speech is to be found ibid., p. 121 (16 June 1640).
66 Ussher to Bramhall, 19 June 1641, in *The Rawdon Papers*, ed. E. Berwick (London, 1819), pp. 81–82. For the dating of the letter see PRONI, T.415, pp. 22–23.
67 Bramhall to the Lords Justices, 6 March 1641: *Hastings papers*, HA 16064.
68 Coke remarked in 1624 that the house of commons 'appear for multitudes and bind multitudes', quoted in Tite, *Impeachment and parliamentary judicature*, p. 158.

lords there experienced a sharp rise in demands for their judgment in the form of appeals and petitions.[69] In Ireland in 1640–1641 both the commons (who had confined themselves to matters of privilege in 1613–1615 and 1634–1635) and the lords began to keep a record of petitions and investigate them in select committees. By June 1641 they had begun to annul privy council decisions.[70] The flood of petitions to parliament (which deserve separate consideration at some other time) did have a bearing on the impeachments. Some of the petitions were clearly launched to run concurrently with the larger proceedings. For example, on 26 February 1641, the day before the impeachment committee was named, the commons entered a petition from the tenants of the dean and chapter of Christchurch against Bramhall.[71] The rent settlement in the case had been reached upon reference from the council board. Again on 1 March, after the prickly debate on bail, Lambart put a petition to the lords against letters patents for lands invalidated by extrajudicial opinions which had been given by Bolton and Lowther.[72] This was reminiscent of a similar two-pronged approach to Buckingham in 1626.[73] A tide of petitions flowed in against the high commission, the provost of Trinity College, the bishop of Down and a number of lower clergy who were not, of course, members of parliament. Bramhall was named again and again and, while the lords were both wary and tardy in compelling the bishops of Cork and Down and Connor to answer, they did order the bishop of Derry to start responding to the 'foulest' of the charges in July 1641.[74]

It is very likely that many of the petitions were intended to serve as material for compiling specific charges and, while this never came to pass, those petitions aimed at the ecclesiastical land settlement were quite successful, because among the concessions

---

69 D. L. Smith, *The Stuart parliaments, 1603–1689* (London, 1999), pp. 36–37.

70 *Commons' jn. Ire.*, i, p. 242 (30 June 1641): 'It is voted upon question that the decree given against the right honourable George, Earl of Kildare, at the Council-Board, at the suit of Henry, now Lord Bishop of Down & Connor, for the towns of Brighe, and the town of Rosglasse in the county of Down, was, and is, extra-judicial and contrary to the Great Charter, and void in law and vacated'.

71 Ibid., p. 184.

72 *Lords' jn. Ire.*, i, p. 169.

73 Tite, *Impeachment and parliamentary judicature*, p. 180. See also the case of Lionel Cranfield, earl of Middlesex, ibid., p. 172.

74 *Commons' jn. Ire.*, i, p. 246 (3 July 1641).

which Charles offered was the return of lands gained by the church since 1633 'by any extrajudicial proceedings upon paper petitions...'.[75] In the instance of the court of high commission, the commons even went beyond royal offers of suspension to vote for its overthrow on twelve points of illegality in its patent.[76] So while impeachment itself fizzled out, it is worth noting that the successful outcome in respect of certain petitions represented both political success and some widening of Irish parliamentary judicature during 1640–1641.

Nonetheless petitioning yielded its own crop of difficulties. Bramhall apart, the lords were not keen on sending their members down to answer petitions lodged with commons' committees. Some of the lords were also wary of joining with the other house in the various declarations and remonstrances. For his part Ormond had tried to take advantage of such uneasiness on 27 February 1641 at the presentation of the charges by maintaining that Audley Mervyn's urging of the peers was an insult.[77] Meanwhile petitioning in Westminster by Irish subjects opened up other, portentous, difficulties. On 3 March 1641, the Irish house of lords received a warrant requiring the bishop of Ardagh to attend at Westminster at the suit of one Teige O'Roddy. They would not permit his departure on the basis of 'the ill consequences which may arise thereby'.[78] By August 1641, when the lords justices would not hand over the Scot, Henry Stewart, the English lords had set up a committee to search the records for evidence of Ireland's dependency on England.[79] Once the English parliament began to adjust its relationship with the crown it was only a matter of time before relations between the Westminster and Dublin bodies came up for scrutiny. In the summer of 1641 Irish politicians still

---

75 *Answer of the King in Council to Irish grievances*, 16 July 1641 (PRO S.P. Ire., 63/260/1).
76 *Commons' jn. Ire.*, i, p. 289 (7 Aug. 1641).
77 *Lords' jn. Ire.*, i, p. 168.
78 Ibid., p. 174, and see also p. 176. The lords had already taken exception to a petition from the Irish judges about the Queries on the grounds that their petition had contained the words: 'and some of the questions concern matters that are now depending and in great agitation in the High Court of Parliament in England'. 'As if', as they said, 'this parliament were subject to the parliament in England': ibid., p. 161 (23 Feb. 1641).
79 C. Russell, 'The British background to the Irish rebellion of 1641' in *Historical Research*, lxi, no. 45 (June 1988), 166 at p. 176.

had the relative luxury of being able to concentrate solely on the relationship between their own parliament and the king.

What sort of thinking emerged from the impeachment proceedings? Patrick Darcy's *Argument*, first heard (no doubt in a much rawer form than the later published version) by the lords on 9 June 1641, is a familiar starting point. It should be noted that twenty years earlier the English parliament had heard the former attorney general for Ireland, Sir John Davies, speak on foot of a bill to restrict the Irish cattle trade: 'Ireland is a member of the crown of England ... This kingdom here cannot make laws to bind that kingdom for they have there a parliament of their own'.[80] This theme was taken up by Sir Audley Mervyn, who offered to 'prove our claim to judicature by the title of coheire with the parliament in England'.[81] The lower courts in Ireland too, he argued, drew their precedents from England; otherwise they would return 'but starved and hungry arguments'.[82] Mervyn also undoubtedly polished up his speeches for publication; but his very practical point about legal precedents came closer to the genuine political feeling in Dublin in 1640–1641 than Patrick Darcy's grand historical legal treatise. Common law was a common inheritance; but Ireland also maintained a parliament which had the capacity to try to behave as its English counterpart did. So the precedents and the very language of the 1620s belonged just as much to Ireland as to England.

Such a commonsense approach was most appealing and Mervyn, Davies and Darcy undoubtedly touched a chord in many new and ancient English hearts. The snag was that it just was not true. It was not true because Poynings' parliament had had the double effect of creating a point in time after which (in spite of the ratification of all previous English statutes for Ireland) the Irish and English statute books had diverged and after which the relationship between the crown and the Irish parliament was modified by the act of 10 Henry VII, chapter 4. This enactment of 1495 created a double problem for impeachment. First of all, it ruled out any precedents from before that date (although Mervyn included a few in his speech of 24 May 1641 anyway).[83] Secondly,

---

80 Quoted in H. S. Pawlisch, *Sir John Davies and the conquest of Ireland: A study in legal imperialism* (Cambridge, 1985), p. 32.
81 *Speech ... concerning the judicature of the high court of parliament in Ireland*, p. 7.
82 Ibid., p. 12.
83 Ibid., p. 13.

Poynings' famous act was not as troublesome as it might first look, because it spoke of certification of 'causes ... considerations, and ... acts'. Bolton had been careful to make mention of the 'Act declaring how Poynings' Act shall be exponed and taken', because it required certification of all 'considerations, causes, and articles of such acts, provisions and ordinances'.[84] The explanatory act was a serious threat to parliamentary judicature by analogy to England. The opinions offered in *Calvin's case* came close as a by-product of deliberation on the king's crowns to the kind of analysis Mervyn and Darcy would offer in 1641; yet the latter referred to it only once – and then not to make any assertions about Irish sovereignty. That part of Edward Coke's opinion which asserted that English parliaments had made laws binding Ireland was best left alone.[85]

The only faint hope of a precedent after 1495 would have been the business of Sir Vincent Gookin in 1634. Gookin had written an open letter to Lord Deputy Wentworth which excoriated Old English, Gaelic Irish and New English alike. In consequence the commons initiated a conference with the lords at which a dispute arose over the precise role of each house. Wentworth himself moved swiftly to block any nascent impeachment by having the offending settler taken into his own custody. Parliament went through the motions for a time; but, having thus miscarried, this case did not offer a very healthy precedent six years later.[86]

'Parliament', Darcy proclaimed, is 'the supreme court, nay, the primitive of all other courts [and] to that court belongs the making, altering, regulating of laws and the correction of all courts and ministers'.[87] This is pure Coke – parliament is the highest tribunal. Darcy cited the petition of right as many times as he cited Magna Carta itself. He expatiated on the terrible dangers of subverting parliamentary rights and the dire outcomes of such a course.[88] Such a high doctrine of parliament was not just a

---

84 3 & 4 Ph. and Mary, c. 4, s. 1.
85 Darcy, *Argument*, p. 71. *Calvin's case* was to become a chief point of Conor Lord Maguire's case when he was on trial for treason in England in 1643: see Orr, 'Sovereignty, state and the law of treason', ch. 4. For Coke's opinion, see Howell, *State trials*, ii, cols. 639–48.
86 Gookin's letter is in PRO, S.P. Ire., 63/270/44. For a brief account see A. Clarke, 'The history of Poynings' law, 1615–41' in *IHS*, xviii (1972), 213.
87 Darcy, *Argument*, p. 113.
88 Ibid., p. 65.

foundation to rest Irish parliamentary judicature upon, nor was it just the rhetorical extravagance of an opposition seeking to push home its advantage. It was both those things, but it was also more. 'England is our mother', said Darcy.[89] Such an assertion of the rights of parliament, inclusive of the right to impeach, was an assertion of the liberties of Englishmen.

As a political ploy the Irish impeachments were only successful as long as they hastened Strafford's end. The subsequent constitutional campaign went nowhere. Yet as an invocation of the spirit of English parliaments and the language of liberty, it did help to keep the opposition together in 1641. Detestation of Strafford launched and sustained the campaign; but the rhetoric of the rights of parliament and of the right of impeachment did for a few months substitute for the many names of the Irish lords and commons – Old English, New English, Gaelic Irish – the common constitutional name of Englishmen.

89 Ibid., p. 96.

'United and knit to the imperial crown': an English view of the Anglo-Hibernian constitution in 1670

J.H. BAKER[*]

ENGLISH LAWYERS HAVE a good precedent for regarding Ireland with respect and affection. Sir Edward Coke, in his *Fourth Institute*, pointed out that 'whilst the liberal sciences in Europe lay in a manner buried in darkness, then did their lustre shine forth most clearly here in Ireland; thither did our English Saxons repair, as to a fair or market of good letters ...'. And as with the church so with jurisprudence, for 'there is no nation in the Christian world,' said Coke, 'that are greater lovers of justice ... than they are, which virtue must of necessity be accompanied with many others; and, besides that, they are descended of the ancient Britons, and therefore the more endeared to us'.[1] Yet it is a foolhardy Englishman who would address the Irish in Belfast on the constitutional relationship between Ireland and England. This particular fool intends only to draw attention to a debate which occurred in 1670, in a case concerning Scotsmen, argued by English lawyers in Westminster Hall: a case which, by secretion in the obscurity of the English law reports, seems to have escaped discussion by the historians of Ireland.

Although the case of 1670 makes extensive use of historical records, this lecture will be less concerned with the facts of Irish history than with the legal analysis of the facts as perceived by seventeenth-century lawyers. What, for them, was the nature of the

---

[*] An edited version of a lecture delivered in the Queen's University, Belfast, on 23 October 1998.

[1] 4 *Co. Inst.* 360–61 and 349. This, and all other quotations below, are rendered into modern spelling, with the punctuation adjusted to suit modern conventions.

union with Ireland? The language of union may, of course, be
traced to the legislation of Henry VIII. We all know that Henry
assumed the title of king of Ireland in 1541.[2] A recent commen-
tator on this measure concluded that it was designed to extend the
crown's sovereign jurisdiction throughout the land by conciliation
rather than conquest, and 'to affirm the sovereign nature of the
constitutional bond between the English crown and Ireland with
a view to having that sovereignty acknowledged among the Irishry'.[3]
It was not intended to effect any constitutional change.[4] But a
more interesting claim had been asserted four years earlier, in the
Irish parliament of 1537. In two of the statutes passed that year,
the land of Ireland was said to depend and belong to the imperial
crown of England,[5] while in chapter 6 it was 'the king's proper
dominion of England, and united, knit and belonging to the imperial
crown of the same realm'[6] – a claim repeated in paraphrase in
chapter 19.[7] No doubt this was not in substance a new claim.
Peter Dillon, a bencher of Gray's Inn, had told a fellow member
of the inn in 1516 that 'Ireland and England are all one' because
their laws were the same;[8] and in the year books for 1488 it is
stated by the justices that Ireland is a member of England (*quasi
membrum Angliae*) and uses its laws.[9] But what, in law, was meant
by 'belonging' to the crown of England? Were appurtenancy to the
crown, dependency, and union, intended as synonyms? And did
Irish statutes have any authority in England?

2   *The statutes at large passed in the parliaments held in Ireland … 1310–1800*
    (Dublin, 1786–1801), i, 176 (33 Henry VIII, c. 1). The proclamation of the
    new style, which had to be used in England as well as Ireland, was enrolled in
    the English king's bench: PRO, KB 27/1122, Rex m. 1.
3   B. Bradshaw, *The Irish constitutional revolution of the sixteenth century*
    (Cambridge, 1979), p. 233.
4   See N. L. York, *Neither kingdom nor nation: the Irish quest for constitutional rights,
    1698–1800* (Washington, 1994), p. 11.
5   *Statutes at large*, i, 76, 90 (28 Henry VIII, c. 2 and c. 5).
6   Ibid., p. 91 (c. 6).
7   Ibid., p. 156 (c. 19): 'the king's land of Ireland is his proper dominion, and a
    member appending and rightfully belonging to the imperial crown of the said
    realm of England and united to the same'.
8   Lincoln's Inn, MS. Misc. 486, unfol. ('Nota que Dyllon dit a moy que Ireland
    et England serront tout un. Mesme le ley est use en ambideux lieux etc.').
    Dillon was presumably of the Anglo–Irish family.
9   Y.B. Trin. 3 Henry VII, fo. 10, pl. 3 ('… dixerunt quod Hibernia est quasi
    membrum Angliae et legibus Angliae utuntur').

Before we examine the case of 1670, we had better glance over the legal authorities bearing on the matter before it came to be argued. The first case seems to have been the *Case of the Waterford merchants* in 1484.[10] The principal question in that case was whether an Irish town was bound by an English statute. All the justices in the exchequer chamber held that, since Ireland had its own parliament which could make and change laws, it was not bound by a statute in England, where it was not represented; but with the important proviso that this principle applied only to matters touching land in Ireland, because in other respects the Irish were the king's subjects and were bound like other subjects, including the inhabitants of Calais and Gascony. No doubt it was partly as a result of this decision that the Irish parliament in 1495 expressly enacted that 'all statutes late made' in England, 'concerning and belonging to the common and publique weal of the same', were to apply in Ireland:[11] a measure which incidentally backfired on the English by showing that English statutes were not thought to apply automatically.[12]

There are a number of other passages concerning Ireland in the early-modern law reports, most notably in *Calvin's Case* (1608),[13] and they are chiefly to the effect that Ireland was a separate kingdom or dominion, annexed to the crown of England by conquest but not part of the realm of England. On the other hand, Coke CJ in *Calvin's Case* held it beyond question that an Irishman was a natural-bom subject, capable of inheriting in England. Allegiance was owed to the king in his natural capacity, not to a place.[14] This would be an important issue in the 1670 case.

10 Y.B. Mich. 2 Rich III, fo. 11, pl. 26; *Select cases in the exchequer chamber*, ed. M. Hemmant (64 Selden Soc., 1948), p. 94, pl. 28. But see *Pilkington's Case* (1440) Y.B. Mich. 19 Henry VI, fo. 8, pl. 18, where Serjeant Portington asserted that a revenue statute did not extend to Ireland because the Irish were not represented in the English parliament; there was disagreement as to whether Ireland was separate (*severé*) from England.

11 *Statutes at large*, i, 56 (10 Henry VII, c. 22).

12 See S. G. Ellis, *Reform and revival: English government in Ireland 1470–1534* (47 Studies in History, Woodbridge, 1986), pp. 152–54.

13 *Calvin v. Smith* (1608) 7 Co Rep 1; Moo 790; 2 St Tr 559; L.A. Knafla, *Law and politics in Jacobean England* (Cambridge, 1977), pp. 184–85 and 202–53; B. Galloway, *The union of England and Scotland 1603–08* (Edinburgh, 1986), pp. 137–60. This case has attracted much learning in the last few years: see K. Kim, '*Calvin's Case* (1608) and the law of alien status' in *J Legal Hist*, 17 (1996), 155 and P.J. Price, 'Natural law and birthright: citizenship in *Calvin's case* (1608)' in *Yale Jnl of Law and the Humanities*, 9 (1997), 73.

14 7 Co Rep at 9b, 22b; W. S. Holdsworth, *A history of English law* (London,

The first extended legal discussion of Ireland occurs in the reports of Sir John Davies, the English serjeant at law serving in Ireland as attorney general.[15] The cases which he chose to report all concerned points of public law, but one may be singled out. It arose in the Irish privy council in 1604.[16] An English merchant had taken a bond for £200 from a Drogheda merchant which was defeasible on payment of £100 sterling in current and lawful money of England at Earl Strongbow's tomb in Christchurch, Dublin; the obligor tendered £100 in mixed money which had been made current in Ireland only by proclamation of 1601; and the obligee brought debt for the penalty. The council held the tender good, inter alia, because Ireland was a member of the imperial crown of England, and therefore money current only in Ireland was correctly described as current money of England.[17] This was an Irish decision reported by an English lawyer, and we should bear in mind that not all of Davies' contemporaries regarded his reports as authoritative.[18]

Most of our other pre-1670 sources would not have been readily available to English lawyers in 1670 and were not cited in the case we are approaching. For instance, in 1621 there was an

1922–66), ix, 81–84. The 'king's two bodies' aspect of the case is fully discussed in Price, 'Natural law and birthright', especially at pp. 83–84, 102–13, 119–20 and 135–36. Coke's views on Ireland are also discussed in B. Black, 'The constitution of empire: the case for the colonists' in *U. Pa. Law Rev.*, 124 (1976), 1157.

15 H. Pawlisch, *Sir John Davies and the conquest of Ireland: a study in legal imperialism* (Cambridge, 1983) is a detailed study of Davies' jurisprudence.

16 *Gilbert v. Brett*, or *Le Case de Mixt Monies* (1604) Dav 18. For the background, see Pawlisch, *Sir John Davies*, pp. 142–57.

17 More important in its consequences, but less relevant to the present purpose, was the great case of *MacBrien v. O'Callaghan*, concerning the custom of tanistry. Here it was concluded that the king of England had acquired a valid title to Ireland according to the law of nations by right of conquest, that the Brehon laws seen as a body of Irish common law had by degrees been replaced by the English common law and in effect superseded, and therefore the Brehon laws continued in force (as local custom) only in so far as they were not repugnant to the common law: *Le Case de Tanistry* (1608) Dav 28, esp. at ff. 29v, 37–39. The same point had already been decided, in principle, in *Le Irish Custome de Gavelkind* (1606) Dav 49. See Pawlisch, *Sir John Davies*, pp. 55–81.

18 Sir William Jones, who served as a judge in Ireland from 1617 to 1620, said that Davies' reports were not 'canonical': *Evans v. Ascough* (*c.* 1625) Latch 234 at p. 238 ('Davies Reports ne sont canonical', which drew from Dodderidge J the remark that 'fueront fait pur le meridian de Ireland solement').

interesting brief interchange in the English house of commons when Sir John Vaughan failed to appear to his summons on the grounds that he had just been created Baron Vaughan of Mullengar in the county of Westmeath,[19] and was therefore discharged. According to Coke, who was present, a peerage could only affect his seat if it was granted under the great seal of England, in which case, whatever its name, it would be an English peerage.[20] As Vaughan's peerage was under the Irish seal, it was effective only in Ireland. Coke apparently founded his opinion on the proposition that, 'though Ireland be held of England yet it is a distinct kingdom of itself and they have parliaments there and do make laws, and the statute laws made now here do not bind them there'.[21]

If Coke indeed said that, without qualification, he might well have deserved beatification in Ireland. For in the 1630s and 1640s, when the relationship between the Irish and English parliaments became a controversial issue in Ireland, a theory was conceived among some Dublin lawyers that Ireland was not legally subordinate to England, and that English statutes did not bind Ireland save when they were merely declaratory of the common law which ran in both countries.[22] However, the two principal tracts arguing for

19 G.E. C[okayne], *The complete peerage* (London, 1913), iii, 7. He was subsequently created earl of Carbery.

20 As evidence that an English peer could be given an overseas title, Coke cited the case of the duke of 'Albermarle' (Aumale), though his facts were garbled. This English dukedom was created in 1397 for Edward, grandson of Edward III, who was already earl of Rutland and of Cork; the earldom of Cork is presumed to have been in the Irish peerage, no instrument of creation having been found: C[okayne], *Complete peerage*, i, 357 (Aumale); iii, 418 (Cork).

21 Manuscript reports of cases in parliament, attributed to Speaker Richardson, quoted (without a reference) in H. Wheeler, '*Calvin's case* (1608) and the McIlwain-Schuyler debate' in *Am Hist Rev*, 61 (1956), 587 at p. 594 ('... and Sir Edward Coke was of that opinion'). But see *Commons Debates 1621*, ed. W. Notestein, F.H. Relf and H. Simpson (New Haven, 1935), iii, 413, *per* Coke MP ('There were parliaments in Ireland and they made a law to bind themselves by our laws [i.e. Poynings' act] but since they are governed by their own ... All the laws of England ran into Ireland, but since otherwise'). All the other reports are very brief: ibid., ii, 431; iv, 422–23; v, 206–07 and 399; vi, 193 and 312. The Yale edition also cites a report of the case in BL, Add. MS 36856, fo. 29r–v.

22 The principal tract, *A declaration setting forth how and by what means the laws and statutes of England from time to time came to be of force in Ireland* (c. 1644) is attributed in two manuscripts to Sir Richard Bolton, chancellor of Ireland, though the editor of 1750 thought it might have been by Patrick Darcy, author of *An argument delivered ... by the express order of the house of commons in Ireland* (Waterford, 1643; Dublin, 1764), which adopted a similar position.

and against this theory were not printed until 1750,[23] and were presumably unavailable to English lawyers in 1670.

The legal authorities were surveyed in detail by Matthew Hale, in his tract *The prerogatives of the king*, written in the 1650s and 1660s. This remained unprinted even longer – until 1976 – and was doubtless equally unknown to those who argued the case of 1670, though it is not impossible that Hale could have been consulted informally. Hale considered the king's dominions to be of two kinds: first, those which the king had as parcel of the crown or annexed thereto, and, second, those which the king had through a title separate from that of England. Ireland was in the former category, together with Wales, Calais and the American colonies. Scotland was in the second category, together with Normandy and France.[24] After tracing the history of the conquest of Ireland, and its subjection to the common law by settlement and capitulation, Hale concluded that Ireland was a distinct kingdom which was nevertheless subordinate to and dependent on that of England.[25] It was subordinate because the great seal of England ran in Ireland, and judgments of the king's bench of Ireland were reviewable by the king's bench in England. Moreover, the parliament of Ireland was subordinate to that of England. Although Ireland was not bound by an English statute without special mention, the year-book cases established that an English statute could be made to bind the Irish, even though they had no peers or elected representatives. Nevertheless, Hale said he would not speculate on the power of the English parliament to repeal an Irish statute, or to impose taxes on the Irish, because he could find no precedents to guide

It provoked a cogently argued reply from Mr Justice Mayart, who said the distinction between declaratory and innovatory legislation was 'a difference without a diversity'. For these tracts and their setting, see J.T. Ball, *Historical review of the legislative systems operative in Ireland* (London and Dublin, 1888), ch. 3; C.H. McIlwain, *The American Revolution* (New York, 1923), pp. 33–43; R.L. Schuyler, *Parliament and the British empire: some constitutional controversies concerning imperial legislative jurisdiction* (New York, 1929), ch. 2, and York, *Neither kingdom nor nation*, ch. 1.

23 *Hibernica*, ed. W. Harris (Dublin, 1747–50), pt. 11. The 'Declaration' seems nevertheless to have been the basis of William Molyneux's better known treatise of 1698 (below, note 77).

24 M. Hale, *Prerogatives of the king*, ed. D.E.C. Yale (92 Selden Soc., 1976), p. 19. He put the Channel Islands in the first category, separate from Normandy, because they had been 'in some kind' subordinated to English jurisdiction.

25 Ibid., p. 35. This very phrase was used in the statute 6 Geo I, c. 5.

him.[26] The reasons for the subordinacy, according to Hale, were, first, that the English courts and parliament had a temporal priority in attaching jurisdiction, since they antedated the creation of the parliament and courts in Dublin on the same pattern; secondly, that it was consonant to natural justice that a newly acquired territory should be subject to the jurisdiction of the country to which it was annexed; and, thirdly, that it was established by long usage.[27] In discussing the American colonies, Hale wrote that upon seizure under the king's commission they became parcel of the king's dominions in right of the crown of England, but not part of the realm of England: 'Presently upon the acquest the English laws are not settled there, or at least are only temporary till a settlement made. And therefore we see that there is in all these plantations administration of justice and laws much differing from the English laws. And thus it was with Ireland. The English laws were gradually introduced by the king without the concurrence of an act of parliament.'[28]

Now at last we may come to the case of *Craw v. Ramsay* in 1670,[29] which raised a fundamental question not considered by Hale or the previous authorities. Could a statute of the Irish parliament have any legal force in England? The question arose in a very indirect manner in a case concerning Scotsmen, naturalised Englishmen, and land in England. None of the parties or their ancestors had any connection with Ireland, and perhaps this explains why the case has not attracted much attention here.[30] It arose thus.

26 Hale, *Prerogatives of the king*, pp. 38–39. 'It is true,' wrote Hale (p. 38), 'that the Irish procured an act of parliament, 10 H. 4, but not enrolled, that statutes made in England should not bind Ireland unless enacted there. But this law thus made in Ireland could not bind the superintendence of the English parliament without consent of the English parliament.'

27 Ibid., pp. 39–40.

28 Ibid., p. 43.

29 *Craw d. Tolmach v. Ramsay* (1670) Vaugh 274; 2 Vent 1; Cart 185; 2 Keb 601; T Jones 10. The name is spelt 'Ramsey' in many of the contemporary sources, but it has here been standardised according to the usual Scottish spelling.

30 It has occasionally been noticed by constitutional historians. The fullest discussion is by McIlwain, *American Revolution*, pp. 96–105, which consists chiefly of quotations from Vaughan. McIlwain acknowledged the importance of the case, but recognised that Vaughan's notes are garbled. There is a brief notice, with a shorter extract from Vaughan's report, in '*The empire of the Bretaignes*', *1175–1688: The foundations of a colonial system of government*, ed. F. Madden (Westport, Conn, 1985), pp. 41–43. See also A.G. Donaldson, *Some comparative aspects of Irish law* (Durham, N.C., 1957), p. 46. Professor

An action of ejectment was brought for the manor of Kingston upon Thames, in Surrey, and the facts found by a lengthy special verdict. Since the plaintiff chose to bring the action in the common pleas, Hale CJ regrettably was not involved.

The essence of the case was that John Ramsay, earl of Holdernesse,[31] had died seised of the manor in 1626 without surviving issue.[32] The earl had been born in Scotland before the Act of Union 1603, but had been naturalised in 1603 (by act of parliament) and was thereby rendered capable of purchasing the manor. However, the inquisition held after his death found that he had died without heir, so that the manor escheated to the crown.

Things were not so straightforward, because the earl had in fact three brothers, Robert, Nicholas and George:

PEDIGREE OF RAMSAY[33]

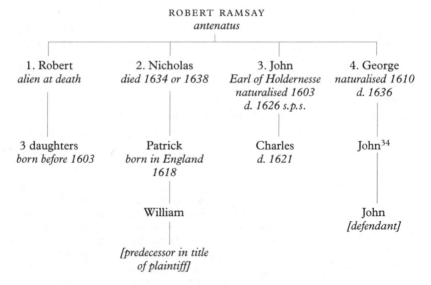

ROBERT RAMSAY
antenatus

1. Robert	2. Nicholas	3. John	4. George
alien at death	*died 1634 or 1638*	*Earl of Holdernesse*	*naturalised 1610*
		naturalised 1603	*d. 1636*
		d. 1626 s.p.s.	

3 daughters	Patrick	Charles	John[34]
born before 1603	*born in England*	*d. 1621*	
	1618		

| | William | | John |
| | | | *[defendant]* |

[predecessor in title of plaintiff]

Osborourgh has pointed out that the case was relied on by counsel for the plaintiffs in *Davies v. Lynch* (1868) IR 4 CL 570.

31 A favourite of James VI of Scotland, he was created a baron in the Scots peerage for killing the earl of Gowrie. He accompanied the king to England in 1603, was admitted to the Inner Temple in 1604, created a viscount in the Scots peerage soon afterwards, and an earl (in the English peerage) in 1621: *DNB*, xviii, 257–58; C[okayne], *Complete peerage*, vi, 534–35.

32 His only son, Charles (*a postnatus*), had died aged three in 1621.

33 Derived from the special verdicts in both the 1661 and 1670 cases: O Bridg at pp. 414–15; Vaugh at pp. 274–76.

34 Lessor of the plaintiff in *Collingwood v. Pace*, below, note 36.

Had this been an English family, there would clearly have been an heir; but all four brothers had been born in Scotland before the Act of Union 1603 and were therefore aliens at birth. However, the youngest brother, George, had been naturalised by act of parliament in 1610, before his father's death. After much litigation in the earlier cases of *Foster v. Ramsay* (1656–59)[35] and *Collingwood d. Ramsay v. Pace* (1656–64),[36] in the second of which the judges of the common pleas sought the advice of the other judges in the exchequer chamber, it was held that George's issue were, by reason of the naturalisation, enabled to inherit from the earl, even though the descent was traced through their father, who was an alien, because inheritance from brother to brother was immediate and could not be barred by the incapacity of their father. On the other hand, Patrick, the English-born issue of the second brother (Nicholas), could not inherit, because he represented his father and his claim would have to be made through his father, who was an alien.

The present case arose from an attempt to overcome this last proposition and claim the inheritance through the second brother, Nicholas.[37] This claim rested on an ingenious argument which despite fifteen years of litigation was not raised by the parties in the two earlier cases,[38] and apparently owed its conception to the redoubtable Serjeant Maynard. Nicholas had died on 1 September 1634,[39] but by an act of the Irish parliament which began at Dublin castle on 14 July 1634, all Scots *antenati* were naturalised

---

35 2 Sid 23, 51 and 148; BL, Hargrave MS 48, ff. 88v, 100v and 104v; cit. O Bridg 447. According to Siderfin, the pleadings were entered in the upper bench, Trin. 1656, m. 1618.

36 O Bridg 410 (from BL, Hargrave MS 55); 1 Keb 65, 174, 216, 265, 535, 579, 585, 603, 670, 699 and 850; 1 Sid 193; 1 Vent 413 (judgment of Hale CB only); 1 Lev 59; Hard 224. According to Siderfin, the pleadings were entered in the common pleas, Hil. 1656, m. 1740.

37 No claim was made through the eldest brother, Robert, presumably because he died before the naturalisation statute of 1634.

38 The Irish statute of 1634 had nevertheless been referred to in argument: O Bridg at p. 459. Moreover, in arguing that acts of naturalisation were not wholly equivalent to actual birth, the three dissenting judges in *Collingwood v. Pace* had observed *obiter* that 'if someone is naturalised by the parliament of Scotland or Ireland, that does not make him capable here in England, and yet a subject born there has capacity in all three countries': 1 Sid at p. 197 (translated).

39 Vaugh at p. 276. This is open to question, since Bridgman's report says he died on 31 May 1638.

in Ireland.[40] The purpose of this statute, as hinted at in the preamble, was to encourage Scots settlers in Ulster rather than to benefit Scotsmen everywhere.[41] Nevertheless, the statute was couched in general terms. It began indeed with a recital that 'your Highness' loving subjects of these your Highness' realms of England, Scotland and Ireland are now growing into one nation, without all mark of difference or distinction'; and it enacted that every Scottish man and Scottish woman born before the king's accession to the crown of England and Ireland – 'crown' is here in the singular – should be:

deemed, adjudged and reputed your Majesty's liege, free and natural subjects of this your Highness' realm of Ireland, and be adjudged, reputed and taken in every respect, condition and degree, to all intents, constructions and purposes, your Majesty's natural and liege subjects of this realm of Ireland, as if they and every of them had been or were born within this realm of Ireland, of English or Irish parents, your Majesty's free-born natural subjects of this realm of Ireland,

with full capacity to purchase or inherit land. Although there was no suggestion that Nicholas had ever set foot in Ireland, it was argued that he was naturalised in Ireland by virtue of this statute, and that therefore he must also be naturalised in England. A person born in Ireland, or in the other dominions belonging to the English crown, was not accounted an alien in England; and so (it was argued) a person naturalised in Ireland should be in the same position as a person born in Ireland; that, indeed, is what the Irish statute expressly provided. The case differed from a naturalisation in Scotland, which did not operate in England, because Ireland was a dominion belonging to the crown of England, whereas Scotland was not.[42] The basic principles of nationality had been much canvassed in *Calvin's Case* (1608), and Coke's report of that case was still the main guide in 1670. However, the question

---

40 *Statutes at large*, ii, 100 (10 Chas I, sess. 3, c. 4). It was well established by this date that acts of parliament took effect in law from the first day of the session, not from the day when they were passed: 109 Selden Soc., lv–lvi.

41 There had already been a massive immigration of Scotsmen in the previous reign: see M. Perceval-Maxwell, *The Scottish migration to Ulster in the reign of James I* (London, 1973); P.S. Robinson, *The plantation of Ulster: British settlement in an Irish landscape 1600–1670* (Dublin, 1984). Neither writer discusses the statute of 1634.

42 Vaugh at p. 278.

raised by Serjeant Maynard was entirely new. Granted that an *antenatus* could inherit by virtue of an English act of parliament, as had been confirmed by *Collingwood v. Pace*, was an Irish act of parliament purporting to remove alien status from a British subject effective to enable a person to inherit land in England?

None of the printed reports of the case is entirely satisfactory. Carter gives the arguments of counsel only; Vaughan's report consists of imperfect notes of his own speech only; Jones reports the speech of Wylde J only; Ventris conflates the opinions on either side into a composite summary; and Keble is a bare note. They nevertheless give us a start in understanding the issues.

We may commence with Serjeant Maynard's argument for the plaintiff, which is reported in some detail by Carter.[43] He began by pointing out that the language of union went back to the thirteenth century, inasmuch as a writ patent of 1246 (twice printed in Coke's *Institutes*)[44] referred to the introduction of English law in Ireland by King John as having been 'for the common utility of the land of Ireland and for the unity of [the king's] lands'.[45] Maynard seems to have suggested that this instrument was an act of parliament.[46] Thus, said Maynard, 'There is in the act *unitas legum et terrarum*', unity both of laws and of lands: 'The two islands are not united geographically, but politically. A political unity hath a political influence. The political efficient is the act; the political form is government; the *materia politica* is the two kingdoms of England and Ireland; the modification and limits are the *leges et consuetudines* ...'.

Maynard's opening apparently led some of the judges to suppose he had based his case on the existence of a constitutional union of the two kingdoms. Indeed, Vaughan CJ found it necessary in his judgment to correct that impression: 'And I must clear my brother

---

43 Cart at pp. 185–89.
44 Pat. 30 Henry III, m. 1; *Co. Litt.* 141; 4 *Co. Inst.* 350; and see Vaugh at p. 296; *Rym. Foed.* i, 442; *Cal. Pat. Rolls, 1232–47*, p. 488. Coke commented (*Co. Litt.* 141): 'Wherein it is to be observed, that union of laws is the best mean for unity of countries.'
45 4 *Co. Inst.* 349, 350: '*Rex Henricus mandavit justiciario suo Hiberniae, etc. Quia pro communi utilitate terrae Hiberniae et pro unitate terrarum provisum est quod omnes leges quae in regno Angliae tenentur, in Hibernia teneantur ...*'.
46 His citation, as reported by Carter, was to *Rot. Parl.*, though this may simply be a misreading of *Rot. Pat.* (as it is correctly cited in Coke). However, he says that Coke treated it as 'a statute, not a grant or concession of the King only'.

Maynard from any mention of an union, as was discoursed, of England and Ireland: nor was it at all to his purpose. If any union, other than that of a provincial government under England, had been, Ireland had made no laws more than Wales.'[47]

What Maynard actually said, after reviewing the case-law, was that 'Ireland is united to England by way of subordination: our laws bind them, though theirs not us. This shows how much they are bound by our law: but the question is, how far the laws of Ireland bind in England?' After exploring the difference between Ireland and Scotland, he came to his two principal submissions. First, the Irish parliament had been given a legislative authority by the English parliament, and that authority must extend to matters of personal status. If the consequence was that a person could inherit in England, it was not because the Irish parliament had purported to alter the English law of inheritance but was merely a consequence of altering the status of an individual.[48] There would be a similar result if the Irish parliament validated a marriage which was void at common law; the issue born after the marriage would be legitimate, and therefore capable of being an heir in England as well as Ireland. His second submission, amply supported by Coke's report of *Calvin's Case*,[49] was that allegiance is owed to a king, not a kingdom: 'Allegiance and subjection relate to the person of the king in his natural capacity, and follow the person of the king; therefore when by the law of England the Parliament of Ireland had power to naturalise, it cannot be restrained to that kingdom, for it follows the person of the king, not as he is king of that kingdom, but as he is king.'

The only report in print derived from any of the participants is that written by Sir John Vaughan, the presiding judge, which ought therefore to be the most reliable. According to his own report,

---

47 Vaugh at pp. 298–99. But see *Treby MS* (below, note 53), p. 323: 'To do my brother Maynard right, I must say, 'tis a mistake to say he affirmed there was any union between the kingdoms ... No question but they are distinct kingdoms, and have distinct parliaments etc.; but that does not prove anything to the question'.

48 But see *Treby MS* (below, note 53), p. 323, *per* Vaughan CJ: 'Nor did [Maynard] affirm that Nicholas inherited as an effect of the Irish act, but as a consequence introduced by the law of England. Ireland did no more than concerned themselves; but the English law added the rest, viz. that he should have here the privilege and benefit of not being an alien.'

49 7 Co Rep at 9b–10a, citing *Cobledike's Case* (temp. Edw. I) from 'Hengham's reports', presumably an early year-book.

Vaughan CJ pointed out the obvious inconvenience of allowing the plaintiff's argument, because it would mean that persons whom the English parliament might be unwilling to naturalise could nevertheless become naturalised in England without the consent of the English nation given in parliament. On the other hand, Vaughan CJ warned that the judges 'must judge according as the law is, not as it ought to be', and 'if inconveniences necessarily follow out of the law, only the parliament can cure them'.[50] However, Vaughan CJ's report is difficult to understand in isolation; and it ends in confusion, with some garbled notes pro and contra as to whether there was a union between Ireland and England.[51] He ends by saying that the court was equally divided and that he and Tyrrell J held for the plaintiff.[52] The puzzles may be resolved by recourse to a very full manuscript report by George Treby of the Middle Temple (the future chief justice of the common pleas), which is now in the Middle Temple library.[53] It accords fairly closely with Ventris, but is much more detailed and distinguishes more clearly between the remarks of the individual judges.

The answer to the final puzzle is that the judges were equally divided on the case as pleaded, because Vaughan CJ did not consider that the defendant had made out a sufficient title to defeat the plaintiff. On the merits, however, Vaughan CJ agreed with the two who favoured the defendant, in other words, that Nicholas could not inherit land in England. Only Tyrrell J, therefore, upheld the plaintiff's claim that Nicholas had been naturalised for the purposes of inheriting land in England.[54] All the judges agreed that English

50 Vaugh at p. 285.
51 But see Vaugh at p. 300: 'Secondly, he [Wylde J] said England and Ireland were two distinct kingdoms, and no otherwise united than because they had one sovereign. Had this been said of Scotland and England, it had been right, for they are both absolute kingdoms and each of them *sui juris*. But Ireland far otherwise, for it is a dominion belonging to the crown of England, and [it] follows that it cannot be separate from it ... Thirdly, that distinct kingdoms cannot be united but by mutual acts of parliament. True, if they be kingdoms *sui juris* and independent upon each other, as England and Scotland ...'
52 This misled McIlwain into thinking that the judges were equally divided on the merits: *American Revolution*, p. 97.
53 There is no call-mark. It is referred to here as *Treby MS*. Quotations are reproduced by kind permission of the treasurer and masters of the Bench of the Middle Temple.
54 He seems to have shifted his ground since *Collingwood v. Pace* (1664), above note 36, when he was one of the three dissentient judges who thought the English act of naturalisation was ineffective to support John's claim, partly on

Line drawing of Sir George Treby, Lord Chief Justice of the
Court of Common Pleas, by Robert White, 1694

law had been introduced to Ireland by King John, subsequently to its conquest; that Serjeant Maynard was wrong in suggesting that this had the sanction of an English act of parliament, though it made no difference because it was a lawful thing for a king to do in respect of a conquered country; and that the Irish parliament thereby had legislative powers similar to those of the English parliament, save that Ireland remained subordinate to England. Whether and to what extent England could legislate for Ireland was not in issue, but there was no question that Ireland could not alter the law of England. So much was agreed by all four judges. What, then, was the point of disagreement?

To understand the difference of opinion, it will be convenient to begin with Tyrrell J's dissenting judgment, though it was the third to be delivered. It was in essence an adoption of Maynard's submissions. He began with the authority of the Irish parliament:

I shall agree that it is a distinct, and also a conquered kingdom ... It being Christian, when it was conquered, their laws continued till such time as an alteration was made of them: *Calvin's case*, 17b. 'Tis not material to inquire what those their laws were; but it appears they were barbarous, uncertain, and bad enough ... And it is agreed, *Calvin's case*, 22, 23, that King John by a charter introduced the English laws into Ireland, and thereby they come to have parliaments there. Now, whether this charter were confirmed by parliament or no, is not now to be questioned. There is a maxim in law which will decide it, *In iis quae diuturnitate temporis confirmantur omnia praesumentur esse solenniter facta* ... Hence, the constitution of the government there being agreeable thus to that of England, the Parliament of Ireland had the same power to make laws as the Parliament of England ... Now, if they have this power to make laws, I may *audacter dicere* that they are not restrained from naturalising men ... Unless the parliament there be unlimited, the laws of the two kingdoms are not alike. In all this, I save the superiority to the king and Parliament of England. The Irish laws (if they appear inconvenient) may be controlled and reformed in the English Parliament; but not by the common law and the judges. For, I say again, we must intend the Parliament of Ireland to be legally and well constituted. Certainly, else, it had never been allowed and taken notice of so long. And it is not necessary to produce the original institution ...[55]

the grounds that an act of naturalisation was not so extensive as de facto birth in a country, and that such legislation ought to be construed strictly: 1 Sid at p. 197 (passages quoted above, note 38, and below, note 59).

55 *Treby MS*, pp. 317–19. This passage is heavily abridged in Ventris.

If, then, the Irish parliament had the power to naturalise, an act of naturalisation there might take effect in England, since it did not work any alteration of English law – which itself recognised the concept of naturalisation – but merely altered the status of individual persons:

2 R. 3. 12: *Hibernia habet parliamentum et faciunt leges*. And in 4 Inst. 452 it is said, they may naturalise an alien; and if they do so, he is all one with an Irish man born. Neither doth it follow from hence, that an act of parliament in Ireland could bind England; it is the law of England cooperating with the act that gives the naturalisation an effect here. The act is but *remotio impedimenti*: as if one were attainted by the parliament there, he should forfeit his lands here, and if that act were repealed, he should be restored to them again; yet neither act were obligative in England: the act of Ireland is *causa remota*, or *sine qua non*; the law of England is *causa proxima* ...[56]

This conclusion was reinforced by the doctrine, derived from *Calvin's Case*,[57] that allegiance was owed to the king's person and not to a place: 'Allegiance is due to the king in respect of his protection and government which is over all his countries and dominions, as well where his writ runs as where not. It is due to the king's person, and is not confined within any place ... He can't be liege in one kingdom and not in the other; for that makes allegiance due to the kingdom and not to the king, which cannot be.'[58] Nevertheless, he added, for good measure:

... admitting naturalisation might be restrained to a place, I think this act, as 'tis penned, does not restrain it to Ireland. It does not exclude England ... and I do not suppose the parliament was ignorant of the consequence of it. Had the act expressly limited it to Ireland, the act had been good but the limitation void; for 'tis not in human power so to limit allegiance. Beside, we are to expound acts liberally, which restore nature, as acts of naturalisation do: for 'tis civil constitutions which exclude men from enjoying and inheriting in certain kingdoms and places where nature made it free for all men ...[59]

Wylde J took a different view, and it may be easiest to set out his argument in his own words:

56   2 Vent at p. 4. This passage is more abridged in *Treby MS*.
57   7 Co Rep at 9b-10a.
58   *Treby MS*, pp. 319–20.
59   Ibid., pp. 321–22. *Cf. Collingwood v. Pace* (1664) 1 Sid 193 at p. 197, where Tyrrell J was one of the three judges who apparently held that 'no statute of naturalisation shall be taken by equity, because it carries with it a prejudice to the subjects in general, by making other sharers with them ... and also subjects may thereby be disinherited of their lands' [passage translated].

I hold that a naturalisation in Ireland does not make a man inheritable in England. The Irish Parliament cannot bind the Englishmen in their real estates or personal estates till they come within that kingdom; which will appear from the relation of that kingdom to the kingdom of England etc. But to make myself more clearly understood, I will reduce my discourse to these five particulars, which are the reasons of my opinion:

1. Ireland is a distinct kingdom from England till Henry II completed the conquest of it. It was distinct in its very laws and government as much as Spain is now. By his conquest, he brought it *infra dominium Angliae* not *infra regnum Angliae*. It being a Christian kingdom, the ancient laws of it remained notwithstanding the conquest, until the conqueror made an alteration of them, as my Lord Coke rightly observes, Libro 7° *Calvin's Case*, fo. 17b. And no such alteration being in the time of Henry II or Richard I, the Irish remained governed by the Irish laws, or the Brehon laws as some call them (but they are angry at that name). Then King John … published the English laws and commanded the due execution of them there, and did order and settle the government there in all points according to the model of the commonwealth of England … so that there is a resemblance in the laws now; and there is an union of sovereignty, but no union of the kingdoms; nor can an union of kingdoms or of laws, as is said 4 Inst. 347, well be without authority of parliament of either side; and my Lord Coke, *ibidem*, says he never read of any union of divided kingdoms, and therefore conceives it to be without precedent. All the royal ensigns of these two kingdoms are distinct; they have several great seals, parliaments, courts of justice, great officers, dignities, etc., and therefore Ireland is truly said to be a distinct dominion and no part of the kingdom of England, 4 Inst. 349. And there was never an act made for the union and consolidation of them, though often endeavoured. In 28 Hen. VIII, c. 25 and 26, and 33 Hen. VIII, c. 1, in the Irish Statutes collected by Bolton, there is an union declared, and Ireland is said to be united and knit to the imperial crown of England; but that must be understood, that they are united under one governor, not into one government …
2. Ireland is an inferior kingdom to England, and therefore incongruous they should bind us. We reverse their errors. Our great seal passes there, theirs not here. The king may command his nobles of Ireland to come to his Parliament of England, 4 Inst. 350, according to the precedent of 8 Edw. II. Such general words in an English act as 'all the king's dominions' extend the act to Ireland, 4 Inst. 351. No parliament is held there but by authority under the great seal of England, and the bills which they pass are kept here …
3. Great mischiefs would ensue upon the introduction of aliens by such means, as, discovering the secrets, perverting the revenue, and betraying the safety of the kingdom etc. *Calvin's Case*,18b. And the Irish would have had it in their power to naturalise all foreigners. Had they enacted that Patrick should enjoy these his uncle George's lands, no man will say this had been good. And shall they do that by a windlass ['windelace'], which they could not do directly? …

4. We have nobody to represent us in an Irish Parliament. Now the reason
   of the great obligatory force of an act of parliament is, because every man
   is personally or representatively there, and may speak for himself in his
   concerns.
5. The difficulty and disappointment of the great endeavours to make the
   Scots inheritable here ... But, were the law as 'tis contended to be in this
   case, King James need not have troubled the English Parliament; he might
   have accomplished his design by such an act of parliament as this in
   Ireland.[60]

Wylde J then went on to answer a number of arguments made on
the other side. It might be objected, he said, that 'the kingdoms
are united in their laws, and that shows an union of the kingdoms,
and it must be intended to be done by act of parliament; for it
can't be without it'. The answer was that 'there is an agreement
and resemblance between their laws, but their laws are not united
and become one':

The last indeed can't be done without act of parliament, but the first may;
for a conqueror may, and in this very case did, establish laws by his
charter.[61] There is no such Irish act appears; and, if it did, it would not bind
us. Beside, if there were an act to unite laws, it would not unite the
kingdoms. But, for doing that, there ought to be express words, as in 27 Hen.
VIII, c. 26, that His Majesty's country or dominion of Wales shall be, stand
and continue for ever from henceforth, incorporated, united and annexed to
and with this his realm of England ...[62]

Archer J delivered an opinion substantially agreeing with
Wylde J, and pointing out that the Irish act did not purport to
make Scotsmen liege subjects of England, but only of Ireland; and
that although native Irishmen were by English law subjects of
England, it did not follow that those naturalised by Irish law
should be in the same position for the purposes of English law.[63]

---

60 *Treby MS*, pp. 309–13.
61 In an endnote (p. 333), Treby adds: 'Agreeable to what is delivered above
   concerning a conqueror's power to give laws to a conquered country, I have
   been acquainted with the opinion of Attorney-General Noy, delivered to King
   Charles I upon a reference to the said attorney concerning Newfoundland, viz.
   that the king alone, without parliament, might makes laws for the governing
   of that place, Newfoundland, it being an acquest. And this opinion was lately
   affirmed by Sir Jeoffry Palmer now Attorney-General ...'.
62 *Treby MS*, p. 313.
63 Ibid., pp. 314–17.

Vaughan CJ undertook the difficult task of moderating between these different views. 'I shall clear my way,' he began,[64] 'by rectifying some mistakes, particularly some committed by my brother Wylde. I do not, as he does, take the question to be a slight question and the case clear.' In particular, Wylde J was wrong in his remarks about union:

> He said there is no other union, but that they are under one sovereign. That were true of Scotland, but not of Ireland; for 'tis a parcel of the royalty of England, follows its crown, and is obliged by its laws.[65] He said there could be no union but by parliaments on both sides.[66] But that is true only of kingdoms independent one upon the other. When Edward I made his war in France for which that great aid was given, upon the peace made Gascony and Guienne were, by parliaments on both sides, united to the crown of England ...[67]

It was also wrong to say that, Ireland being a distinct kingdom, it could not make any law obligative to England, because on that argument England could not make any law obligative to Ireland. However, Wylde J had recovered his position by rightly saying that Ireland was in a subordinate position, and that it would be inconvenient if the subordinate parliament could bind the superior.[68] Although it is said that parliament can do anything, that is only true within its sphere of legal competence. Parliament can make a woman a man for civil purposes, for instance by qualifying her to be a barrister or a mayor; but it could not enable a man to bear a child or to be born in a country where he was not born:

---

64 Ibid., p. 322.
65 *Cf.* Vaugh at p. 300: 'Secondly, he said England and Ireland were two distinct kingdoms, and no otherwise united than because they had one sovereign. Had this been said of Scotland and England, it had been right, for they are both absolute kingdoms and each of them *sui juris*. But Ireland far otherwise, for it is a dominion belonging to the crown of England, and [it] follows that it cannot be separate from it ...'.
66 *Cf.* Vaugh at p. 300: 'Thirdly, that distinct kingdoms cannot be united but by mutual acts of parliament. True, if they be kingdoms *sui juris* and independent upon each other, as England and Scotland ...'.
67 *Treby MS*, p. 323.
68 Vaugh at pp. 299–300: 'But he recover'd it by saying that Ireland was subordinate to England and therefore could not make a law obligatory to England. True; for every law is coactive, and it is a contradiction that the inferior, which is civilly the lesser power, should compel the superior, which is the greater power'. *Cf. Treby MS*, p. 323: 'An inferior power cannot compel a superior; and all law is compulsion'.

Nor can they do anything out of their power, as it would be for the Irish Parliament to do anything in France or England. England may make an act which will reach Ireland, but Ireland can't make an act which will reach England. Regularly, a man who is once an alien in England can't be made a liegeman but by English act of parliament. To say, yes he may, by being naturalised in Ireland, is to prove the question by the question ... No fiction shall do anything which concerns the people of England without their consent. By such a naturalisation in parliament a man shall be a subject as to all civil relations, but not as to nature, as to which they have no power ...[69]

The plaintiff's proposition, according to Vaughan CJ, rested upon a logical fallacy:

The syllogism into which the argument of the other side is formed carries a great appearance of strength and reason with it. But I will give a full answer to it by detecting the fallacy, and that is done by putting in a term or addition in the second proposition, which ought to be put in, viz. *by the law of Ireland*. For then it would be thus: he that is a natural born subject of Ireland is a natural born subject of England; he that is naturalised in Ireland is a natural born subject of Ireland *by the law of Ireland*. Ergo what? Certainly, the syllogism has not nor can have any conclusion ... The same argument and syllogism urged before would hold as to Scotland (as well as to Ireland), he that is a natural born subject of Scotland etc. And yet it is not denied, but that the consequence of that would be very dangerous, because we cannot control or alter their laws ...[70]

The Irish parliament, according to Vaughan CJ, simply did not have the power to bind in England:

I will not say that the Irish Parliament have no power to naturalise; though it is certain that naturalisation is one of the great reserves which the king's power does not extend to: and if the king have it not, how can he grant the power of doing it to others? Since this act there have been some particular naturalisations in Ireland, but I did never hear of any there before; though, as I said, I will not deny it to be law. But we know who governed then,[71] and it was a plausible thing to naturalise the *antenati*. Though they have a parliament in Ireland, yet they are not *sui juris*, and that in many particulars; and their own acts confess they are a conquered country. King James asked Mr Selden whether an English act would bind in Ireland, and he answered that it would, and gave him his reasons. By act of parliament of England, any

---

69 *Treby MS*, pp. 325–26.
70 Ibid., p. 328. The same passage is somewhat abridged in Vaugh at p. 288, which raises the possibility that Vaughan's report is merely a draft from which he spoke at greater length.
71 Treby adds a note of explanation: 'Viscount Wentworth'.

part of England or belonging to England might be aliened, as in the case of Gascony; but the like does not hold of an act of parliament of Ireland. An act of parliament of Ireland can't transfer the sovereignty of Ireland to the king's youngest son; for England has an interest in it. So if they should make an act that English acts should not bind them, or that no writs of error should go from hence; it would be void. They may make laws to alter their own property etc., but not the kingdom of Ireland or any part of it, for all that belongs to the kingdom of England. 'Tis like a corporation or foreign plantation; they bind themselves, but not the state of England ...[72]

Therefore, but for the defect in the defendant's pleading, judgment would have been given for the defendant. It seems that the even division prevented any final judgment from being given. However, if we may speak of a *ratio decidendi* in such circumstances, it was not, perhaps, altogether surprising. Naturalisation by statute is a species of legal fiction, and fictions cannot be allowed to cause inconvenience; nor can they work miracles beyond the power of the legislature which passed the statute. The Irish parliament had the power to naturalise aliens for the purposes of Irish law, but not in such a way as to make them non-aliens in England. For what the comparison is worth, it so happens that the same result was reached independently by the English Court of Appeal in 1920, when it held that a former Prussian national who had been naturalised in Australia under an Australian statute of 1903, and who had thereupon taken the oath of allegiance to King George V, was nevertheless an alien in England.[73] Counsel seem to have been unaware of our 1670 case, which was not cited.

Craw v. Ramsay is, to modern legal eyes, more about the conflict of laws and the law of nationality than about Ireland as such. While the law of nationality had been largely settled in 1608, the case shows us that what we perceive as 'conflicts of law' as to personal status were not yet addressed in those terms. And yet the case is of interest to legal historians as showing the considerable sophistication of the arguments, and indeed of the historical research, which could be brought to bear on such matters in the time of Charles II,[74] even by judges of less distinction than Hale.

---

72 *Treby MS*, pp. 331–32.

73 *Markwald v. Attorney General* [1920] 1 Ch 348. In 1842, the colonial office (on the advice of James Stephen) had disallowed a Canadian naturalisation statute which was inconsistent with imperial legislation: see D.B. Swinfen, *Imperial control of colonial legislation 1813–65* (Oxford, 1970), p. 74.

74 *Cf.* the arguments made seventy years later in *Campbell v. Hall* (1774) Lofft

For instance, most or all of the familiar constitutional arguments of the eighteenth century concerning the position of the American colonies, *vis-à-vis* the British parliament, were evidently common currency in Westminster Hall a hundred years earlier – and in a case apparently innocent of any immediate political considerations.[75]

It may also be of some small interest in the legal history of Ireland, as showing what the seventeenth-century judges in England understood by the language of union. They unanimously rejected the suggestion that the Irish legislation of Henry VIII had effected a constitutional union by implication. Union could be achieved by explicit legislation of the English parliament, as in the cases of Wales and Scotland, and with differing legal consequences as set out in the statutes; but Ireland, though having the same common law, remained very different. The relationship was triangular: England and Ireland were both united to the crown of England, but not to each other. Ireland was a distinct dominion and kingdom, albeit subordinate to the kingdom of England by reason of the undisputed conquest by Henry II.[76] The effect of this subordination was that the English parliament could make laws for Ireland, if it did so by express language, and subject to various disputable qualifications found in the year-book cases, whereas the Irish Parliament could not make laws which took effect in England. The first half of that proposition was necessarily

655, especially at pp. 686–88, where counsel was able to refer to Molyneux's treatise (below, note 77), Harris's *Hibernica* (above, note 23), Thomas Leland, *The history of Ireland from the invasion of Henry II* (London and Dublin, 1773) and Lord Lyttelton, *The history of the life of King Henry II* (London, 1767–71) – not to mention *Craw v. Ramsay* (at p. 694).

75 McIlwain, *American Revolution*, pp. 54–55 drew attention to the 'greatest importance' of *Calvin's Case* and *Craw v. Ramsay* for American historians. However, McIlwain's book has been heavily criticised for a simplistic view of the Anglo-Hibernian relationship: see Schuyler, *Parliament and the British empire*; Wheeler, '*Calvin's Case* and the McIlwain-Schuyler Debate', p. 587; Black, "The constitution of empire' (where it is suggested at p. 1172 that McIlwain was wrong with a 'touch of rightness'). See also J.P. Reid, *In a defiant stance* (University Park, Penn., 1977); D.T. Konig, 'Colonization and the common law in Ireland and Virginia, 1569–1634' in J.A. Henretta *et al.* (ed.), *The transformation of early American history: Society, authority and ideology* (New York, 1991), pp. 70–92.

76 This assumption, however, is less than straightforward: see J. Hill, 'Ireland without Union: Molyneux and his legacy' in J. Robertson (ed.), *A union for empire* (Cambridge, 1986), 271, at pp. 278–84; A. Carty, *Was Ireland conquered? International law and the Irish question* (London, 1996).

more controversial than the second, though it is not obvious that the English judges were yet aware of the contrary case. The controversy would flare up again in 1698, when the Dublin arguments of the 1640s were restated by William Molyneux,[77] and the flames were fanned by the British parliament in 1720, when it declared that the kingdom of Ireland had been and was 'subordinate unto and dependent upon the imperial crown of Great Britain, *as being inseparably united*[78] *thereto'*, with the consequence that the British parliament could pass statutes binding in Ireland.[79] But that is another story, the course of which is better known.[80]

77 W. Molyneux's treatise, *The case of Ireland's being bound by acts of parliament in England stated* (Dublin, 1698) was immediately answered by W. Atwood, *The history, and reasons, of the dependency of Ireland upon the imperial crown of the kingdom of England* (London, 1698) and J. Cary, *A vindication of the parliament of England* (London, 1698). For a biography of Molyneux, see J.G. Simms, *William Molyneux of Dublin, 1656–1698* (Dublin, 1982). For the impact of his treatise, see Hill, 'Ireland without Union'.

78 For the language of union, see also 1 Will & Mary, stat. 1, c. 9 (1689), which declared that Ireland was 'annexed and united to the imperial crown', and that therefore Irish parliaments held without royal authority were illegal and void.

79 *An act for the better securing the dependency of Ireland upon the crown of Great Britain*, 6 Geo 1, c. 5 (repealed 1782). The immediate occasion was the case of *Annesley v. Sherlock*, in which the British house of lords denied the appellate authority of the Irish house of lords, a determination confirmed by s. 2 of the act.

80 For the story from 1688 to 1720, see M.S. Flaherty, 'The empire strikes back: *Annesley v. Sherlock* and the triumph of imperial parliamentary supremacy' in *Columbia Law Rev*, 87 (1987), 593. See also Hill, 'Ireland without Union'.

Edmund Burke and the law

R.B. McDOWELL*

EDMUND BURKE, BORN in Dublin in 1729, grew up in a very practical legal environment. His father, Richard Burke, was an attorney in the court of exchequer. Richard had been born a catholic but had conformed, otherwise he would have been debarred from the legal profession. However, as it seems that much of the law business in Dublin was handled by 'new converts',[1] Richard Burke would not have been unpleasantly conspicuous for his change of denomination. Indeed his catholic connections may have been useful when it came to building up a practice. In any event, according to Edmund Burke, his father was 'for many years not only in the first rank but the very first man of his profession in point of practice and credit' and, after maintaining for years a high standard of living and 'some heavy losses by the banks', he was able to leave a substantial sum to his family.[2] Richard's eldest son, Garrett, enrolled as an attorney, working with his father. The second son was Edmund. The third, Richard, after an adventurous but unprofitable career, was called to the English bar when he was forty and through his brother Edmund's influence was elected recorder of Bristol. To go back in the seventeenth century, Edmund Burke was remotely connected through his mother, Mary Nagle, with James Nagle, attorney general of Ireland under James II, and to go forward to the later eighteenth century, Edmund's son Richard was called to the bar in 1780.

Edmund Burke entered Trinity College, Dublin in 1744, was elected a scholar in 1746 and graduated in 1748. In his senior sophister year he was introduced to jurisprudence, Pufendorf being one of the prescribed authors. Pufendorf (1632–94) was praised by Mackintosh – with significant qualifications: 'Without

---

* The text of an address delivered in The Queen's University, Belfast on 24 October 1998.
1 H. Boulter, *Letters written by His Excellency Hugh Boulter ... to several ministers of state* (Oxford, 1769), i, 226.
2 *The correspondence of Edmund Burke*, ed. T.W. Copeland (Cambridge, 1958–1978) [hereafter referred to as *Correspondence*], i, 274.

the genius of Grotius', Mackintosh wrote, 'and with very inferior learning' Pufendorf treated natural law 'with sound sense, with clear method, with extensive and accurate knowledge and with a copiousness of detail, sometimes indeed tedious, but always instructive and satisfactory'.[3] Pufendorf taught that the Creator, besides giving to mankind divine law, had implanted in men an awareness of the rules that should govern them in their relations to one another – rules which taken together comprised natural law, an essential element in all legal systems. The conviction that law fundamentally was of divine origin must have awakened a ready response in a religiously-minded youth such as Burke.

For two years after graduating Burke stayed on in Dublin, enjoying the entitlements of his scholarship, dabbling in journalism and reading widely. He could have attended the lectures of the regius professor of laws and of the professor of oratory and history, assuming they were delivered. But the holders of those chairs at the end of the 1740s were undistinguished senior fellows. In 1750 Burke left Dublin to read for the bar. He had already been entered as a law student in the Middle Temple in 1747 when still an undergraduate. This step suggests that his father, a successful attorney presumably concerned with upward mobility, was keen that his bright son should join the senior branch of the profession and, a masterful man, he was ready to subsidise his son generously as a law student. How far Burke himself was eager to embark on a career at the bar is hard to say. He had already a number of other intellectual interests and aspirations. But reading for the bar provided him with an immediate objective and left him fairly free to have a stimulating life in London. It is also impossible to say which bar, the English or the Irish, he intended to practice at, since as a prelude to admission to the Irish bar a law student had to spend 'eight terms commons' in an English inn of court.[4] So the fact that Burke entered the Middle Temple leaves the matter open. Of course if he had been called to the Irish bar, his father controlling a supply of briefs could have given him a good start.

In the Middle Temple it was required that every person should keep commons in hall for twelve terms before being called to the

---

3 J. Mackintosh, *The miscellaneous works of the right honourable Sir James Mackintosh* (London, 1846), i, 355.
4 C. Kenny, *King's Inns and the kingdom of Ireland: the Irish 'Inn of Court' 1541–1800* (Dublin, 1992), p. 179.

bar – the only requirement except, of course, the prescribed fees.[5] It is easy to sneer at the system of eating one's way to a professional qualification. But a barrister's clients were hard-headed attorneys, and a law student who hoped to earn his living as a barrister, in addition to dining, read systematically and attended the courts taking notes and even perhaps worked in an attorney's office to gain some knowledge of procedure. Burke certainly made an effort to prepare himself for the bar. After rather more than a year in London, referring to his legal studies, he wrote: 'I read as much as I can (which is however but a little), and I am just beginning to know something of what I am about, which till very lately I did not; this study carries no difficulty to those who already understand it and to those who will never understand it, and for all between those extremes (God knows) they have a hard task of it'.[6] Burke writes modestly, but he was possessed by a driving determination to master intellectually any subject he was engaged with and in his efforts to comprehend the law he must have been encouraged by the admiring and cheerful companionship of his cousin, William Burke, also a student at the Middle Temple, who was called to the bar in 1755.

Burke was soon distracted from his legal work by other interests – poetry, history, philosophy, general literature – 'the fatal itch that makes me scribble still', travel and London life. So, after some years he came to the conclusion that the law 'has been confined and drawn up into a narrow and inglorious study … insomuch that the study of our jurisprudence presented to liberal, well-educated minds, even in the best authors, hardly anything but barbarous terms, ill explained; a coarse but not plain expression; an indigested method, and a species of reasoning the very refuse of the schools'. 'Young men', he added, 'were sent away with an incurable and, if we regard the manner of handling rather than the substance, a well-founded disgust'.[7] One young man was ready to broaden the English legal mind. At the age of about twenty-eight, Burke, who seemed to have already lost interest in a career at the bar, decided to embark on a history of the English law, a work of which only a few introductory paragraphs survive. English lawyers,

---

5   W. Holdsworth, *A history of English law* (London, 1922–66), xii, 24.
6   *Correspondence*, i, p. iii.
7   *The writings and speeches of Edmund Burke*, ed. P. Langford (Oxford, 1981–)
    [hereafter referred to as *Writings and speeches*], i, 323–24.

he wrote, laboured under two misapprehensions – that the English law had remained very much 'in the same state from antiquity' and that it was entirely English in origin, 'in every respect peculiar to this island'.[8] He intended to show that the English law had evolved through the centuries, drawing from a variety of sources, Anglo-Saxon custom, Norman law, canon law and civil law.

That Burke had been greatly stimulated by his legal studies emerges in a work he wrote at the outset of his political career. When at the beginning of the 1760s he was private secretary to William Gerard Hamilton, the Irish chief secretary, Burke drafted a sweeping attack on the penal laws against the Irish catholics which, in addition to citing some of the standard arguments for the modification or complete abolition of the laws – that they hindered Irish economic development, introduced discord into family life, reflected an anachronistic intolerance and discriminated against a loyal section of the community – he endeavoured to show in a few paragraphs studded with quotations from Cicero, Philo, Suarez and the Digest, that they were against 'the acknowledged principles of jurisprudence'. They challenged, Burke contended, the two great principles on which law was based – equity, which 'grows out of the great rule of equality which is grounded upon our common nature', and utility, 'that is to say general and public utility'. The consent of the people, actual or implied, he wrote, was absolutely essential to the validity of a law. Admittedly, the people were presumed to consent to whatever the legislature ordained for their benefit and should 'acquiesce in it ... as an act of homage and just deference to a reason which the necessity of government has made superior to their own'. But the exclusion of a great body of men from the common advantages of society could not be intended for their good and could not be ratified even by an implied consent. Indeed, he stated, if the people, or presumably, a majority, consented to a law prejudicial to the whole community, it would be against 'the principle of a superior law ... I mean the will of Him who gave us our nature and impressed an invariable law upon it'. Finally, 'it would be hard to point out any error more truly subversive of all the order and beauty, of all the peace and happiness of human society, than the position that any body of men have a right to make what laws they please'.[9]

8 Ibid., p. 323.
9 *Writings and speeches*, ix, 453–58 and 462.

This is a suitable point to stress to what an extent Burke's reverence for law was closely connected with his religious beliefs. An evangelically-minded youth, attending a quaker school at an impressionable age, a loyal and devoted member of the Church of England, he was tolerant of other christian denominations and had a measure of respect for other great religions, 'the synagogue, the mosque, the pagoda'.[10] Throughout his political career he frequently referred to Providence, apparently not as a synonym for inevitable or vague destiny, but as denoting a merciful and just Creator, keeping a concerned watch over humankind. Law, 'beneficence acting by a rule',[11] was God's gift to man, and we were all born in subjection 'to one great immutable, pre-existent law, prior to all our devices, prior to all our contrivances, paramount to our very being itself, by which we are knit and connected in the eternal frame of the universe, out of which we cannot stir'.[12] Law, rightly conceived, representing the Creator's intentions, was, along with other institutions and customs, prejudices and traditions, an important element in binding society together. Broadening down from precedent to precedent, it vividly illustrated how the rules governing human behaviour in society evolved. Indeed, when Burke wanted to illustrate how greatly Englishmen were indebted to past generations, he employed a legal metaphor: we 'derive all we possess as an inheritance from our forefathers' – 'an entailed inheritance'.[13] Moreover one very significant legal principle, prescription, part of the law of nature, was of essential social value, because it protected private property, inherited and acquired, the great guarantee of independence and happiness.[14] So anxious was Burke to preserve property rights, that he went so far as to imply that parliamentary interference with those rights could be quashed by the courts: 'we entertain', he wrote, 'a high opinion of legislative authority, but we never dreamt that parliament had any right whatever to overrule prescription or force a currency of their own fiction in the place of that which is real and recognised by the law of nations'.[15]

---

10 *Correspondence*, iv, 85.
11 *Writings and speeches*, viii, 109.
12 *Writings and speeches*, vi, 350.
13 *Writings and speeches*, viii, 81–84.
14 *Writings and speeches*, ii, 65 and viii, 220; *Correspondence*, vi, 42–44.
15 *Writings and speeches*, viii, 221.

Law was not only a cohesive element in British society. It was, Burke declared, 'a similitude ... of religion, laws and manners'[16] which bound the nations of Europe together. Europe, Burke considered, was a Commonwealth, 'virtually one great state', based on the general law derived from German customary law and feudal law, all 'improved and digested into a system' by Roman law.[17] Going much further afield in 1788, during Hastings' impeachment, he emphasised that in Asia as in Europe the same law of nations prevailed: 'the same principles are continually resorted to, the same maxims sacredly held'.[18] All civilisation, in short, was underpinned by the same legal fundamentals. This was well illustrated, Burke pointed out, during the American war of independence by the respect 'civilised states' paid to the rules of war, established not 'in black letter by statute and record' but by reason, 'by the convention of parties', and by the authority of writers, who took the laws and maxims not from their own invention and ideas but from the consent and sense of ages and from precedent. One of the rules was that the private property of individuals in a conquered territory was immune from seizure. After all every monarch, even a conqueror, was bound to respect property rights – 'a principle inspired by the Divine Author of all good'.[19]

In the 1790s, French developments forced Burke to face an important question in international law. In what circumstances was it justifiable for a foreign power or powers, 'the potentates of Europe', to interfere in the domestic affairs of another country? Burke had to admit that the rules relating to this question were uncertain. But fortunately from his point of view, it seemed that jurists were agreed that when 'a country was divided [between warring factions] other powers were free to take which side they pleased' – a position upheld by 'a very republican writer', Vattell. Burke also justified the allied invasion of France by citing Roman civil law, pointing out that 'the law of neighbourhood', an important head of praetorian law, would not permit a man to carry out operations on his own property detrimental to his neighbour.[20] It

---

16 *Writings and speeches*, iii, 195.
17 *Writings and speeches*, ix, 248–49.
18 *Writings and speeches*, vii, 317.
19 *The parliamentary history of England from the earliest period to the year 1803* (London, 1806–20)[hereafter referred to as *Parliamentary history*], xxii, 228–30.
20 *Writings and speeches*, viii, 74 and ix, 250; *Correspondence*, vi, 317.

should be added that, when optimistically looking forward to the restoration of the *ancien régime* in France, Burke revealed his ingrained respect for law. Though, he stated, 'bloody and merciless offenders' must be called to account, no man should be punished until after a trial 'carried on with all that caution and deliberation which has been used in the best times and precedents ... of the French jurisprudence'. In addition, anything which could be brought forward in mitigation of an offence was to be taken into consideration: 'Mercy is not a thing opposed to justice'.[21]

In dealing with domestic questions Burke displayed the same reverence for law he showed in the international sphere. Shortly after he entered the house of commons, Burke pronounced that 'whatever the sacred seal of judicature impressed upon it, let it rest inviolate for ever'.[22] How concerned he was to protect the sanctity of the law was illustrated a few years later by his attitude to the juries bill of 1771. As an opposition Whig he supported the demand that in a trial for libel the jury should be entitled to give a general verdict on the whole issue, and he wished the question to be settled by an act empowering the jury to give such a general verdict. But he was definitely against a declaratory act enunciating that the judges had been wrong in restricting juries to finding only on the fact of publication: a declaratory act, 'a measure which tended to blacken the character of the judges', was, he wrote, 'utterly impracticable'.[23]

On crime and punishment Burke's views were enlightened and humane, but not excessively sentimental. As a schoolboy, discussing the situation of an acquaintance facing the possibility of a murder charge, Burke wrote that 'human sufferings call for human compassion'; thirty-five years later, as an influential MP, he emphasised that justice should be tempered with mercy.[24] But he also stressed that it was wrong to yield to the compassion which was rooted in 'a flimsy, prevaricating, petty, peevish morality, incompatible with the dignity of public justice'. There is nothing, he remarked, 'so immoral as perverted morality'.[25] This insistence on the importance of controlling compassion was, it is scarcely

---

21 *Writings and speeches*, viii, 495–96.
22 *Writings and speeches*, ii, 225.
23 *Correspondence*, ii, 187.
24 *Correspondence*, i, 22; *Parliamentary history*, xxi, 388.
25 *Parliamentary history*, xxx, 981.

surprising, a reaction to what Burke regarded as misguided sympathy for Warren Hastings in his impeachment ordeal.

Admitting that punishment was 'a melancholy necessity'[26] and was usually greater than the offence merited, Burke emphasised that the penalty should be proportionate to the offence and should operate as a deterrent rather than as a torment. Considering in 1789 that 'the whole system of the penal laws in this country is radically defective' and requiring revision, he was strongly against the multiplication of offences. The existing laws would often meet the case if the magistrates were less negligent in enforcing them. He also suggested that, where possible, instead of creating a criminal offence a civil remedy should be provided – the damage could be assessed by a jury and the injured party receive compensation.[27] Naturally he was highly critical of conventional reliance on capital punishment. Experience had shown, he declared, that capital punishment was not more certain to prevent crimes that inferior penalties, and with the excessive use of the death penalty 'the laws lose their terror in the eyes of the wicked and their reverence in the eyes of the virtuous'.[28]

A capital sentence was often commuted to transportation, which to Burke was an acceptable penalty – 'an unpleasant remedy, but still a remedy in a desperate disease'.[29] But he considered it should not be inflicted for trivial offences and that the convicts should not be transported to an unhealthy zone, such as Gambia, 'the capital seat of plague, pestilence and famine'. Burke saw transportation as a desirable substitute 'for the butchery which we call justice', and as a means for keeping the wicked from being let loose on the world and for rendering those of mischievous disposition useful.[30] Referring to a well-known confidence trickster about to be transported, Burke painted transportation in glowing colours:

He goes to a place [Botany Bay] where he is not oppressed by the judgment he has suffered and where none but honest ways of life are open to him. The climate is good, the soil is not unfavourable. There is even some choice in the society. God knows that they who have suffered, and even deservedly suffered, by the sentence of the law, are very far from the worst or most

---

26 *Correspondence*, iv, 134.
27 *Parliamentary history*, xxviii, 146.
28 *Writings and speeches*, iii, 338–39 and 614.
29 *Correspondence*, viii, 328.
30 *Correspondence*, iii, 252.

disagreeable men in the world. I assure you that if I were to fall into a misfortune of this sort, and have youth and vigour of body and mind, I should think this change of place a thing to be desired, and not shunned.[31]

A substantial category of the prison population who were not criminals but debtors, detained by their creditors, aroused the sympathy of many peers and MPs, including Burke, who on one occasion wrote to an undistinguished poet imprisoned for debt that 'some mistakes in conduct are natural or almost inevitable to men of lively imaginations and narrow circumstances, particularly during the warmth and openness of youth'. It was inhuman, Burke argued, to keep thousands in a state of slavery, detained not by the judgment of a court but at 'the arbitrary discretion of a private, nay interested and irritated, individual'. Moreover, in addition to those debtors in prison there was a multitude of insolvents hiding in terror, 'a deadweight on the community'. A modification of the law, Burke argued, would protect credit by making lenders more cautious.[32]

Burke's belief that punishment should be tempered by well-measured leniency is illustrated by his attitude during the aftermath of the Gordon riots (riots in which he was in considerable personal danger). He urged the government, while discouraging violence, 'to avoid an injudicious severity'. 'The appetite of justice', he declared, 'is easily satisfied and is best nourished with the least possible blood'.[33] He strongly deplored 'long strings of executions'.[34] Instead, after carefully examining all the cases of convicted rioters, the government should select a small number, at the utmost six, 'sufficient to mark and discountenance the general spirit of tumult', to be executed in the most solemn manner that could be devised. All the other malefactors were to be sent to the hulks or enlisted in the navy. Incidentally, he was inclined to be more lenient to the 'common plunderers' than to those rioters who had been led into crime 'by a false or pretended principle of religion'. Naturally enough, as a zealous advocate for the repeal of penal laws against the catholics, Burke blamed anti-catholic propaganda for the riots, and as a member of the parliamentary opposition, he

31 *Correspondence*, viii, 328.
32 *Correspondence*, iii, 231; *Writings and speeches*, iii, 636; *Parliamentary history*, xxix, 512–13.
33 *Writings and speeches*, iii, 618.
34 *Correspondence*, iv, 255.

asserted that the government's failure to take firm measures had encouraged the rioters.[35]

Though Burke gave serious attention to crime and punishment and occasionally expressed his opinion on issues relating to the subject, he never participated in a major campaign to reform the criminal law. In fact, it might be said that his efforts in that direction were few and ineffective. In 1776, he introduced a bill to prevent the plundering of shipwrecks, 'a barbarous practice'. But his plan for levying compensation from the area in which the crime was committed, 'a remedy' which, he remarked, 'may be justified by the violence of the disease', aroused considerable opposition. Also it was asserted that, given the legislation already in force, the bill was unnecessary. Understandably, then, it never reached the statute book.[36] Burke was eager to abolish the pillory. After an outburst of mob violence had resulted in two pilloried criminals being killed, the pillory had, he declared, been transformed from 'a punishment of shame' into 'an instrument of death', 'a death of torment'.[37] He initiated a discussion in the house of commons, but does not seem to have taken the question further and the pillory was not abolished until 1837. In 1785, Burke informed the house that he intended to propose a series of resolutions on the treatment of convicts awaiting transportation;[38] but he does not seem to have persevered, possibly because from 1787 convicts were steadily being transported to Australia. Finally, near the end of his parliamentary career, in 1791, he expressed regret that he never had an opportunity of bringing forward the question of imprisonment for debt, and offered his services to those 'who might bring it up'.[39]

In one sphere, the law of marriage (or 'family law') he enunciated firm views, reflecting profound convictions. In 1781, he opposed Fox's attempt to remove the bar on minors marrying without parental consent. Matrimony, Burke emphatically declared, was instituted not for 'mere animal propagation', but for 'men's nutrition, their education and their establishment' and for answering all the purposes of a rational and moral being. Men, he pointed

---

35 *Writings and speeches*, iii, 612–18.
36 Ibid., p. 225; *Correspondence*, iii, 141; *Parliamentary history*, xviii, 1298–1302.
37 *Writings and speeches*, iii, 585.
38 *Parliamentary history*, xxv, 391–92.
39 *Parliamentary history*, xxix, 512.

out, were well qualified for propagation before they were sufficiently qualified by 'mental prudence and by acquired skill in trades and professions for the maintenance of a family'. Surely, to allow someone 'to introduce citizens into the Commonwealth before a rational security can be given that he may provide for them and educate them, as citizens ought to be provided for and educated, is totally incongruous with the whole order of society'.[40] And he called on the house of commons to have mercy on the youth of both sexes and protect them from their youth and inexperience. Ten years earlier, in a debate on divorce, having declared that 'the foundation of all the order, harmony, tranquillity and even the civilisation that is amongst us turns upon two things, the indissolubility of marriage and the freedom of the female sex', he strongly but unsuccessfully supported the proposal that a clause should be inserted in all divorce acts forbidding the marriage of adulterous parties and providing that their children should not be legitimised. This, he said, would not punish adultery but make it inconvenient. The stronger the marriage tie, he explained, the 'more easy it was for women to move freely in polished society'.[41] Naturally, then, at the end of the century he denounced both the French national assembly for declaring that marriage was a civil contract, dissoluble by mutual consent and on a number of other grounds and the assembly's successor, the convention, for placing bastards on the same footing as legitimate children. The new French approach to divorce aimed not at 'the relief of domestic uneasiness' but at 'the total corruption of all morals, the total disconnection of social life'.[42]

At a late stage in his political career, Burke, who in early manhood had turned away from the bar, found himself playing the role of a prosecuting counsel as the leader of the managers appointed by the house of commons to conduct the impeachment of Warren Hastings. From the early 1780s, Burke had been intensely interested in Indian affairs, and, having examined a vast mass of manuscript and printed material and having examined a number of witnesses, he had decided that Hastings, the governor-general, a man actuated by 'avarice, rapacity, pride, cruelty, ferocity, malignancy of temper, haughtiness and insolence' was 'the scourge of

---

40 *Parliamentary history*, xxii, 410.
41 *Writings and speeches*, ii, 357–58.
42 *Writings and speeches*, ix, 243–45.

India',[43] and he pledged himself 'to God, to his country and to the unfortunate and plundered inhabitants of India that he would bring to justice the greatest delinquent that India ever saw'. There were, he explained to the house of commons, three modes by which state delinquents could be proceeded against – a bill of pains and penalties, which Burke rejected as unfair to the accused; a prosecution in the king's bench which, as it would involve a very large indictment, would overwhelm the court, blocking all its normal work; or an impeachment, the prosecution of a great state offender by the house of commons, 'the great inquest of the nation', before the house of lords, 'the most high and supreme court'.[44]

Impeachment, an historic and impressive process, was, according to Burke, 'the cement that binds the constitution together'.[45] But though the threat of impeachment was still part of parliamentary rhetoric and was in 1787 imbedded in the American constitution, it was falling into disuse. Viewed retrospectively, most impeachments had in their inception and progress reflected violent partisanship and better methods for bringing ministers and high officials to account were being developed. So by the mid-nineteenth century a great legal historian could refer to impeachment as 'a cumbersome and unsatisfactory mode of proceeding', and, having Hastings in mind, add that it was 'monstrous that a man should be tortured, at irregular intervals, for seven years, in order that a singularly incompetent tribunal might be addressed ... by Burke and Sheridan, in language far removed from the calmness with which an advocate for the prosecution ought to address a criminal court'.[46] But in 1788 Burke was convinced that an impeachment accorded with the status of the offender and the magnitude of the cause – involving as it did grave crimes, relations between Great Britain and India and the principles which should govern imperial policy.

There was, too, a practical reason for proceeding by impeachment. The house of lords, Burke argued, in a cause within its original jurisdiction, should follow 'the laws and usage of parliament' and should not feel obliged to follow the rules of pleading observed in the inferior courts at Westminister or indeed the rules

---

43 *Writings and speeches*, vi, 275 and v, 476.
44 *Parliamentary history*, xxv, 1060–68; *Writings and speeches*, vi, 51 and 56–57; W. Blackstone, *Commentaries on the laws of England* (5th ed., Oxford, 1773), iv, 259.
45 *Writings and speeches*, vi, 272.
46 J.F. Stephen, *A history of the criminal law of England* (London, 1883), i, 160.

of Roman civil law. At the beginning of his opening speech he reminded the house that 'Your lordships are not bound by any rules whatever, except those of natural, substantial and immutable justice', and he hoped that 'the liberality and nobleness of the sentiments to which you were born' would not, by any abuse of the forms and technical course of the proceedings, deny justice to India.[47] But the peers, conscious perhaps that they were living in an enlightened age and that most of the precedents relating to impeachment were drawn from periods of ruthless civil strife, readily consulted the judges when legal issues arose during the Hastings impeachment, and the judges delivered their opinions privately to the house. The managers bitterly complained that this practice left them in doubt about matters on which they desired to have every light; but, of course, by not stating their opinions publicly the judges deprived the managers of opportunities for challenging them – probably at interminable length.[48] Burke indignantly pointed out that by allowing the judges to decide what evidence should be admitted, the lords were reducing themselves to the level of mere jurors, seriously upsetting the constitutional balance. In 1789 Burke boldly asserted that, though the house of lords was a supreme court of justice, the house of commons, 'the watch, the inquisitor, the purifier of every judicial and executive function', had a degree of control over the upper house in its judicial capacity – 'one of the seeming paradoxes of our constitution', he remarked.[49] Wisely, however, he refrained from attempting to express this paradox in action, an attempt which would presumably have led to a major clash between the two houses.

In a long defence of the managers' conduct of the Hastings prosecution, Burke pleaded eloquently for a flexible approach to the rules of evidence, paying particular attention to the rules relating to circumstantial evidence.[50] In the civil law, he pointed out, many attempts involving much subtle reasoning had been made 'to reduce to rule the principles of evidence or proof' and in ancient times the English common law courts had tended to

---

47 *Writings and speeches*, vi, 276.
48 *Parliamentary history*, xxxi, 315.
49 *Parliamentary history*, xxviii, 1032–34.
50 The report of the committee of managers, which was very largely or wholly the work of Burke, is printed in *Commons' jn.*, xlix, 504–37, and in *Parliamentary history*, xxxi, 287–373 (and see also *Correspondence*, vii, 540).

observe 'a rigid strictness in the application of technical rules'. But, as Burke was quick to point out, human actions were not of 'a metaphysical nature' and could not be 'subjected (without exceptions which reduce it to almost nothing) to any certain rule'. Fortunately, 'the genius of the law of England' permitted 'the general moral necessities of things and the nature of the case' to override even those rules which 'seem to be the very strongest'. Rules which savour of the schools, Burke argued, should yield to experience, observation, good sense, manly reason and human sagacity. He commended Hardwicke and Mansfield for their readiness to enlarge the rules of evidence and disregard useless technicalities, Mansfield being outstanding for his efforts to make the law 'keep pace with the demands of justice'. In short, the need to track down and punish crimes which were difficult to detect 'superseded the theoretic aim at perfection and obliged technical science to submit to practical experience'.[51]

Besides deploring an uncritical and unreasonable adherence to the rules of evidence, Burke also warned against an excessive deference to precedent. Precedents, he stated, should have been created in 'good constitutional times' and be agreeable to the general tenor of legal principles, and he denounced lawyers as 'hunters after precedents' and 'scratchers of parchment'. 'In a question which concerned the safety and welfare of the people', he declared, 'every consideration except what has a tendency to promote these great objects became superseded, *salus populi suprema lex*' (a maxim he would have heard with distaste if advanced in defence of Hastings).[52]

Legal reformers would have highly approved of Burke's fervent concern that legal forms, sometimes archaic, should not obstruct the quest for truth. Unfortunately, however, his reasoned and erudite plea for a common-sense approach to the laws of evidence and the use of precedent was seriously weakened by his disregard for the rights of the accused and his passionate determination to secure Hastings' conviction.

During the impeachment years Burke, much as he esteemed and respected the law, displayed at times a degree of contempt for the English bar. Though he declared in the house of commons

51 *Parliamentary history*, xxxi, 326–42.
52 *Parliamentary history*, xxviii, 1130–33.

that he had for the legal profession 'a degree of veneration, approaching almost to idolatry', he went on to say that he could not help feeling that its members were 'very apt to be influenced by a very natural prejudice, which the French called *esprit de corps*'. This, for instance, explained the antipathy of lawyers to impeachment, a procedure by which those who 'called all others to account' might themselves be brought to trial.[53] In fact, he approved of the country being governed by law, but not by lawyers.[54] Writing to Lord Hailes, the well-known Scottish judge, historian, antiquarian and Christian apologist, Burke remarked that he never thought 'of some of you Scotch gentlemen of the robe without being a little ashamed for England. Our bar does not abound in general erudition – and I am every day more and more convinced that they are not the better professional men from not being more extensively learned'.[55] Two years later he characterised Chief Justice Kenyon, a learned if limited lawyer and a strong supporter of Hastings, as 'a violent, hot-headed vulgar man, without the least tincture of liberality or generous erudition and, though of some low acuteness, is void of anything like enlarged sense'.[56] A few years later, chatting with a young Irish barrister with intellectual inclinations, Burke discussed the legal profession in more general terms. He thought that the law as a profession was 'not calculated to develop the highest powers of the human mind', though he granted that there were several exceptions to this. A barrister's work and studies might sharpen his understanding and give a degree of logical precision to his thinking; but the general effect was 'to reduce the mind from a wholesale to a retail dealer in subordinate and petty topics of information'.[57]

There is an embarrassed fascination in observing Burke, an admirer and ardent defender of historic institutions and well-established corporations, appearing in the guise of an exasperated critic of traditional legal procedures and of the English bar. Burke, of course, could insist that he always distinguished between reform, which was good and innovation, which would probably

---

53 *Parliamentary history*, xxviii, 1234.
54 Ibid., p. 1169.
55 *Correspondence*, vi, 468.
56 Ibid., p. 3.
57 J. Prior, *Memoir of the life and character of ... Edmund Burke* (2nd. ed., London, 1826), ii, 531.

prove disastrous. But his attitude in the late 1780s and 1790s to the legal profession and their procedures can, of course, be largely explained by the course of the Hastings impeachment. The house of lords in its judicial capacity 'corrupted by the Indian malady', the judges whom it consulted, some lawyers in the commons, Hastings' powerful legal team and Thomas Erskine, the great Whig advocate who had appeared for the defence when a pamphleteer was prosecuted for his support of Hastings – all were in Burke's eyes leagued to preserve Hastings, 'the head, the chief, the captain general in iniquity'[58] from the punishment he so richly deserved and consequently to deny justice to the people of India.

It is also possible that Burke may have been influenced by memories of a somewhat domineering, if generous, father, pressing him to enter a profession which, if seriously pursued, would have to a great extent cut him off from enthralling intellectual interests. Moreover, towards the end of his life, he was saddened and puzzled by the 'astonishing and unmerited want of success' at the bar of his brother and his son.[59] Family feeling rendered him oblivious to defects which must have interfered with their careers. Richard, his brother, though undoubtedly intelligent, was convivial and feckless, the very model of a cheerful but almost briefless barrister. His son, though able, industrious and high-minded, was opinionated, over-fluent and rather insensitive to other people's reactions.

Finally, even in a man of outstanding intellectual gifts, personal set-backs can colour ratiocination. In 1784 Burke took an action for libel against the *Public Advertiser* which had accused him of misapplying public money, claiming £5,000 damages. The jury, because they thought 'my only view was to clear myself of the imputation which had been thrown upon me', awarded him only £100. 'A more direct encouragement', he exclaimed, 'could not be given to such practices. £100 is as nothing to the stock of that paper.' In 1797, when he was suing a printer for literary piracy, he angrily complained that the courts 'seemed to be in league with every kind of fraud and injustice', proceeding as if they had an intricate settlement of £10,000 a year to discuss when dealing with 'an affair which might be as well decided in three weeks as in three hundred years'.[60]

58 *Writings and speeches*, vi, 276.
59 *Correspondence*, vii, 596.
60 *Correspondence*, v, 159–60 and 165; ix, 245–46.

Circumstances in fact provoked Burke at times to pronounce that the law was an ass.[61] But though he may, during short bouts of irritation, have impulsively expressed intense exasperation with lawyers, their practices, procedures and prejudices, Burke nevertheless remained convinced that the law, with all its limitations, must be regarded with reverence and that lawyers, with all their faults, performed functions of the utmost value to the community.

61 Mr Bumble's particular grievance (see Charles Dickens, *Oliver Twist* (1838), ch. 51) was removed by the Criminal Justice Act 1925, s. 47.

Manor courts in the west of Ireland before the Famine

RICHARD McMAHON[*]

THE GENERAL BACKGROUND

THE MAJORITY OF MANOR courts in Ireland operated under patents granted in the seventeenth century, when manorial jurisdictions were set out in connection with land grants.[1] Others were established through the individual petitioning of the crown by landlords or by 'prescription',[2] that is, without a royal patent – initiatives which suggest that landlords 'found the courts useful enough to establish them themselves'[3] as a means of regulating their estates.

The manor court operated in two main forms, as a court leet and as a court baron.[4] The court leet was generally held twice a

---

[*] This paper is derived from the author's thesis on 'The courts of petty sessions and the law in pre-Famine Galway', for the degree of Master of Arts in the National University of Ireland, Galway in 1999. I would like to thank Dr Niall O Ciosáin who supervised the thesis on which this paper is based, and Professor Desmond Greer for his valuable editorial work. I alone am responsible for errors.

1 R. Gillespie, 'A manor court in seventeenth-century Ireland' in *Ir Econ Soc Hist*, xxv (1998), 80 at p. 82. But a number of manor courts were of earlier origin. For instance, courts baron had been held in the manor of Karte (or Crebilly) in Co. Antrim from 'time immemorial ... the O'Hara family being in possession of this manor since King Henry 2. first invaded Ireland', and the charter of the manor of Timoleague (or Tagmalog) in Co. Cork 'was granted in the 17th year of the reign of King Edward the second, and in the year of our Lord, 1324': *Select committee appointed to inquire into the operation of the small debt jurisdiction of manor courts in Ireland, the abuses which may exist therein, and the remedies proper to be applied: Minutes of evidence*, pp. 301 and 357, H.C. 1837 (494) xv, 305 and 361 (hereafter cited as Manor courts committee, *Minutes of evidence 1837*).

2 For example, 'The manor of Cloyne [Co. Cork] is by prescription; its existence is recognised in the oldest record in Cloyne registry, which is of the 14th century': Manor courts committee, *Minutes of evidence 1837*, p. 346.

3 Gillespie, 'A manor court', p. 82.

4 There was also a court of piepowder (from the French *pied poudre*, dusty feet) which sat during fairs or markets within the manor to administer justice on the spot to buyers and sellers – see e.g. W.H. Crawford and B. Trainor (ed.), *Aspects of Irish social history, 1750–1800* (Belfast, 1969), p. 131.

year, to hear and determine criminal charges in relation to offences which had occurred within the estate. It also dealt with an array of administrative matters relating to the running of the manor, which the landlord set out in his charge to the leet jury.[5] For instance, the leet court could serve as a form of register where the inheritance or transfer of property within the manor was recorded.[6] It could also have a role in regulating both agrarian practices and the market-place. In 1800, for example, the leet jury in Clonmel placed 'agents on the different roads in the vicinity ... in order to buy up the corn, potatoes, milk, or other articles of provision coming into the public market'.[7] The court baron, on the other hand, was held on a three-weekly basis to determine various minor civil cases, primarily small debts and claims of trespass, which arose within the manor. The difference between the courts leet and baron was, however, often blurred, as the leet *de facto* also dealt in practice with petty cases of debt, trespass and, indeed, gossip.[8]

In civil cases, the manor courts had a three-fold jurisdiction.[9] First, the charter may have conferred a 'common law' jurisdiction which could range from five marks[10] to £200; in such cases, the manor court 'proceeded according to the rules of the common law ... as in the superior courts'.[11] Secondly, the charter generally conferred the jurisdiction of a court baron normally limited to

---

5 Gillespie, 'A manor court', pp. 86–87.
6 R. Gillespie, *Colonial Ulster: the settlement of East Ulster 1600–1641* (Cork, 1985), pp.157–58.
7 R. Wells, 'The Irish famine of 1799–1801: Market culture, moral economies and social protest', in A. Randall and A. Charlesworth (ed.), *Markets, market culture and popular protest in eighteenth-century Britain and Ireland* (Liverpool, 1996), 163 at p. 177.
8 Gillespie, *Colonial Ulster*, p. 156 and 'A manor court', p. 83.
9 For a legal commentary on manor courts see especially J. Napier, *Practice of the civil bill courts and courts of appeal*, ed. R. Longfield (Dublin, 1841), ch. viii. See also J. Napier, *Digest of the civil bill and manor court statutes* (Dublin, 1836) and D. Kinahan, *Digest of the statutes regulating proceedings by civil bill before judges of assize, assistant barristers, chairmen of the county, the Recorder of Dublin, the Mayor of Waterford, and seneschals of manors* (Dublin, 1826 (1st ed.) and 1837 (2nd ed.)).
10 Since one mark was worth two-thirds of an English pound, five marks amounted to £3. 6s. 8d.
11 Such cases involved 'regular pleadings ... in which declarations and pleas were filed' and proceeded 'by either attachment against the goods, or a capias against the person': Manor courts committee, *Minutes of evidence 1837*, p. 2 (Fogarty). By the 1830s, however, most manor courts had 'discontinued their common law jurisdiction': ibid., p. 5.

forty shillings and 'exercised by summons to be tried before the seneschal and a jury'.[12] Thirdly, there was from 1785[13] a statutory jurisdiction over the recovery of small debts by way of civil bill.[14]

The landlord had the responsibility of presiding over the manor court; but it was more usual for him to appoint for this purpose an agent known as a seneschal, remunerated from court fees.[15] The

12 Ibid.
13 *An act for the more speedy and easy recovery of small debts, in the manor courts within this kingdom, and for regulating the costs of proceedings for that purpose therein* (25 Geo III (Ire.), c 44)(hereafter cited as Small Debts (Manor Courts) Act (Ire.) 1785).
14 A civil bill was a short document containing the names of the plaintiff and defendant, a short statement of the plaintiff's cause of action, and the date and place on and at which the defendant was to appear to answer the plaintiff's claim. A general jurisdiction to hear and determine cases begun by civil bill was also transferred from the judges of assize to the newly-created assistant barristers at quarter sessions in 1796: see generally D.S. Greer, 'The development of civil bill procedure in Ireland' in J.F. McEldowney and P. O'Higgins (ed.), *The common law tradition: essays in Irish legal history* (Dublin, 1990), p. 28 and Napier, *Practice of the civil bill courts.*
15 The appointment of James Foley as seneschal of the Manor of Arturmon in Co. Sligo read as follows: 'To all to whom these presents shall come: I, Sir Robert Gore Booth, bart., of the manor or manors of Arturmon, send greeting: Know ye that I, the said Sir Robert Gore Booth, bart., have given, granted and confirmed, and by these presents, as far as in me lies, and that I may lawfully, do give, grant and confirm unto James Foley, in the county of Sligo, the office and place of Seneschal of all and singular the said lordships and manors; and do hereby constitute, ordain, nominate and appoint him, the said James Foley, seneschal of the said manors, there to keep and hold all courts baron and courts leet, and all other courts belonging to said manors, as the same have been accustomed to be held in, used and kept within said manors, in such sort, manner and form, and at such places and days and times as they have heretofore usually kept and holden, together with the correction, government, amotion and appointment of all inferior officers of the said courts; to have, hold, execute, use, occupy, possess and enjoy the office and place of the said manor of Arturmon, and all the powers and privileges aforesaid, to the said James Foley, or his sufficient deputy, and to take and receive all and singular the fines, amerciaments, profits, fees, reward, wages, advantages and emoluments to the said office of seneschal belonging or in anywise appertaining, or at any time heretofore used and accustomed to be paid, rendered for or by reason of the said office of seneschal, for and during the time, will and pleasure of Sir Robert Gore Booth, and his heirs, to the said James Foley, and his heirs, in such office of seneschal of said manor of Arturmon. In witness hereof, I said Sir Robert Gore Booth have hereunto set my hand and seal this 24th January 1813. (signed) *Robert Gore Booth*. Signed, sealed and delivered in presence of *Peter Henry*': Manor courts committee, *Minutes of evidence 1837*, pp. 452–53.

office was open to catholics and protestants.[16] It was the duty of the seneschal to direct the business of the court. He was responsible for authorising the serving of summonses and for issuing and signing the decrees and dismisses of the court; he could also have a power of attachment, which meant that a defendant's goods could be held before the trial in cases where it was suspected that he or she would attempt to remove them from the manor. In addition to his judicial role, a seneschal might play an active role in the local community, particularly with regard to the regulation of the market place. For instance, in 1800 the seneschal of Granard, Co. Longford, although given 'written evidence' that the 'Government did not countenance [his] interference [in the market]', retorted that he acted for the common good, 'the tempers of Juries' being such 'that he did not fear damages for striking a man, who refused to sell corn at the price he had fixed'.[17] This case serves to show, incidentally, the extent to which seneschals could act independently of the central administration.

It is important to recognise also that, as this incident demonstrates, the ultimate decision in a case lay not with the seneschal, but with a jury selected from the more 'respectable' tenants living on the estate.[18] It is very likely that these jurors had in most cases a personal knowledge of the litigants, and it was on the basis of their verdict that the seneschal issued either a decree or a dismiss. A decree in the plaintiff's favour was, however, subject to appeal to the next going judge of assize.[19] This appears to have been the only effective 'outside' control on the exercise of the seneschal's jurisdiction.

By the 1830s there were still some 200 manor courts in operation in Ireland, mainly in Ulster.[20] Gillespie has estimated that these courts represented 'only a fraction of what had existed earlier' and he suggests that they had, by this time, 'degenerated into small debts

---

16 N. Garnham, *The courts, crime and the criminal law in Ireland, 1692–1760* (Dublin, 1996), p. 261.
17 Wells, 'The Irish famine of 1799–1801', p. 178.
18 J.A. Sharpe, *Crime in early modern England 1550–1750* (London, 1984), p. 83 says that '… an analysis of those serving as leet jurors … frequently provides a roll-call of the village notables'.
19 Small Debts (Manor Courts) Act (Ire.) 1785, s. 5.
20 In 1842, there were 100 or so seneschals in Ulster, as compared to 21 in Munster, 19 in Leinster and 18 in Connaught: *Return of the name of each seneschal of a manor in Ireland, with the date of his appointment, and the person by whom he was appointed*, H.C. 1842 (35), xxxviii, 361.

courts ...' stripped of their more wide-ranging functions.[21] Indeed, McCabe claims that the courts and their procedures were largely anachronistic by the 1830s.[22]

By this time, the manor courts were in effect in competition with the assistant barristers at quarter sessions, whose civil bill jurisdiction was in 1836 extended to include a wider range of cases involving sums of up to £20.[23] There may also have been rivalry, on a more local level, with the courts of petty sessions which were established on a national basis in 1823 and which had a civil jurisdiction up to five pounds over claims of trespass and to six pounds in cases relating to wages and hiring.[24] From an official point of view, the petty and quarter sessions were clearly the preferred venue for 'small claims' litigation, the manor courts having developed a reputation among the authorities for being 'disorderly and dangerously informal'.[25] They had for many years operated with a great deal of autonomy from the central administration,[26] although the Irish parliament in the 1780s had attempted to regulate some aspects of their procedure and to limit the costs of proceedings therein.[27] In the 1820s, however, the

21 Gillespie, 'A manor court', p. 81. The courts also continued to operate in England in the nineteenth century, although many of their functions were usurped by quarter and petty sessions: see D. Eastwood, *Governing rural England: tradition and transformation in local government 1780–1840* (Oxford, 1994), p. 44.

22 D. McCabe, 'Law, conflict and social order: County Mayo 1820–1845' (unpublished Ph.D. thesis, University College Dublin, 1991), p. 408.

23 Civil Bill Courts (Ire.) Act 1836 (6 & 7 Will IV, c. 75), s. 1, amending Civil Bill Courts Act 1796 (36 Geo III (Ire.), c. 25). Petty sessions were not given jurisdiction over small debt cases until the manor courts were abolished in 1859 by the Manor Courts Abolition (Ire.) Act (22 Vict, c. 14), ss. 1 and 5.

24 Under the Impounding of Cattle (Ire.) Act 1826 (7 Geo 4, c. 42), the Malicious Trespass Act 1829 (1 Geo 4, c. 56) and the Recovery of Wages (Ire.) Act 1814 (54 Geo 3, c. 116) respectively. See e.g. McCabe, 'Law, conflict and social order', pp. 424–25 and McMahon, 'The courts of petty sessions', ch. 3

25 R. B. McDowell, *The Irish administration, 1801–1914* (London, 1964), p. 118.

26 *Select committee appointed to inquire into the operation of the small debt jurisdiction of manor courts in Ireland, the abuses which may exist therein, and the remedies proper to be applied: Minutes of evidence*, p. 57, H.C. 1837–38 (648) xvii, p. 6 (evidence of Mr George Mathews of the Chief Secretary's office). Mathews referred to the office of inspector or surveyor of the King's manor courts which had been held by the Hon Mr Westenra prior to its abolition in 1837. The duties of this office are not explained, but Mathews comments that it had become a sinecure: 'I suppose, having always been so'. There was also the practical difficulty that, notwithstanding the requirements of section 12 of the act of 1785, 'the seneschals of the manor courts make no returns of their judicial proceedings': ibid.

27 Small Debts (Manor Courts) Act (Ire.) 1785; *An act to render more effectual an act, entitled An act for the more speedy and easy recovery of small debts in the manor courts, etc* 1787 (27 Geo III (Ire.), c. 22).

government began to take a greater interest in the operation of these courts. Two regulatory acts were passed in 1826 and 1827[28] and, as 'very frequent' complaints began to arrive in the chief secretary's office,[29] the courts were the subject of a detailed select committee inquiry in 1837 and 1838.[30] Yet, even at this juncture, there was some doubt as to the power of parliament to interfere, since the courts had been established by royal charter and the seneschals were not appointed by the government.[31]

The lack of control over the manor courts was also a bone of contention for the legal profession who, according to Osborough, 'came to regard with ill-disguised antipathy the fashion in which the manor courts functioned'.[32] Napier, later to become lord

---

28 *An act to amend the laws for the recovery of small debts, and the proceedings for that purpose, in the manor courts in Ireland* (7 Geo IV, c. 41)(hereafter Manor Courts (Ire.) Act 1826) and *An act for further amending the laws for the recovery of small debts, and the proceedings for that purpose, in the manor courts in Ireland* (7 & 8 Geo IV, c. 59)(hereafter Manor Courts (Ire.) Act 1827).

29 Manor courts committee, *Minutes of evidence 1837–38*, p. 6 (Mathews), who explained that the chief secretary had taken no action,'it being supposed they were about to be controlled by some legislative enactment'.

30 Appointed in March 1837, the Committee had by July taken evidence from twenty witnesses when 'the sudden termination of the session ... rendered it impossible to pursue the inquiry further': Manor courts committee, *Minutes of evidence 1837*, p. 1. After the election, the Committee was reappointed in December 1837 and took evidence from a further eleven witnesses before issuing a two-page report in July 1838: *Select committee appointed to inquire into the operation of the small debt jurisdiction of manor courts in Ireland, the abuses which may exist therein, and the remedies proper to be applied: Report and Minutes of evidence*, H.C. 1837–38 (648) xvii, 1 and 7 (hereafter cited respectively as Manor courts committee, *Report* and Manor courts committee, *Minutes of evidence 1837–38*).

31 Manor courts committee, *Minutes of evidence 1837–38*, p. 60 (Mathews). If a seneschal exceeded his authority, the attorney general could apparently bring either the lord of the manor or the seneschal before the queen's bench; but Mathews knew of no occasion on which this had been done. The autonomy granted to some seneschals may be seen in the patent of the manor of Dunkieron, Co. Kerry, in which George I gave Henry, earl of Shelburne, his heirs and assigns 'the fines, issues, amerciaments, forfeitures, perquisites, profits, commodities and emoluments' generated by the manor court 'without ever giving or yielding unto us, our heirs or successors, any account for the same; and that without the molestation, disturbance, disquiet or grievance of us, our heirs or successors, or of the justices, escheators, sheriffs, bailiffs, or other officers or ministers of us, our heirs or successors': Manor courts committee, *Minutes of evidence 1837*, p. 419.

32 W.N. Osborough, 'The Irish legal system, 1796–1877' in C. Costello (ed.), *The Four Courts: 200 years* (Dublin, 1996), 33 at p. 58 and reproduced in the author's *Studies in Irish legal history* (Dublin, 1999), 239 at p. 255.

chancellor of Ireland, was a particularly severe critic: 'Manor courts are not the most perfect form of judicature. They were anciently, in fact, the most systematic nuisances; and now that the legislature has intervened to protect the public from the oppressive exactions of these privileged plunderers, the Courts are still deserving of aught but praise, many of the former evils continue, and no effectual remedy can be devised but the total abatement of the nuisance.'[33]

The courts also attracted the attention of the newspapers of the time. The *Dublin Monitor*, in 1839, called for the abolition of 'these fragments of feudal absurdity', claiming that seneschals were clearly biased against defendants.[34] The *Mayo Constitution*, writing in reply, claimed that trial by jury in the courts was 'as valuable and as likely to uphold the right, as trial by any one man – even a "learned" [assistant] barrister'.[35]

Manor courts clearly had a controversial place in the Irish legal system in the pre-Famine period, and were eventually to be abolished in 1859. Whatever the merits and status of these courts, however, there are two related points which can be made about their role before the Famine. First, their operation varied considerably from place to place and was shaped and influenced by local conditions. Secondly, they remained largely autonomous. These two factors contributed to the often diverse and distinctive roles that the courts could play in different areas. The primary aim of this paper is to identify the part that these courts had by this time come to play in the particular context of the west of Ireland.

MANOR COURTS IN THE WEST OF IRELAND

The main source for any investigation of manor courts in any part of Ireland in the early nineteenth century is the evidence given to the select committee in 1837 and 1838. A number of witnesses gave details of the operation of the courts in the west of Ireland, particularly in the counties of Mayo, Roscommon and Clare, and

---

33 *Practice of the civil bill courts*, p. 138. Philip Fogarty, an assistant barrister, advised the select committee that 'On general principles ... the exercise of a judicial office by a person who is nominated by a private individual and ... responsible to no one ... is objectionable': Manor courts committee, *Minutes of evidence 1837*, p. 9.
34 As reported in *Tuam Herald*, 10 Aug. 1839.
35 *Tuam Herald*, 17 Aug. 1839.

to a lesser extent, Galway. The committee was also provided with returns made by a number of seneschals – but unfortunately these are not complete. We know, for instance, that the seneschal of the manor court of Castlebar, Mr Sinclair O'Malley, did not make a return, although there was clear evidence that his court was still 'in active operation'.[36] Thus, it is necessary to bear in mind that while these returns offer us very useful information on the courts, they may not reflect the full extent of manor court activity at this time.

According to the evidence at our disposal, there were in 1837 nineteen seneschals conducting thirty-four manor courts in five counties in the west of Ireland.[37] A number of seneschals obviously had control over more than one manor. For instance, Joseph H. Roughan presided over courts in the manors of Inchiquin, Corcomroe, Burren and Killone, all in Co. Clare,[38] while J.J. Bricknell, a justice of the peace of Loughrea, Co. Galway and the seneschal of the marquis of Clanricarde, presided over five courts.[39]

In keeping with the overwhelming majority of manor courts in the country, most of the courts in the west of Ireland functioned under charters granted in the seventeenth century.[40] The courts generally had a pecuniary jurisdiction limited to £10 'Irish',[41] but

36 Manor courts committee, *Minutes of evidence 1837–38*, p. 111 (MacDonnell).
37 Counties Clare and Mayo each had six active seneschals, Co. Galway had four, Co. Roscommon two and Co. Sligo one (two seneschals from Sligo made returns to the committee, but only one was still holding a court): Manor courts committee, *Minutes of evidence 1837*, appendix and McCabe, 'Law, conflict and social order', p. 407. But see *Return of the name of each seneschal ...* H.C. 1842 (35), xxxviii, 361, which suggests a higher number; however, some of those listed in this return do not appear to have been active.
38 Manor courts committee, *Minutes of evidence 1837*, pp. 328–31.
39 Ibid., pp. 409–10. The courts were held in Portumna, Killimore, Woodford, Kilconnell, Claregalway and Currendulla.
40 Manor courts committee, *Minutes of evidence 1837*, appendix. Charters which deviated from this pattern included those for the manor of Newport Pratt, Co. Mayo (1789), Frenchpark, Co. Roscommon (1711) and possibly Castlemore, Co. Mayo ('reign of Elizabeth').
41 Ibid. The 'old' Irish £1 was worth twelve-thirteenths of the English £1, making £10 Irish the equivalent of £9. 4s.7d. English; the two currencies were amalgamated in 1826: see e.g. C. Ó Gráda, *Ireland: A new economic history 1780–1939* (Oxford, 1994), pp. 46–51. Courts with a lower financial limit, expressed in Irish pounds unless otherwise stated, included those at Tomgrany and Killaloe, Co. Clare; Clare, Co. Galway, and Killalla, Co. Mayo

some had a much higher limit, at least in theory.[42] The geographical jurisdiction of a court could range from 'not more than four miles' (the manor of Castlebank in Co. Clare) to as much as thirty miles (the manor of Boyle in Co. Roscommon). However, as the seneschal of the manor of Boyle pointed out in his return, the majority of litigants lived within eight miles of the court.[43]

In assessing the extent to which litigants used the courts it is important to recognise that the manor court process went through three stages – (i) the issuing of a summons or process, (ii) entry of the case for trial, and (iii) the actual trial. Table 1 suggests that the number of processes issued normally exceeded – often greatly exceeded – the number of cases entered for trial.

Table 1: Incidence of cases settled before trial[44]

	No. of processes issued	No. of cases entered	No. of cases tried	No. of decrees	Aggregate value of decrees
Co. Clare Manor of Castlebank (Oct 1835-April 1837)	393	58	52	nk	£74
Co. Galway Clanricarde manors (Dec 1836-May 1837)	1,218	413	278	235	£492
Co. Mayo Manor of Castlemore (Jan 1834-March 1837)	3,552	nk	888	nk	£1,300

(£2), Newport Pratt, Co. Mayo (£6 Eng.), Boyle, Co. Roscommon (£3. 6s. 8d.) and Markree, Co. Sligo (£5). On the other hand, the manor court at Frenchpark, Co. Roscommon had the higher limit of £20.
42 For example, the patents creating the Inchiquin manor courts in Co. Clare set no financial limit to their jurisdiction; by the 1830s, however, these courts did not in practice deal with cases involving more than £10: Manor courts committee, *Minutes of evidence 1837*, p. 328.
43 Ibid., p. 451.
44 The figures in this Table are taken from Manor courts committee, *Minutes of evidence 1837*, pp. 325 (Castlebank), 409–10 (Clanricarde) and 441–43 (Castlemore).

Such out-of-court arrangements were not peculiar to the west. The seneschal at Stranorlar, Co. Donegal, for example, claimed that 'nine-tenths of the cases were settled without trial in [his] court'.[45] More spectacularly, Richard Smith, seneschal of Ballyhooly and Newmarket, Co. Cork, claimed 'with confidence ... that the number of cases tried [in his court] did not amount to one out of every 100 processes issued ...'.[46] Thus, it is worth bearing in mind that use of the manor courts may have been more extensive than is indicated by the actual number of cases entered for trial.

The amount of business enjoyed by the manor courts in the west of Ireland varied from area to area and, indeed, from county to county. In Co. Sligo, the availability of alternative procedures clearly affected the amount of litigation in the county's manor courts. James Foley, seneschal of Arturmon, claimed that 'since the commencement of the petty sessions, manor courts have considerably fallen off, and I have not held a court for some years ...'.[47] McCabe has similarly argued that changes both in the court system and in landlord-tenant relations led to a marked and, indeed, terminal decline in the operation of manor courts in Co. Mayo.[48] The returns made to the select committee suggest, however, a somewhat higher usage than Co. Sligo. Castlemore, the busiest manor court in Co. Mayo, issued close to 1,100 summonses, and tried some 273 cases, per year in the mid-1830s.[49] This level of business compares favourably to the figures available for petty sessions courts at this time. For instance, the Crossmolina petty sessions issued 1,059 summonses (for both civil and criminal cases) in 1835.[50] When compared to litigation at quarter sessions, however, it is evident that the more official courts enjoyed a

45 Ibid., p. 366.
46 Ibid., p. 353.
47 Ibid., pp. 452–53.
48 McCabe, 'Law, conflict and social order', p. 408.
49 Manor courts committee, *Minutes of evidence 1837*, pp. 441–43. At the manor courts of Dayne and Ballynock, there were, on average, 213 cases entered per annum; at Newport, an average of 142, and at Killalla, only 42 cases entered per year.
50 *Returns of courts of petty sessions in Ireland, 1835*, p. 151 H.C. 1836 (415), xlii 613 (hereafter cited as *Petty sessions returns, 1835*). The other petty sessions courts in Co. Mayo for which figures are available had a lower level of business – Ballycastle, 345 civil summonses; Newport, 780 summonses and Cong, 560 summonses (ibid., pp. 148, 153 and 150); unless otherwise indicated, these figures include both civil and criminal business.

considerably higher level of business. The busiest quarter sessions in the county, at Clare, decided an average of 1,246 civil bills per annum, and quarter sessions in the county as a whole dealt with a yearly average of 5,143 civil bills between 1829 and 1833.[51]

Table 2: Manor courts in Co. Roscommon[52]

	Boyle	Frenchpark
1834		
No. of cases entered	876	62
No. of cases tried	116	61
No. of decrees	88	32
Total amount awarded	£221	£88
1835		
No. of cases entered	965	83
No. of cases tried	92	83
No. of decrees	80	26
Total amount awarded	£180	£45
1836		
No. of cases entered	1,048	120
No. of cases tried	114	120
No. of decrees	97	63
Total amount awarded	£230	£96

Manor courts in other parts of the west, however, had a more substantial workload. The level of business at Boyle manor court in Co. Roscommon exceeds that of all but one petty sessions court in the county at this time – the sessions at Roscommon town which had the slightly higher figure of 1,086 cases on its civil books in 1835.[53]

51 *A list of the assistant barristers in Ireland ... [and] the number of civil bills decided by each barrister, etc*, pp. 27–28, H.C. 1834 (383), xlviii, 573 at pp. 599–600 (hereafter cited as *Civil bill returns, 1834*). These figures are based on returns made from quarter sessions in Co. Mayo for the period 1829–1833; they include all the *ordinary* civil bills decided during this period (i.e. excluding civil bill ejectments).
52 Manor courts committee, *Minutes of evidence 1837*, pp. 451–52 and 488.
53 *Petty sessions returns, 1835*, p. 186. The other courts of petty sessions for which information is available are Elphin petty sessions (627 civil summonses), Leearrow (568) and Four Roads, near Mount Talbot (950): ibid., pp. 183 185 and 186.

The quarter sessions in Boyle, with an average of 1,323 civil bills per annum,[54] did enjoy a higher level of business than its more informal counterpart; yet the fact that the manor court in the town managed to attract even a comparable level of litigation would seem to indicate that it was far from anachronistic even by the 1830s. It should also be recognised that the number of cases at manor courts in Co. Roscommon was on the increase at this time (albeit from a modest base). In contrast, the level of quarter sessions activity in the county, although much higher, was in decline – from 6,059 cases in 1830 to 4,493 cases in 1833.

It is to counties Clare and Galway that we must look for the most active manor courts in the west. The level of manor court activity in Co. Clare would seem to be the highest of any county in the region.

Table 3: Manor courts in County Clare, 1834–1836[55]

	Cases entered for trial	Cases tried	No. of decrees
Bunratty	767	698	527
Castlebank	116	104	nk
Clonroad	659	633	490
Crovreaghan	1,470	1,446	1,240
Doonass	2,705	2,654	2,411
Ennistimon	329	296	244
Inchiquin	974	nk	830
Killaloe	573	451	381
Kilrush/Moyarta	3,582	3,501	nk
Moy-Ilrickane	1,551	1,440	1,242
O'Brien's Bridge	970	970	647
Tomgrany	1,087	1,024	662
Total	14,783	13,217+	8,674+

54 *Civil bill returns, 1834*, p. 27.
55 Figures taken from Manor courts committee, *Minutes of evidence 1837*, pp. 324–33 and 474–75. Please note that the figures for Castlebank are estimates only, that those for Inchiquin, O'Brien's Bridge and Tomgrany include the first few months of 1837, and that the return for Inchiquin in any event is 'exclusive of petty actions'.

Table 4: *The manor courts of Castlebellew and Clare, Co. Galway*[56]

	Castlebellew	Clare(mont)
1834		
No. of cases entered	2,431	nk
No. of cases tried	442	831
No. of decrees	288	714
Total amount awarded	£1,292	nk
1835		
No. of cases entered	2,700	nk
No. of cases tried	465	812
No. of decrees	302	672
Total amount awarded	£1,576	nk
1836		
No. of cases entered	2,822	nk
No. of cases tried	578	798
No. of decrees	402	706
Total amount awarded	£2,185	nk

During the period 1834–1836, the annual number of cases entered for trial in the manor courts of Co. Clare averaged 4,928. This is marginally higher than litigation at quarter sessions, where an average of 4,877 civil bills were dealt with annually between 1829 and 1833.[57] It is vital to recognise, however, that in manor courts throughout Co. Clare – with the exception of the manor of Kilrush – business was in decline, whereas civil business in the quarter sessions was on the increase.[58] Furthermore, where quarter sessions and manor courts existed in the same towns – as was the case, for example, in Kilrush and Ennistimon – the official courts enjoyed more business.[59] On the whole, however, we must acknowledge the relative vibrancy of manor courts in Co. Clare;

---

56 Manor courts committee, *Minutes of evidence 1837*, pp. 409–12 and 482–83. It is stated that the amount awarded by the manor court at Clare was, on average, '£150 monthly': ibid., p. 411.
57 *Civil bill returns, 1834*, p. 6.
58 The number of civil bills dealt with rose from 4,372 in 1829 to 5,281 in 1833: *Civil bill returns, 1834*, p. 6.
59 Ibid. Kilrush quarter sessions dealt with an average of 1,484 civil bills per year; that at Ennistimon with an average of 541 cases.

the fact that they attracted such litigation close to forty years after quarter sessions gained a civil bill jurisdiction and well over ten years after the introduction of petty sessions must indicate that the manor courts could still play a prominent part in the socio-economic life of the county.

A relatively high level of manor court litigation also appears to have existed in Co. Galway. We have already seen that in the Clanricarde manors 413 cases were entered for trial, and 278 cases were tried, during the five month period from 1 December 1836 to 1 May 1837.[60] As Table 4 suggests, the courts at Clare (or Claremont) and Castlebellew were busier; but business in the fourth court, at Eyrecourt, was much lighter.[61]

Litigation at individual manor courts in Co. Galway seems quite high when compared to the figures available for petty sessions in the county. In 1835, for instance, Tuam petty sessions issued 403 summonses for civil cases, less than half the number of cases actually tried at Claremont manor court in the same year. At Gurteen petty sessions (also in east Galway) there were just over 1,800 civil cases entered for trial over the seven and a half years from 1838 to 1845 – a significantly lower level of civil disputes than at the manor courts in the county (with the exception of the manor of Eyrecourt).[62]

In spite of a geographical remit which extended only over a radius of eight miles, the manor court at Castlebellew appears to have been the busiest court in the whole region. Between January 1834 and December 1836, it had 7,953 cases on its books – an average of 2,651 cases per year. By comparison, the busiest quarter sessions in the west of Ireland, at Galway town, dealt with an average of only 1,978 civil bills during the years 1829 to 1833.[63] It should be recognised, however, that in the county generally quarter sessions dealt with a higher level of business – an average of 6,200 civil bills per annum,[64] as compared to the 5,000 or so cases entered for trial in the manor courts during the period 1834 to 1836.

---

60 See above, Table 1.
61 The total number of cases entered over the period from 1834 to early 1837 was only 486, of which 256 were tried: ibid., pp. 411–12.
62 *Petty sessions returns, 1835*, p. 86 (Tuam); *Registry of civil proceedings at Gurteen petty sessions, June 1838-December 1845*: NAI Petty Sessions collection.
63 *Civil bill returns, 1834*, pp. 12–13.
64 Ibid.

Although it would thus appear that the official courts of petty and quarter sessions handled a higher level of litigation in the region as a whole during this period, it is also abundantly clear that manor courts were far from obsolete and, indeed, were prospering in some areas. How, then, did these manor courts actually operate?

For a fuller understanding of the working of the manor courts we need, at this stage, to turn to the evidence given by various witnesses to the select committee.[65] In examining the work of this committee, it is important to recognise that, across the political spectrum, there was a growing commitment to greater uniformity and regularisation in the administration of justice in Ireland. The Whig government of the day was certainly placing a greater emphasis on the centralisation of the system of law and order than had been the case in previous administrations.[66] There was also a greater willingness on the part of the government in the late 1830s to entertain complaints against the manor court seneschals than had hitherto been the case.[67] Although the committee did not, in any direct sense, represent the views of government, it may still have been inclined to look for negative aspects in the operation of manor courts which were still informal, highly localised and largely outside state control.

The evidence to the committee came mainly from seneschals, jurors, attorneys and magistrates and, to a lesser extent, from government officials and employees. Little or no evidence was taken from litigants who had used the courts in the west of Ireland, and it is therefore difficult to establish their attitude to

---

65 The committee was chaired by Morgan John O'Connell, MP for Co. Kerry 1835–1852 and a nephew of Daniel O'Connell. Three of the fifteen members were from the west of Ireland – Andrew H. Lynch (Galway, repealer), Fitzstephen French (Roscommon, liberal) and Hewitt Bridgeman (Ennis, reformer). Bridgeman played a full role in the work of the committee, but Lynch and French did not. The government's chief representative appears to have been Stephen Woulfe, the attorney general for Ireland; but he does not appear to have attended any meetings at all. After the election of 1837, the committee was reappointed with a modified membership, but still under the chairmanship of O'Connell. A two-page report was published in July 1838, but no action was taken before the Famine to implement the committee's recommendations.

66 See e.g. M.A.G. Ó Tuathaigh, *Thomas Drummond and the government of Ireland, 1835–41* (O'Donnell Lecture, Galway, 1978); V. Crossman, *Politics, law and order in nineteenth-century Ireland* (Dublin, 1996).

67 Manor courts committee, *Minutes of evidence 1837–38*, p. 58.

these courts. Those witnesses who did give evidence may not have been best placed to judge popular opinion, or, indeed, may have had an interest in distorting this opinion to justify their own view of the courts. Thus, any attempt at gauging popular attitudes must be undertaken with a degree of caution. Accordingly, we will be primarily concerned with attempting to establish some of the factors which influenced the working of the courts and, through a cautious reading of the evidence at our disposal, to assess the significance of the courts for people in the west of Ireland before the Famine.

Two witnesses from Co. Mayo gave evidence to the committee – the Revd Joseph Seymour JP, seneschal of Castlemore, and Mr Edward Patrick MacDonnell, who had served on the jury in Seymour's court and had attended a number of other courts in the county. Frederick Cary, seneschal of Frenchpark, gave evidence on the operation of his court in Co. Roscommon. Two witnesses offered evidence from Co. Galway. John Jagoe from Co. Cork had attended a court at Oughterard, fifteen miles north-west of Galway town; he lived mainly in Cork, but had travelled throughout the country as part of a parliamentary commission on fisheries and had attended a number of manor courts as 'an inquirer'.[68] Charles Staunton Cahill JP, a magistrate who presided over the petty sessions at Corrafin in Co. Clare, had experience of the manor court in Oranmore, about four miles east of Galway town. According to Cahill, the practices in the manor courts of Oranmore and Corrafin were 'nearly the same thing'.[69] Evidence concerning the manor court at Corrafin was also given by Timothy Fitzpatrick, who had served as a juror in the court and who was born and had lived all his life 'within a mile and a half of Corrafin', and Mr Joseph Roughan, seneschal of a number of manor courts including that at Corrafin.[70] Other evidence relating to Co. Clare was given by Mr Michael Cullinan, an attorney in Ennis, and Mr Denis Leonard, an attorney in Kilrush. The evidence offered by these witnesses should offer us an insight into both the operation of the manor court system and the *dramatis personae* of the courts in the region.

68 Manor courts committee, *Minutes of evidence 1837*, p. 39. The commission in question was the Inquiry into the state of the Irish fisheries, which reported in 1836.
69 Manor courts committee, *Minutes of evidence 1837*, p. 57 (Cahill).
70 Ibid., p. 114 (Fitzpatrick).

THE MANOR COURT PROCESS

Jurisdiction

A manor court could deal with a case within its monetary jurisdiction only where (i) the cause of action arose, and (ii) the defendant was resident, within the manor.[71] The royal patent which set
out the territorial limits of a manor court could sometimes give
rise to a degree of controversy as to the precise area within the
jurisdiction of the court. For instance, the charter of the court at
Corrafin was a source of considerable argument because the
names of many of the townlands in the patent had been changed
since the seventeenth century.[72] Seneschals could also have some
difficulty reading their patents, which were written in Latin. Mr
Cullinan, the Ennis attorney, had, for instance, seen 'a seneschal
unable to read his patent before a judge of Assize...'.[73] The Revd
Seymour in Co. Mayo also admitted that his patent was 'written
in very contracted Latin, and it is not very easy to decipher'.[74]

In fact, most successful appeals from a seneschal's decision
probably stemmed from the fact that 'the defendant did not reside
in the manor'.[75] However, even when the judge of assize had ruled
that a particular area was *not* within the manor, a seneschal might
continue to issue summonses against those residing there. When
asked if he indulged in this practice, Roughan, the seneschal at
Corrafin, replied that he did because '[he had] known [the areas]
were in the manor'. He also claimed that 'very few appeals' were
lodged in such instances.[76] The seneschal at Oranmore is said to
have claimed that 'he could spread his jurisdiction over every foot
of land which belonged to the Clanricardes, at any time', an area

---

71 Napier, *Practice of the civil bill courts*, p. 139, citing in particular the Small
    Debts (Manor Courts) Act (Ire.) 1785, s. 3, *Macauley v. Thompson* (1841) Ir
    Cir Rep 43 and *White v. McConnell* (1841) 2 Cr & Dix CC 115. Not
    everyone agreed with (ii) – Cary told the select committee that an action may
    be brought against a person residing outside the manor, provided the
    summons can be served, and property taken, within the manor: Manor
    courts committee, *Minutes of evidence 1837*, p. 171.
72 Manor courts committee, *Minutes of evidence 1837*, p. 59 (Cahill).
73 Manor courts committee, *Minutes of evidence 1837–38*, p. 41.
74 Manor courts committee, *Minutes of evidence 1837*, p. 178.
75 Manor courts committee, *Minutes of evidence 1837–38*, p. 41 (Cullinan).
    Mathews told the committee that 'non-residence' of the defendant was the
    chief complaint made to the chief secretary's office concerning the manor
    courts: ibid., p. 60.
76 Manor courts committee, *Minutes of evidence 1837*, p. 278.

which would encompass a significant proportion of east and south Galway.[77] Thus, the courts could potentially enjoy jurisdiction over a considerable area of land.[78]

Although manor courts could, in principle, exercise an extensive pecuniary jurisdiction,[79] most in practice were limited to claims not involving more than £10 Irish and utilised primarily for the recovery of small debts.[80] The 1785 Act, however, refers to a wider range of contract and tort actions by way of civil bill;[81] it also tied the civil bill jurisdiction to the monetary limit set by the charter, if this was less than £10. In 1826, however, legislation provided 'a most extraordinary increase of jurisdiction' by extending the court's civil bill limit to that set out in the charter, which meant that some courts could deal with cases involving up to £200.[82]

There is also reason to believe that many of the powers of a court leet were still in active use in the 1830s. In Kilrush, Co. Clare, for example, the court leet was in operation until 1836 and,

77 Ibid., pp. 59–60 (Cahill).
78 Another example is the manor of Castlemore, Co. Mayo, which extended over the barony of Costello, estimated to have contained over 40,000 inhabitants: ibid., p. 178 (Seymour).
79 One seneschal, Mr Sinclair O'Malley, is reported to have said, with regard to the pecuniary jurisdiction of his court at Castlebar, Co. Mayo, that 'his power [was] unlimited': ibid., p. 115 (MacDonnell).
80 Manor courts committee, *Minutes of evidence 1837*, p. 176 (Cary). It is likely that even this jurisdiction was rarely exercised to its full amount. For instance, Cary (ibid.) claimed that he had dealt with claims for £9 or £10 on only three or four occasions in five or six years.
81 In particular, breach of contract actions such as *assumpsit* and *insimul computassent*, and tort actions of trespass, trover and detinue: Small Debts (Manor Courts) Act (Ire.) 1785, s. 1. Patents were drawn in similar terms. For example, the patent to John French, of Frenchpark, Co. Roscommon gave jurisdiction over 'all actions of debt, covenant, trespass, trover and detinue, and all other causes and matters whatsoever, which in debt or damage exceed not the sum of £20 sterling, current money of Great Britain, happening, arising, done or perpetrated within the said manor, and to hear, determine and execute within the said court all such and the like actions, causes and matters whatsoever, as are accustomed or ought to be heard, determined or executed in any court baron within our said realm of Ireland': Manor courts committee, *Minutes of evidence 1837*, pp. 165–66 (Cary). The wide range of actions covered by the term 'trespass' was, for example, held in *M'Laughlin v. Williamson* (1839) 1 Cr & Dix CC 265 to include an action for loss of services for seduction.
82 Manor courts committee, *Minutes of evidence 1837*, p. 3 (Fogarty), referring to Manor Courts (Ire.) Acts 1826, s. 1 and 1827, s. 6. Where a manor court had an *unlimited* common law jurisdiction, however, the civil bill jurisdiction remained subject to the £10 limit.

although the petty sessions had usurped its criminal jurisdiction, it played a significant role in the rural economy by regulating 'the amount and value of the damages in the manor committed, the number of beasts constituting what is called a collop; the grazing of land is let by so much a collop, and they regulate the number constituting a collop ...'. Indeed, the leet 'goes so far as to regulate the markets'.[83]

The court leet also determined 'what amount of debt a person could decree on his own oath, and so instituted the action called the petty action of the court'. Mr Leonard, the local attorney, thought that by doing so the leet was taking on 'the functions of the Legislature with regard to the law for the recovery of small debts within the manor'.[84] The tenants of the manor were also obliged to follow these rules under the terms of their leases. In this way, the courts probably played a pivotal role in regulating the practices of the local communities in which they were still established. Leonard also pointed out that although the leet had not sat in a year and a half the regulations it laid down were still in force. He also believed that this was the 'general practice' in the country. Such regulations were largely determined by representatives of the tenants, usually the 'most substantial farmers' who served as jurors and were 'always very punctual in their attendance on the inquiry, for their own sakes'.[85] It is probable that this group could use such regulations to suit their own interests and that this may also have led to some abuses in the operation of the jurisdiction of manor courts.

Commencing proceedings: summons and attachment

The usual method of commencing proceedings in a manor court was by means of a summons issued by a seneschal upon complaint made to him and then served on the defendant in sufficient time to enable him or her to make an appearance in court on the appointed day.[86] In some cases, however, on receipt of a complaint, the

---

83 Manor courts committee, *Minutes of evidence 1837–38*, p. 72 (Leonard).
84 Ibid.
85 Ibid., pp. 72–73. He pointed to Kerry as an example of an area where he knew this was the case.
86 Three days for a claim not exceeding £10, seven days for a claim of £10–£100 and fourteen days for a claim in excess of £100: Manor Courts (Ire.) Acts 1826, s. 3 and 1827, s. 1.

seneschal could instead issue an attachment against the goods of the defendant in order to compel his or her appearance.[87]

The summons was a short statement of the plaintiff's claim much the same as a civil bill, and its use does not appear to have given rise to any particular problems. The same cannot, however, be said for the seneschal's power of attachment, which involved the seizure of the defendant's goods pending the trial. This procedure gave an immediate and necessary remedy when the defendant was in danger of leaving the manor and taking his goods with him or her; but in other cases it could be manipulated by unscrupulous or vindictive plaintiffs and operate unfairly against defendants, particularly if they did not normally reside within the manor.[88]

The attachment was usually issued by the seneschal on payment of the appropriate fee upon receipt of a sworn affidavit of a debt owed to the plaintiff; it does not appear to have been necessary for the plaintiff to swear in the affidavit that the defendant was about to remove his or her goods from the manor. Goods of the defendant to the appropriate value were then seized and, unless 'bailed' by the defendant, kept in custody pending the trial. The whole process involved much more expense than proceeding by means of a summons.[89]

The power of attachment was used in most courts, but not in all.[90] It appears to have been used 'very much' in the court at Oranmore, and was claimed to have been oppressive since the common people knew 'little or nothing of the law, and very little of the English language' and accordingly mistook an attachment for a final decree. But it was not only the lower orders who suffered,

---

87 Napier, *Practice of the civil bill courts*, pp. 140–42.
88 A number of witnesses complained about the procedure. According to Cullinan, it was a 'constant' practice for a plaintiff to obtain an attachment, 'run away' with the defendant's goods and then, without obtaining a decree, to sell them: Manor courts committee, *Minutes of evidence 1837–38*, pp. 49–50. Fogarty thought that attaching goods was 'liable to very great abuse', and Jagoe agreed, saying that the practice had been discontinued at Bantry: Manor courts committee, *Minutes of evidence 1837*, pp. 6, 40 and 42.
89 Charles Ruthven, an attorney and sessional crown solicitor for Co. Down, gave a detailed description of the procedure and estimated that a case which proceeded to trial in this way incurred costs of about £2: Manor courts committee, *Minutes of evidence 1837*, pp. 258–59.
90 Ibid., p. 179, where Seymour claimed that he had never issued an attachment.

since 'a horse belonging to a gentleman at Oranmore was seized under one of these attachments. The bailiff who had the power of taking bail refused to do so, and the gentleman had no remedy but to issue a Chancery replevin, which cost several pounds'.[91]

Attachment of a defendant's goods could not only lead to inconvenience and expense; it could also provoke violent resistance. This appears to have been the case at Corrafin where there was 'often murder ... very nearly committed in consequence of it'. One defendant, for instance, who thought it was 'a hardship to see his cattle taken', managed to get a crowd to support him. The plaintiff also had '30 or 40 people with him'. This led to a fight, as a result of which the 'poor man [presumably the defendant] died ... from the beating he got [and] there were some of the other people nearly killed also'.[92] It appears that Roughan, the seneschal at Corrafin, could also be quite negligent in the manner in which he issued attachments. For instance, he did not 'always' take an affidavit and he also admitted that 'for about three or four years' after his appointment he 'used to leave some of them ... with [his] name signed in blank, with a man of the name of Hynes, [but when he] found the custom was bad, [he] gave it up'.[93] Despite an often laissez-faire approach to issuing attachments, the seneschal claimed that the lower orders could benefit from them.

This certainly seems to have been the situation in a case which the attorney, Mr Cullinan, reported. He represented a shoemaker, Mr Maher, who brought a case against a Mr Bridgeman, who was the second husband of Lady De Burgho, a member of the powerful Galway landowning family. Bridgeman was visiting the seaside when his carriage was seized under attachment by Maher, who claimed that Lady De Burgho's first husband owed him fourteen shillings for shoes. When a decree was subsequently issued against him at the manor court, Bridgeman appealed to the judge of assize; but his case failed on a technicality, and he was left with costs of 'a couple of pounds' and the loss of his carriage.[94]

The power of attachment could also be used to thwart the operation of the criminal law. The attorney Cullinan, for instance, claimed to have represented a man who had been charged with

91 Ibid., p. 58 (Cahill).
92 Ibid., p. 120 (Fitzpatrick).
93 Ibid., p. 276.
94 Manor courts committee, *Minutes of evidence 1837–38*, p. 49.

MANOR OF GILFORD,
TO WIT.

James McConville of Ballynaganick farmer

Plaintiff;

Bernard McConville of Ballynaganick

in said Manor, *farmer* Defendant.

Reilly, Printer, Lurgan.

At a Court held at the Court-House in said Manor, the *Third* day of *March* 1843 pursuant to Notice.

It appearing to the Court, that the Defendant was duly served with Process to appear at this present Court, and is justly indebted to the Plaintiff in the Sum of *Six Shillings and Six pence Sterling for Cash lent*

It is therefore Ordered and Decreed by the Court, that the Plaintiff shall have and recover from the Defendant the said Sum, together with Five Shillings and Six Pence, the Costs of this Decree; and I do hereby authorize and empower the Bailiff of said Manor and his Assistants, at the Plaintiff's peril to take in Execution the Defendant's Goods, and them to Sell and dispose of to pay Plaintiff or his Assigns, his said Debt and Costs.

Given under my Hand and Seal of Office, this *Fourth* day of *March* 1843

Debt, ... £0 . 6 . 6
Costs, ... 5 . 6
Total £0 . 12 . 0

To the Bailiff of said Manor and his Assistants, these to execute.

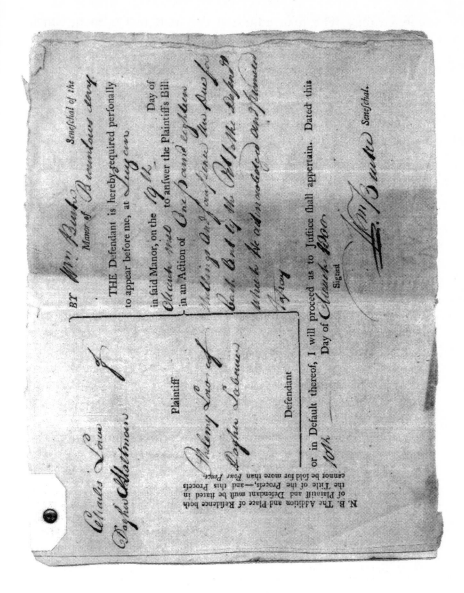

(*opposite*) A decree of the manor court of Gilford, Co. Down, 4 March 1843.
(*above*) Process from the Brownlow manor court, Lurgan, Co. Armagh, 10 March 1800.

cow-stealing. The man admitted the theft to Cullinan, which surprised him because of the man's 'station in the country, and the quantity of land [he held]'; but the defendant was confident that he could avoid conviction by claiming that he had taken the cattle under an attachment, which he could procure and have antedated. On the morning of the trial, he got an attachment from the daughter of a local seneschal, Mr Whitestone. Whitestone's daughters, one 'the wife of a captain in the army and the other the wife of a medical man', regularly signed and sold distringases, which gave the power of attachment. This proved a successful ploy by the man charged with theft and he was acquitted at the assizes. Cullinan did not think this was a regular occurrence; but he did know of other cases where distringases were signed by people other than the seneschal, on his behalf.[95]

It seems, therefore, that the power of attachment could certainly be oppressive and could also lead to violent resistance against the decisions of the seneschal and the manor courts. This indicates that the courts may have been resented and distrusted by sections of the community. It is also clear that they could be used by the lower orders against those of a higher rank and, indeed, against the elite in society. It is difficult, however, to establish to what extent this was a regular occurrence. The power of attachment could also be irregularly obtained to avoid conviction in the criminal courts. This demonstrates, perhaps, the dangers of seeing the law as operating in a standard or uniform way throughout the court system. It is clear, at least in the cases that we have encountered here, that the procedures in one court could be used to counter the operation of the law in another court.[96]

95 Ibid., pp. 48–49. The story may well have been apocryphal, since Cahill and Roughan gave similar evidence concerning two men charged with sheep stealing who thereby secured their acquittal and were saved from transportation: Manor courts committee, *Minutes of evidence 1837*, pp. 58–59 and 276. But as Roughan said, even if such an 'occurrence' had not taken place, 'it was certainly possible'.
96 Another example is provided by M O'Dowd, 'Women and the Irish chancery in the late sixteenth and early seventeenth centuries' in *IHS*, xxxi (1999), 470 at p. 480: in one case, 'the chancellor was asked to assist a widow in having decisions taken in a common law court implemented. Constance Stafford of Wexford reported that she had secured her dower through a writ of dower in the court of common pleas. Her husband's heir, however, had sufficient influence with the seneschal of the county to prevent the implementation of the writ. She asked the chancellor to issue an injunction against them. He obliged.'

Such practices certainly brought the power of attachment in manor courts into official disfavour. There was by this time, in any event, a 'great diversity of opinion' even as to its legality, at least in cases involving less than ten pounds.[97] The issue was resolved in 1848, when the court of queen's bench held in *Costelloe v. Hooks*[98] that the 1785 Act clearly meant that attachment was to cease in all cases where civil bill process was now available. It was only in cases exceeding the £5 or £10 limits set out in the Act that process by attachment was still to continue.

The hearing

It appears that manor courts were held mostly between eleven or twelve o'clock and five or six o'clock, in order to facilitate litigants travelling to and from court. They were, according to one witness, 'invariably' held in public-houses,[99] and tended to be 'very crowded and noisy'. The court at Corrafin in Co. Clare, for example, had for many years been held in a private house; but due to the cholera epidemic of 1832, it had been moved to a public house – apparently in preference to the town-hall and the market-house.[100] In Mayo, the seneschal, Revd Seymour, shared a court-house with the local petty sessions; but he did use a public house for one of his other courts.[101]

The jury usually sat on one side of a table with the seneschal sitting at the end of it, around which the 'suitors and crowd ... pressed' and were 'at liberty to make any observations they pleased'.[102] One witness claimed that the crowd were able to lean over the jury and were allowed to take part 'constantly'.[103] According to Mr Leonard, the Ennis attorney, this led to 'the greatest uproar and confusion; [with] the parties blaspheming and abusing each other' and up to a dozen people at a time addressing

---

97 Manor courts committee, *Minutes of evidence 1837*, p. 259 (Ruthven).
98 (1848) 11 Ir Law Rep 294 at p. 304 (Blackburne CJ).
99 Manor courts committee, *Minutes of evidence 1837*, p. 179. Not surprisingly, the select committee recommended that 'in no case shall a court be held in a house where spirituous liquors are sold': Manor courts committee, *Report*, p. 2.
100 Manor courts committee, *Minutes of evidence 1837*, pp. 54 (Cahill) and 267 (Roughan). According to Roughan, Sir Edmund O'Brien refused to allow the market-house to be used for this purpose.
101 Ibid., p. 179 (Seymour).
102 Ibid., p. 40 (Jagoe).
103 Ibid., p. 115 (Fitzpatrick).

the jury in English and Irish in what he terms a 'regular tower of Babel'.[104]

Part of the reason for the less than orderly state of the courts may have been the fact that the police did not attend. Joseph Roughan, the seneschal, made 'frequent application[s] for the police to attend', but these were refused on the grounds that the police should not be brought 'in contact with the country people'. The police had attended the court for the 'first three or four years' after Roughan's appointment in 1808 and during this time there was 'no noise or bustle'. But since then he 'could not control the tempers of persons'.[105] The police did attend the petty sessions at Corrafin, probably with the intention of marking it out as the more 'official' court. They attended the Revd Seymour's manor court in Co. Mayo, but this was only done as 'a favour' to a seneschal who was also a magistrate. Seymour also had a jury box in one of his courts and in another he had a railing around the jury – a degree of formality which may also have helped to maintain order.[106] It is likely, however, that such provisions were the exception rather than the rule in manor courts in the west of Ireland.

Execution

Manor court decrees could be enforced by execution against the body of the defendant (by arrest and imprisonment) or by seizing his or her goods found within the manor.[107] But there could be no execution against the body unless the court was expressly authorised by charter to issue such execution; most manor courts did not have such a power, and those which did rarely, if ever, exercised it.[108]

The usual practice was to seize goods within the manor belonging to the defendant and, after due notice (presumably to

104 Manor courts committee, *Minutes of evidence 1837–38*, p. 67.
105 Manor courts committee, *Minutes of evidence 1837*, p. 268.
106 Ibid., pp.190–91.
107 Small Debts (Manor Courts) Act (Ire.) 1785, s. 3.
108 Several seneschals explained that the power had been exercised prior to 1826 by committing the defendant to a local prison within the manor; but these prisons had then been abolished by the Prisons (Ire.) Act 1826 (7 Geo IV, c. 74). The act went on to provide that a person committed by a manor court was to be sent to a county gaol, apparently at the expense of the seneschal personally. As a result, they now 'rarely' signed decrees against the body. Under the Manor Courts (Ire.) Act 1827, a creditor could also be ordered to pay a weekly allowance to a debtor in prison. The only reported case from the west of Ireland arose from contempt of court; one person was committed to Ennis gaol 'for a few hours' for 'rioting' in Clonroad court-house, being drunk and insulting the seneschal: Manor courts committee, *Minutes of evidence 1837*, p. 326.

give the defendant the opportunity to pay the amount due), to sell them by auction and use the proceeds to pay the judgment debt.[109] A bailiff who wilfully neglected or delayed execution, or having executed, refused to pay money over to the plaintiff, was liable on civil bill at quarter sessions for the amount of the judgment debt and damages. To assist poor debtors, however, the law provided that if the decree did not exceed forty shillings, the jury could direct that payment could be made by weekly or monthly instalments within such time, not exceeding three months, as the jury thought fit; if the defendant agreed to this arrangement, execution was stayed *pro tempore*.[110]

Appeals

The 1785 Act provided that any person aggrieved by a manor court decree could appeal to the next going judge of assize – provided he entered into a bond with the plaintiff with sufficient security in double the sum awarded by the decree.[111] A plaintiff, however, had no right of appeal against a dismiss.[112]

In general, the rate of appeal, at least in the west of Ireland, appears to have been low, and many appeals which were lodged were never heard.[113] According to the evidence given to the select committee, the courts with the highest number of appeals were Moy-Ilrickane and Kilrush/Moyarta, both in Co. Clare. In 1835–1836, when the court at Moy-Ilrickane issued 732 decrees, 45 appeals were lodged – an appeal rate of six per cent;[114] in Kilrush/

109 Manor courts committee, *Minutes of evidence 1837*, pp. 4–5 (Fogarty).
110 Manor Courts (Ire.) Act 1827, s. 2.
111 Small Debts (Manor Courts) Act (Ire.) 1785, s. 5. The procedure on appeal, as amended by subsequent legislation, gave rise to considerable case law – see generally Napier, *Practice of the civil bill courts*, pp. 147–52. *Semble*, the 1785 act applied only to the civil bill jurisdiction of the manor courts; an appeal in common law cases lay by way of certiorari or writ of error to the courts in Dublin: Manor courts committee, *Minutes of evidence 1837*, pp. 3 and 8 (Fogarty). The select committee recommended that appeals should lie to quarter sessions: Manor courts committee, *Report*, p. 2.
112 *Barry v. Montgomery* (1839) 1 Cr & Dix CC 83; *Flinn v. Flinn* (1839) 1 Cr & Dix CC 331.
113 But there was evidence from Co. Cork that appeals were more frequent from courts in which attorneys practised: Manor courts committee, *Minutes of evidence 1837*, p. 153 (Hume).
114 Only twelve of the appeals were tried, and of these only four were successful: ibid., p. 332. The highest *rate* of appeal seems to have been from the court at Newport Pratt in Co. Mayo, where eight appeals were lodged

Moyarta, a much busier court, only fifty appeals were lodged in the period 1834–1836.[115] The number of appeals from decrees of the other courts was much lower; for instance, Revd Seymour claimed that in his court, there had been 'but two [appeals] for the last 23 years',[116] while in some courts there were no appeals at all.[117]

The low rate of appeal may be explained in part by the fact that the process was expensive,[118] and could involve considerable travel to the nearest assize town. But seneschals were also said actively to discourage appeals by insisting upon the defendant having the necessary recognizances ready 'at the moment' when the case was decided.[119] The seneschal at Oranmore is reported to have claimed that 'unless the plaintiff was present, and had the appeal ready drawn up, he would not take it afterwards; he did not conceive he was bound to take it'.[120] Thus, defendants would almost need to have been convinced that they were going to lose the case before it came to trial and have the appeal prepared (probably by an attorney or an agent) beforehand.

It may be that seneschals simply preferred not to have the proceedings scrutinised by a higher court. On the other hand, there is evidence that many appeals were vexatious, designed simply to gain time for the payment of the decree.[121] Roughan, the seneschal at Corrafin, for example, testified that he would not grant an appeal if he felt it was just a ploy by the defendant to gain time.[122] The

against the 26 decrees issued between December 1836 and April 1837; but only one decree was reversed: ibid., p. 443.

115 The court heard 3,501 cases during this period, but the number of decrees is not given. Only 23 of the appeals were tried, and in only two cases was the decree reversed: Manor courts committee, *Minutes of evidence 1837–38*, pp. 129–30.

116 Manor courts committee, *Minutes of evidence 1837*, pp. 333 and 441.

117 See e.g. Ennistimon (no appeals from 244 decrees) and Killaloe (one appeal lodged but not tried from 381 decrees): ibid., pp. 327–28 and 331–32.

118 Jagoe said that the cost of an appeal to a poor man was 'extremely vexatious': ibid., p. 44.

119 Ibid., p. 11 (Fogarty).

120 Ibid., p. 60 (Cahill).

121 Both Cary and Seymour claimed that vexatious appeals could be discouraged by proper application of the requirement to lodge an appeal bond: ibid., pp. 169 and 184. But the select committee considered that an appellant should also be required to swear 'an affidavit ... of belief in the justice of the appeal': Manor courts committee, *Report*, p. 2.

122 Manor courts committee, *Minutes of evidence 1837*, p. 273. But Cahill claimed that Roughan 'endeavours to evade granting [appeals] as much as he can': ibid., p. 61.

right of appeal might, therefore, be dependent on the whim of the particular seneschal.[123] This again serves to emphasise the degree of autonomy that these courts could enjoy. Indeed, if the procedures followed by the seneschal in respect of an appeal were incorrect his initial decree would not in practice be reversed. Hence, 'the greater the incompetence of the seneschal, the greater the difficulty in reversing his decree'.[124]

When appeals were heard by the judge of assize, it appears that they seldom succeeded – unless, perhaps, the appellant could prove that the seneschal had exceeded his jurisdiction. On the whole, however, appeals were rare and it is probable that this was due to the difficulty of appealing rather than to a high rate of satisfaction with the courts' decisions. Resistance to those decisions was, in fact, far more likely to come from outside the legal system. For example, Fitzpatrick at Corrafin claimed that 'a man might say, though the decree was granted, it was robbery, and he would not let his cattle go [with the bailiff]'.[125]

'DRAMATIS PERSONAE' OF THE MANOR COURTS

The seneschals

As already mentioned, seneschals were appointed by the lord of the manor and paid from court fees.[126] It appears that the majority of seneschals in the west of Ireland either came from the ranks of the middle classes or the lesser gentry or were related to the lord of the manor or worked on the lord's estate. In Corrafin, for example, the seneschal, Joseph Roughan, owned property and was 'one of the middling gentlemen', and the seneschal at Oranmore was a professional man who had previously been an attorney.[127] The seneschal of Frenchpark, Frederick Cary, had acted as 'the keeper of accounts ... for the receiver of rents' on the

123 An attempt to circumvent a seneschal's decision to 'prevent' a defendant from appealing was rejected in *Fox v. King* (1843) 3 Cr & Dix CC 38.
124 Manor courts committee, *Minutes of evidence 1837–38*, p. 70, where Leonard says that the seneschal at Kilrush impeded appeals by his incompetence in drawing up the appeal papers 'informally'.
125 Manor courts committee, *Minutes of evidence 1837*, p. 117.
126 In some cases, as in Brookeborough, Co. Fermanagh, they might also be paid in part by fees from tenants under a covenant in their leases: ibid., pp. 36–37 (Taylor).
127 Manor courts committee, *Minutes of evidence 1837*, pp. 54 and 56 (Cahill).

estate.[128] In Co. Mayo, the seneschals other than Revd Seymour were members of the grand jury; in particular, the seneschal of Westport was 'a magistrate and one of the wealthiest men in the country'; when Seymour himself had taken over the position from his father, one of the other two men who sought the post was a tenant 'to the amount of £500 a year'.[129] The evidence suggests that, even in Mayo, the office of seneschal was essentially a position which a middle class man would seek either to achieve a moderate living or to supplement his income.

No professional qualification was necessary; rather, one of the key attributes was the 'respectability' of the applicant or his family. For instance, in Cloughnakilty, Co. Cork, an ex-navy man who came from a 'very respectable family' served as the seneschal although he was 'perfectly blind'.[130] This led to a number of complaints being made about the operation of his court. In an attempt to bring the holders of the office under some degree of regulation, the 1826 act had provided that every seneschal not being a barrister of at least three years' standing had to enter into a recognizance, with two 'good and sufficient' sureties, in such sum as the assistant barrister at quarter sessions or the judge of assize 'shall think sufficient' and 'conditioned for the true and faithful performance of the duties of the office'.[131] A principal purpose of this recognizance was to satisfy any action which might be brought against the seneschal for neglect, misconduct or breach of duty in his office. However, as Napier pointed out, 'the utility of this enactment is not very apparent, as it has been decided that the seneschal cannot be sued in the civil bill court or by civil action for misconduct, and the only remedy is by information in

---

128 Ibid., p. 175. Cary was, at the time of the report, working as an accountant and cashier in the Boyle branch of the Agricultural Bank.
129 Ibid., pp. 192–93. Seymour's father had 'a great objection' to his son taking office, but Seymour felt obliged to accept when it was presented to him by Lord Dillon.
130 Manor courts committee, *Minutes of evidence 1837*, p. 8 (Fogarty).
131 Manor Courts (Ire.) Act 1826, s. 6. The penalty for failing to enter into such a recognizance was £500. This requirement only applied on appointment, and the sums required varied from £500 (as in the case of Roughan) to £50 (Cary): *Return of the name of each seneschal ...* H.C. 1842 (35), xxxviii, 4 and 11. The Manor courts committee, *Report*, p. 1 recommended that no appointment of a seneschal should be final until it had been approved by the next going judge of assize.

the Queen's Bench, or by putting the recognizance in suit'[132] – presumably expensive proceedings likely to be out of all proportion to the amount at issue.

The office was in practice normally held for life and this could induce a certain degree of lethargy in the holder. In Frenchpark, for example, before the appointment of Frederick Cary, a court had not been held for at least three years, due to the 'infirm health' of his predecessor who had remained in office in spite of his infirmity.[133] If the seneschal chose to stay in office, he could be removed only on the grounds that he had stepped outside what was considered to be 'good behaviour'. Mr Cullinan, the attorney from Ennis, had seen a man who had since become a seneschal, 'very constantly drunk in the daytime, before dinner...' and believed that it was his 'habit to be so in his court'. The lord of the manor attempted to remove the man on the grounds that he held office only at the pleasure of the patentee; but the seneschal retorted that he could not be removed during good behaviour and that his drinking was not 'inconsistent' with such behaviour. Another Clare seneschal, Mr Whitestone, was a 'very good judge when he was sober'; this, apparently, was 'very seldom', as he was 'almost constantly drunk'.[134]

The fact that such seneschals continued to hold office would seem to indicate that once appointed they had a great deal of autonomy not only from the central administration but also from the lord of the manor. This may have been particularly the case where the landlord was an absentee. It was also possible for the lord of the manor to sell part of his estate, but still retain the manorial rights. This was the case in Corrafin, where Sir Edward O'Brien bought part of the estate and wanted to appoint a relative, Colonel O'Brien, as seneschal in place of the incumbent, Joseph Roughan. Roughan successfully resisted this by continuing to hold his court, there being a 'general appeal' for him to do so.

---

132 Napier, *Practice of the civil bill courts*, p. 138. See e.g. *Wyly v. Gannon* (1840) 1 Cr & Dix CC 349.
133 Manor courts committee, *Minutes of evidence 1837*, p. 173 (Cary).
134 Manor courts committee, *Minutes of evidence 1837–38*, pp. 46–47. Whitestone is reported to have 'thrown an ink-bottle at Mr Aston Green ... which struck him on the forehead'. Green, an attorney, had managed to insult the seneschal in the course of his address which led to 'a great deal of abuse between the gentlemen'.

When Colonel O'Brien recognised that Roughan had a good deal
of popular support, he gave up trying to hold a court himself and
paid back the price of the summonses he had issued. It appears as
if O'Brien did not have 'so strong a backing as [Roughan]'
towards whom there was 'a good deal of good nature' shown.
Indeed, it was only the fact there was 'frost and snow on the
ground' that prevented 'bonfires and illuminations' in celebration
of Roughan's success.[135] Evidently, seneschals, although at times
clearly incompetent, could also act with a great deal of independence and could win a degree of popular support from a sizeable
section of those who appeared before the court.

The manor court jury

By law, a seneschal was required to summon 'sufficient' jurors to
enable him to empanel a jury of twelve to hear and determine all
contested cases.[136] Although it remained in some doubt whether
a juror could be fined for non-attendance,[137] lack of numbers does
not seem to have been a problem. In some cases, however, juries
were simply selected from bystanders present in the court. This
was certainly the case in Corrafin, where the seneschal had not
summoned jurors for 'a great many years'. He felt that this would
lead to interference with the jury before the court was held, and
he was content to select jurors from the 'most respectable part of
[the crowd]'.[138]

The parties could object to particular jurors 'on account of
relationship, ... pre-expressed opinions, [or] often ... country
persons [could] have a spleen against each other, and one would
say, [he] should not like that such a man should be on the jury'. In

135 Manor courts committee, *Minutes of evidence 1837*, p. 289.
136 Small Debts (Manor Courts) Act (Ire.) 1785, s. 2. Strictly speaking, this
provision applied only to civil bill cases; but a jury was also required in
other cases 'by the ancient common law of the country, by which no
decision could be come to by any tribunal upon a matter of fact without the
intervention of a jury': Manor courts committee, *Minutes of evidence 1837*,
p. 4 (Fogarty).
137 Small Debts (Manor Courts) Act (Ire.) 1785, s. 2 provided only that
seneschals had 'the like powers ... to enforce ... attendance ... as such
seneschals ... now have by law ...'. But in some manors, such as
Frenchpark, jurors might be bound by a clause in their leases to attend the
manor court, on penalty of a fine for non-attendance: Manor courts
committee, *Minutes of evidence 1837*, p. 171 (Cary).
138 Manor courts committee, *Minutes of evidence 1837*, p. 268 (Roughan).

such instances, the seneschal 'always' removed the juror.[139] Once selected, the jurors had to swear an oath to give a 'true verdict'.[140]

As in other courts, the jury was supposed to consist of twelve persons. But it seems clear that some juries consisted of nine, seven or even five, particularly where the seneschal was unable to find twelve 'respectable' men.[141] Such practices gave rise to judicial concern, however, and the select committee were informed that after a number of decrees were reversed by the judge of assize on account of incomplete juries, 'greater attention' has been paid.[142]

Although it seems likely that the majority of manor court jurors were drawn from the ranks of shopkeepers and small farmers, opinion was divided on the quality of the persons concerned. Some witnesses regarded many jurors as 'totally unfit',[143] while others suggested that they were of the highest quality.[144] As seneschal, Joseph Roughan attempted to get 'some respectable shopkeepers or the better order of persons' to sit as jurors in his court. It appears, however, that the jury was open to anyone residing in the manor and that it could often be made up of the same people at each court. One such juror was a man, by the name of Shehan, whom the seneschal considered to be 'a very proper man, though he is a tailor'. He also claimed that he 'never saw the sign of drink upon [Shehan]'.[145] This was clearly in

---

139 Manor courts committee, *Minutes of evidence 1837–38*, p. 112 (MacDonnell). See also McCabe, 'Law, conflict and social order', p. 404.

140 Small Debts (Manor Courts) Act (Ire.) 1785, s. 2. The oath of the jurors in Seymour's court went as follows: 'You shall true verdicts give, according to the evidence which shall be given before you in the cases which shall come before you this day': Manor courts committee, *Minutes of evidence 1837*, p. 191.

141 Cahill 'seldom saw more than three, five or seven [jurors]' and Roughan considered himself justified in proceeding with a jury of less than twelve, having seen it done at quarter sessions: Manor courts committee, *Minutes of evidence 1837*, pp. 54 and 269; Leonard reported that a full jury at Kilrush was 'very rare': Manor courts committee, *Minutes of evidence 1837–38*, p. 66. The select committee recommended that a jury of seven should in all cases be considered sufficient, reducing to five or even three with the consent of the parties: Manor courts committee, *Report*, p. 2.

142 Manor courts committee, *Minutes of evidence 1837–38*, p. 45 (Cullinan).

143 According to Fogarty, the 'universal belief' was that persons who serve on manor court juries were 'totally unfit', while Jagoe said that jurors were 'not of that class which ought to compose a jury': Manor courts committee, *Minutes of evidence 1837*, pp. 10 and 41.

144 According to Seymour, some of the jurors at Castlemore were magistrates and others were gentlemen who had acted 'on special juries at the assizes': ibid., p. 188.

145 Ibid., p. 269.

response to evidence given by the local magistrate, Cahill, who claimed that both Shehan and another man, a 'public-house keeper' called Kease, were 'constantly in attendance [and appeared] to be people given to whiskey'.[146]

Having heard the case, the jury sometimes retired, and sometimes stayed in court. If the jury did not retire to a separate room,[147] there might well be a 'debate', in which bystanders might take part, as to what the verdict should be; but this did not apparently prevent the jury reaching a 'true' verdict.[148] There was some evidence that juries waited until the end of the court day before announcing any verdicts; they then gave their verdicts altogether 'in a heap' – a practice condemned as making the trial 'nothing short of a mockery'.[149]

It seems to have been 'pretty general' for the jury to receive payment from the successful party either in the form of money or whiskey. The jury would say that they were to give a verdict for a certain party and that he or she was to give them '...1s. or 2s. 6d; or a pint or a quart of whiskey'. This payment was referred to as the 'Cob' and was given in open court before the seneschal.[150] According to Cahill, this enabled the seneschal to exercise a good deal of control over the court and in some cases to rule 'as if the jury were not present at all'. He claimed that the jury at Oranmore included 'two or three men who [were] notorious drunkards [who travelled] 10 or 12 miles to be upon the jury' and who would

---

146 Ibid., p. 54. In Cahill's opinion, most of those who attended court as jurors did so for the purpose of getting drink.

147 In some cases, as at Brookeborough, Co. Fermanagh, the public were excluded from the court-room – and the door locked – while the jury deliberated: ibid., p. 34 (Taylor).

148 Ibid., pp. 40–41, where Jagoe goes on to say that he had never heard a verdict which was 'flagrantly unjust'. Cullinan said that juries 'seldom' retire, but 'most generally pronounce their verdict without much hesitation': Manor courts committee, *Minutes of evidence 1837–38*, p. 46.

149 Manor courts committee, *Minutes of evidence 1837*, p. 34 (Taylor, referring to Brookeborough) and p. 25 (Kelly).

150 Ibid., p. 41 (Jagoe). The use of drink, in particular whiskey, was common in the pre-Famine period as a means of sealing a deal. It was also often given to intermediaries 'who ... helped to settle [an] argument' between buyers and sellers at fairs to symbolise the legitimacy of the agreement. The manor court custom may, in fact, have had its origins in the court of piepowder which sat at fairs and settled arguments between buyers and sellers: see J.R. Barrett, 'Why Paddy drank: the social importance of whiskey in pre-Famine Ireland' in *J of Popular Culture*, xii (1977), 155 at p. 159.

sometimes 'go [on the] circuit with [the seneschal]'. The jury was in general made up of what Cahill termed 'a low description of people; persons to whom the drink they got appeared to be the great object', and he believed that by selecting the jury and ensuring that they got drink the seneschal could expect them to do 'exactly what he liked'.[151]

There is evidence to suggest, however, that the seneschal did not have the level of control over the jury which Cahill assumed. Timothy Fitzpatrick, who occasionally served on the jury at Corrafin, gave a different account of the relationship between the seneschal and the jury. He agreed that some of the jury 'never would [attend] if they did not get the shilling or the whiskey';[152] but he denied that such practices gave the seneschal control of the jury. In his experience, the jury 'generally agreed' with the seneschal's opinion and there was no need to retire; the promise of drink or money played no part in reaching the verdict – rather it was given afterwards by the successful party. Whatever their verdict, the jury was guaranteed some form of compensation. Joseph Roughan, the seneschal of the court, went further; drink was only given to the jury on rare occasions and then only as a form of refreshment at the end of the day. He denied that money was given to the jury in his court, although he did admit that before his time it 'was considered a matter of right'.[153]

Fitzpatrick also recalled an incident where the jury refused to give a verdict to the seneschal when they were not given drink by the successful party. In order to placate the jury the seneschal himself had to give them 'a glass of punch or something of that sort'.[154] This incident demonstrates that, whatever their motives for attending, jurors could assert their authority in the court. Indeed, Frederick Cary, the seneschal at Frenchpark, Co. Roscommon, claimed that he gave no assistance to the jury 'because the business is principally agricultural, matters arising out of agricultural trans-actions, and the jurors being all farmers, understand such things perfectly'.[155]

---

151 Manor courts committee, *Minutes of evidence 1837*, p. 57.
152 Ibid., p. 116.
153 Ibid., pp. 270, 273 and 284.
154 Ibid., p. 115.
155 Ibid., p. 167.

It is clear, however, that juries did not make the decision in all cases. Roughan admitted that, as seneschal, he had 'decided without the jury'; but this was done only where the parties agreed that he should act as 'an arbitrator between them'.[156] There was evidence that most seneschals themselves decided cases under five shillings, since these were usually based on an IOU (promissory note) and there was little doubt as to the validity of the plaintiff's claim. Indeed, there was often no defence. It was generally only in defended cases over five shillings that the jury would make the decision.[157] In such instances the jury had not been known ever to 'deliberate longer than half an hour, or three quarters of an hour'.[158]

The overall impression conveyed by the evidence is that the manor court jury, drawn mainly from the more comfortable element of the lower orders, played a relatively substantial role in the decision-making of the court.

Agents and attorneys

Agents who were not qualified lawyers were often hired to provide informal representation for litigants before the manor courts. The role of the agent, according to the seneschal at Corrafin, was to read out the summons to the court.[159] This was, however, a role that the seneschal could fulfil himself without charging a fee. It is unlikely, therefore, that litigants would go to the extra expense of hiring someone if agents did not play a wider role in the court in terms of questioning witnesses and addressing the jury. But the evidence of their true role remains sketchy.

One example may be provided by the Doyles, a family who operated in the court at Corrafin. Mrs Mary Doyle, the widow of an ex-bailiff, apparently exercised considerable influence on the proceedings of the court. For a fee of one shilling, she 'did the business' making out accounts and speaking 'a little to the court or jury, sometimes' by saying 'as much as she could in favour of the party who employed her'.[160] Another witness saw her as

156 Ibid., p. 273.
157 Manor courts committee, *Minutes of evidence 1837–38*, pp. 44 (Cullinan) and 64–65 (Leonard).
158 Manor courts committee, *Minutes of evidence 1837*, p. 170 (Cary).
159 Ibid., p. 274, where Roughan commented: 'The only agency I allow is merely to state the nature of the process, or read it over, and then to fill up the decree, leaving me to fill up the special bailiff's name and sign it'.
160 Ibid., p. 56 (Cahill).

having a slightly more extensive role. He claimed that she interfered with witnesses by 'asking them questions relating to the case,
as any attorney would do'. Both of Mrs Doyle's sons were bailiffs
and process-servers in the court, and it seems that she acted as an
agent only when they were involved in a case. Fitzpatrick believed
that she did not receive a fee, but rather got 'plenty of drink'; in
addition, if she was successful, her sons would get to execute the
decree. By the time of the select committee report she was '50 or
60 years of age' and had been practising in the court 'just the
same' during her husband's lifetime.[161]

Joseph Roughan, the seneschal of the court, however, declared
'solemnly' that Mrs Doyle played no such role in the court. He
accepted that she was present on court days, but asserted that her
role was merely 'to collect money for the processes served in the
court for her son, or for her husband...'. He also claimed that he
had to remove her on occasion from the court because 'she would
sometimes be drunk, and make a great noise'. He admitted that
she 'might have done anything she liked at the lower end of the
room, or in the street' which may have had some influence on the
jury. However, Roughan also seems to admit that Mrs Doyle did
on occasion address the court. He claimed that she was 'a most
incorrigible woman when she was drunk' and 'interrupted everything' and he admitted that she would talk to him and the witnesses,
the jury and even 'the lord lieutenant if he was there'. He claimed,
however, that he did not pay attention to what she said as she 'did
not care what she said or did' on such occasions.[162] Mrs Doyle's
role, while not strictly speaking that of an attorney, was probably
more substantial than that of a drunken nuisance.

Those who operated as agents often came in for strong criticism,
especially from licensed attorneys who tended to take a dim view
of lay people acting as advocates. For instance, when the attorney
Denis Leonard arrived in Kilrush he put a stop to people who
were not attorneys practising in the court. He declared that such
people were 'the most horrible ruffians' and that they were clerks
who had 'been discharged by their employers' and 'drunken
fellows of the village'.[163]

---

161 Ibid., p. 117 (Fitzpatrick).
162 Ibid., pp. 274–75 and 288.
163 Manor courts committee, *Minutes of evidence 1837–38*, p. 68. Cary, the
   seneschal at Frenchpark, also claimed to prohibit lay persons from acting as
   agents: Manor courts committee, Minutes of evidence 1837, p. 173.

It is unclear to what extent barristers and attorneys practised in manor courts. It seems that attendance by counsel was rare, but not unheard of.[164] Representation by solicitor was more frequent, but the evidence is somewhat contradictory. Edward McDonnell claimed that 'attornies constantly attended' the court in Castlebar, and he referred to the advantages of their doing so.[165] On the other hand, Cullinan said that 'respectable' attorneys did not practice in manor courts 'except on particular occasions, for respectable clients', and Fitzpatrick asserted that attorneys were only willing to attend when there was a 'matter of some importance' or 'some irregularity in the proceedings'.[166] The manor courts were said to be unpopular with attorneys in part because they were in out-of-the-way places and in part because of the low level of fees.[167]

Bailiffs

Decrees issued by a manor court were, if necessary, enforced by the court bailiff.[168] By law, a manor court bailiff was required, on appointment, to give a security, with two sufficient sureties, of £50 'for the faithful discharge of his office';[169] the select committee was told, however, that such sureties could in practice be 'men of straw not worth a penny'.[170]

The office was clearly open to a wide range of applicants and their influence was not necessarily restricted to matters of execution. There is evidence, for example, that bailiffs could have an influence on the decisions of the jury. Mr Cullinan, the Ennis attorney, claimed that '… if the bailiff says, I know so and so, that goes further in some instances with the jury than the oath of a

---

164 Thus, Fogarty knew of only one manor court (Charleville) where counsel were employed, and then only occasionally: Manor courts committee, *Minutes of evidence 1837*, p. 5.
165 Manor courts committee, *Minutes of evidence 1837–38*, p. 116.
166 Ibid., p. 46 (Cullinan) and Manor courts committee, *Minutes of evidence 1837*, p. 117 (Fitzpatrick).
167 Ibid., p. 76 (Warren, a seneschal in Co. Cork). Solicitors were more generally used in Ulster, though practice in manor courts there was 'considered to be rather derogatory': ibid., p. 233 (Mr Sausse, barrister-at-law).
168 A bailiff might also be appointed by the plaintiff personally: ibid., p. 277 (Roughan).
169 Small Debts (Manor Courts) Act (Ire.) 1785, s. 11.
170 Manor courts committee, *Minutes of evidence 1837–38*, p. 50 (Cullinan).

respectable witness, and they will interfere in that way constantly'.[171] The bailiffs at Corrafin had a particularly bad reputation. The seneschal admitted that there had been a number of complaints of malpractice by them,[172] and the local magistrate testified that the bailiffs did 'everything in the most oppressive way, unless they got money'.[173] He also claimed that one of the bailiffs could not be trusted as a witness and, indeed, that Gahagan, the bailiff at Oranmore, 'would not be much believed either'.

Bailiffs and agents could also work in tandem. In Corrafin, a man by the name of Conway had acted as a bailiff while his son operated as an agent. As well as carrying out the duties of a bailiff by seizing goods, Conway acted as 'a kind of registrar to the court and filled up decrees'. His son would charge up to two shillings for carrying out his duties as an agent.[174] Given that bailiffs were paid a fee for each execution, they would probably have been anxious to obtain work, while agents would have been equally eager to be involved in the trial. Both would normally have been acting for plaintiffs, and it is not difficult to imagine that they each had an interest in assisting the other.

Litigants

In manor courts, as in other civil courts, costs followed the event in the sense that the successful party was entitled to be reimbursed in respect of the cost of litigation. These costs, at least in cases commenced by civil bill, were fixed in 1785 at 5s. 11^{1}/2d. Irish, the equivalent of 5s. 6d. new currency, 'and no more'.[175] The select committee heard evidence, however, that the statutory scale was frequently exceeded, and that costs could be higher than for

---

171 Ibid., p. 46.
172 Manor courts committee, *Minutes of evidence 1837*, p. 277 (Roughan). Under the Small Debts (Manor Courts) Act (Ire.) 1785, s. 11, a bailiff who wilfully neglected or delayed execution of a decree or, having levied the same, refused to pay the plaintiff, was liable to an action by civil bill.
173 Manor courts committee, *Minutes of evidence 1837*, p. 59 (Cahill).
174 Ibid., p. 56 (Cahill).
175 Small Debts (Manor Courts) Act (Ire.) 1785, s. 3. This sum was made up of court fees payable to the seneschal and a fee of two shillings for an attorney who attended the hearing. The 1785 act did not apply to common law cases, and the costs in such cases could amount to 'as much as £10 upon a single case'; if used in small debt cases (as in Charleville), the costs for cases under forty shillings could be £2 or £3: Manor courts committee, *Minutes of evidence 1837*, pp. 5–7 (Fogarty).

similar cases at quarter sessions.[176] On the other hand, it became 'lawful' after 1826 for a seneschal to withhold all or part of the costs when issuing a decree for a sum not exceeding forty shillings.[177]

The cost of manor court litigation suggests that many plaintiffs would have come from a social class above that of the labouring poor. Labourers were unlikely to have been able to afford even modest costs and, in any event, were unlikely to be in a position to offer credit. No doubt some benefitted from the seneschal's discretionary power to reduce the cost of litigation; but there is nothing to suggest that the practice was widespread or well publicised.[178] It should also be remembered in this context that successful suitors were often expected to pay an additional sum of one shilling to each member of the jury.

Cases could be brought before the court by 'large commercial creditors' such as 'agricultural and national banks, [and] loan fund societies'.[179] It is probable also that a number of cases involved shopkeepers and 'country people'.[180] It seems, however, that the business of the court 'chiefly [involved] transactions between farmers and their labourers, or between small farmers themselves'.[181] Cases between tenants and labourers may, in fact, have been the mainstay of business in the courts; there is evidence, for instance, that areas of Galway had no need for the courts in places where the land was held by 'independent people' in large tracts.[182] Many

176 According to Fogarty, 'costs are generally much larger than the proceedings before assistant barristers, and ... vary ... from 7*s*. 6*d*. to 9*s*. 6*d*. upon a decree': Manor courts committee, *Minutes of evidence 1837*, p. 8. Fitzpatrick commented that manor court costs were 'nearly double' those at quarter sessions, and Roughan noted that decrees had been reversed by judges of assize on account of excessive costs: ibid., pp. 117 and 274. Cary, on the other hand, stated that costs allowed by the Frenchpark manor court were 'more moderate' than those at quarter sessions: ibid., p. 173.
177 Manor Courts (Ire.) Act 1826, s. 5. William O'Brien, seneschal of the manor of Bunratty in Co. Clare, for example, normally charged 2*s*. 6*d*., and in Dayne and Ballynock, Co. Mayo, 'in many cases costs were not charged for various reasons, persons not having means to recover their debts; seneschal has forgiven costs and given processes to such persons as had no means to recover the small debts': Manor courts committee, *Minutes of evidence 1837*, pp. 325 and 442.
178 In particular, Seymour stated that he was in the habit of advancing money to those too poor to obtain redress in his court; but he also admitted that he did not publicise the fact: ibid., pp. 181 and 184.
179 McCabe, 'Law, conflict and social order', p. 406.
180 Manor courts committee, *Minutes of evidence 1837*, p. 189 (Seymour).
181 Ibid., p. 172 (Cary).
182 Ibid., p. 169 (Cary).

of these cases would have arisen from what were termed 'time-bargains' which involved labourers who bought potatoes 'at a very high rate in the months of March and April' and then could not afford to repay the debt and interest the following September.[183] There was evidence that the rate of interest could be quite 'usurious'; but this was denied by a number of seneschals, one of whom claimed that 'the jury never allow anything more than a trifling interest, what they think fair'.[184] Edward MacDonnell, the Co. Mayo juror, also declared that in cases of time-bargains juries acted 'as a sort of arbitrators [*sic*] between [the parties], and [gave] them fair play on both sides. I have hardly ever seen a defendant go away dissatisfied ...'.[185]

Since it would have been primarily the labouring class who needed such loans, it seems likely that they made up the majority of defendants before the manor courts. It has already been noted that many cases were settled out of court; this may indicate that many defendants felt that they had little chance of success if the case went to trial. The returns to the select committee (as summarised in the Tables above) suggest that the success rate of manor court plaintiffs in the west of Ireland seldom fell below 80 per cent and could be as high as 96 per cent.[186] These results would seem to support the view that manor courts generally favoured the complainant. A key factor which emerges in the course of the evidence is that this may have been due to the jury being of the same social class as the plaintiffs.

An interesting example of conflicting evidence on this issue comes from Corrafin and the role of one Patrick Keefe in the court. According to Mr Cahill, a local magistrate, Keefe 'was in the habit of giving out potatoes and money at most exorbitant interest – small sums to the peasantry; and he was always sure to

---

183 Ibid., p. 41 (Jagoe).
184 Ibid., p. 172 (Cary). See also *Poverty before the Famine: County Clare 1835: First report from His Majesty's Commissioners for inquiring into the condition of the poorer classes in Ireland*, ed. M. Comber (Ennis, 1996), p. 49.
185 Manor courts committee, *Minutes of evidence 1837*, pp. 112–13.
186 Ibid., appendix B, especially the Manors of Dayne and Ballynock, Co. Mayo (96 per cent). See also Crovreaghan (86 per cent), Doonass (91 per cent) and Moy-Ilrickane (86 per cent) in Table 3 above, and Boyle (82 per cent) in Table 2 above. Notable exceptions were two of the busiest courts, namely Castlebellew, Co. Mayo, where, on average, 67 per cent of the cases tried in 1834–1836 resulted in decrees (Table 4 above), and O'Brien's Bridge and Tomgrany, Co Clare, where Table 3 above yields a 'success' rate of 65–66 per cent.

go to the seneschal's court and get decrees'. Indeed, he was known
to have '40 or 50 summonses in the seneschal's court'. Mr Cahill
also claimed that manor courts were generally biased in favour of
the plaintiff, with a rich man having '99 chances out of 100 in his
favour'.[187] The juror, Mr Fitzpatrick, agreed that Keefe 'was a
regular visitor, [who] generally got verdicts in his favour'. This was
due mainly to the fact that the jury thought of him as 'the best
that used to come into the court' as he 'used to do a good deal of
business there'. Fitzpatrick also claimed, however, that it was the
general opinion of the people that 'no persons will have any
business in the court except those who cannot recover their debts
at the [quarter] sessions'. Furthermore, Keefe himself, although
having '30 or 40 summonses a day ... would not bring them to the
seneschal's court, if he thought he could recover at the sessions'.[188]

Joseph Roughan, the seneschal of Corrafin, admitted that Keefe
used the court. But he declared that 'there were more dismisses
against [Keefe] than verdicts in his favour', and that the latter
were reached only after the correct procedures of the court had
been followed. Indeed, Roughan claimed that he reduced the price
Keefe charged for barley and potatoes and only gave him 'a fair
rate of interest'. When he eventually discovered that Keefe was
involved in fraud, he made an effort to have him banished from
the court. Keefe nonetheless continued to use the court for 'six to
eight months; [but] he was very cautious; he knew he was watched'.
Roughan also took to informing the jury of his 'suspicions as to
the character of the man' and he believed that the jury had in any
event as 'great a knowledge' of Keefe as he had – and that it was
for these reasons that Keefe had begun to bring cases before the
quarter sessions again.[189]

This evidence suggests that some members of the more
'comfortable' farming class attempted to exploit the vulnerability

---

187 Manor courts committee, *Minutes of evidence 1837*, pp. 53 and 55. Cahill
     also claimed that Keefe 'was once before the magistrates for detaining a
     poor man's bed for a loan of 16*s*., all of which had been paid except 4*s*., he
     had the man's bed, and made him work a day every month, and pay him 4*s*.
     a year discount ... [when calculated] ... it came to 200 per cent'.
188 Ibid., pp. 116 and 120. Fogarty also claimed that parties go to manor courts
     'who despaired of succeeding in other places', in reliance on 'want of
     sufficient knowledge' in the seneschal, and 'to the fact of the jury ... having
     the friends of such party upon it': ibid., p. 10.
189 Ibid., pp. 269–71.

of the labouring classes through the courts. The question it fails to answer, however, is whether or not the courts facilitated such actions or whether they worked against or at least limited the harshness of these cases. We have seen that manor courts could have a role in fixing prices and even in regulating the market, measures which could benefit those from the lower orders by ensuring that they had a food supply in times of need. There is also evidence that juries could establish a fair rate of interest to the satisfaction of the defendant. It is also clear, however, that both the jury and the seneschal could benefit substantially from the high rate of participation of plaintiffs, such as Keefe, and that plaintiffs did indeed enjoy a high success rate. Thus, it is possible that the court could be used in an oppressive way against the labouring classes. It should be noted, however, that a plaintiff like Keefe used the quarter sessions as well as the manor courts and may in fact have preferred the former as being more 'secure'.[190] In this sense, the manor court can be seen as being used on occasion, when it was expedient, in a wider conflict of interests between labourers and farmers rather than being seen as simply a forum which created and/or facilitated such conflicts to any greater extent than the more official courts of petty and quarter sessions.

CONCLUSIONS

There remains, at this juncture, one crucial question to be addressed: to what extent were these courts significant in the lives of the people in the west of Ireland before the Famine? Both the number of seneschals and of active manor courts probably diminished markedly in the first half of the nineteenth century. It is clear that some of their key functions, particularly with regard to criminal proceedings, were usurped by the petty and quarter sessions. The overall level of civil litigation enjoyed by petty and quarter sessions also exceeded that of the manor courts in the region. This would seem to indicate that the manor courts were in rapid and terminal decline at this time. There is certainly evidence of this from Co. Sligo and to a lesser extent from Co. Mayo. But there is also evidence, particularly from counties Clare, Galway

---

190 Manor courts committee, *Minutes of evidence 1837–38*, p. 115 (MacDonnell), claiming that the assistant barrister's court was more reliable in terms of having 'a decree put in force at once'.

and Roscommon, that where the courts were still active they could deal with a very high level of business. Indeed, we have seen that the busiest court in the entire region was the manor court of Castlebellew, which handled well over two thousand disputes a year in the mid-1830s. If this constituted a decline in the level of business, it is difficult to conceive what the previous rate of participation had been.

There is also evidence to suggest that if a case failed at petty or quarter sessions it could be brought, with a reasonable chance of success, before the manor court.[191] Indeed, it appears as if manor courts would deal with cases which a regular court of law would not entertain.[192] Moreover, the fact that seneschals could sometimes act as magistrates – as was the case, for example, with Revd Seymour, seneschal for the Castlemore manor – may indicate that the courts could co-exist with the official courts in some areas. It would be a mistake, therefore, to see the operation of the lower courts in the pre-Famine period simply in terms of the inevitable rise of petty and quarter sessions and the corresponding decline of manor courts. On the whole, it seems as if the manor courts could still be widely used and could often be regarded as a useful alternative to the sessions.[193]

It should also be acknowledged that manor courts were controlled largely by the middle classes and were used primarily by the middle and lower orders. This is not to suggest that these courts simply reflected their concepts of justice. The courts were clearly affected by wider societal pressures; but they do offer an insight into how these groups could use and manipulate the law when there was minimal intervention from the social elite and when they

---

191 Manor courts committee, *Minutes of evidence 1837*, p. 120 (Fitzpatrick).
192 Ibid., p. 53 (Cahill).
193 The select committee considered, however, that if the assistant barrister's court could be held more frequently and in more convenient localities, 'the necessity of courts of inferior jurisdiction [i.e. the manor courts] might probably be avoided, unless in considerable towns'. Until such changes could be made, steps should be taken to place the manor courts on a more satisfactory footing. In particular, the practice of all manor courts should be rendered uniform, 'so that a person acquainted with the law as administered in any one such court shall be in no danger of running into error as to the administration of the law in any other such court ...': Manor courts committee, *Report*, pp. 1–2. But nothing was done to implement the committee's recommendations before the Famine, and thereafter the government preferred the course of outright abolition.

enjoyed a great deal of autonomy from the central administration. In this sense, the operation of manor courts offers an important contrast to the standard view of the law in the pre-Famine period – that it was an essentially repressive force which was rejected by the mass of the people. Popular participation in the manor courts indicates that law, in particular the civil law, could be utilised by ordinary people in important and significant ways in their daily lives.

R.R. Cherry, lord chief justice of Ireland, 1914–1916

DAIRE HOGAN*

RICHARD ROBERT CHERRY held office as lord chief justice of Ireland for three years, from February 1914 to December 1916. He had first been appointed to judicial office as a lord justice of appeal in December 1909, having been attorney general for four years before that, as a member of the Liberal government under, successively, Sir Henry Campbell Bannerman (1905–1908), and H.H. Asquith as prime minister, and a Liberal member of parliament. His official and judicial career will be outlined in the second part of this paper, but his earlier career at the bar, as a legal author and in politics, is of interest and sets the scene for the more official part of his career. Even after his appointment as lord chief justice he was to find his old political friends endeavouring to call upon his presumed goodwill and loyalty to them in order to seek his resignation and create a judicial vacancy, to help them out of a long-running political difficulty.

The Cherrys were a family of Huguenot origin. Richard was born on 19 March 1859 in Waterford. He was the youngest son of Robert William Cherry, a solicitor, and a brother became a solicitor also. Richard was proud of his connection with the city, of which he was made a freeman in 1910. He entered Trinity College in November 1875. He took an active part in athletics and in rowing, and obtained first class honours and a double gold medal in mental science and history and political science. He was elected as the auditor of the college historical society ('the Hist') in 1882. Cherry's daughter wrote that he regarded his election as auditor of the Hist as one of the two proudest occasions in his life, the other being his election as a member of parliament.[1] His training in

---

* The edited text of the presidential address delivered on Friday, 10 October 1997 at the Public Record Office of Northern Ireland, Belfast, and an extended version of the text previously published by the Society in pamphlet form.
1 M.H. Cherry, *A short memoir of the right hon. Richard Robert Cherry, sometime lord chief justice of Ireland* (Dublin, 1924).

debate in the Hist served him well at the bar and, as will be seen, on the hustings in Liverpool about twenty years later.

He was called to the bar in 1881 and joined the Leinster circuit. This circuit, despite its name, included Waterford, and when the freedom of the city was conferred on him, he said that 'the solicitors of Waterford, not merely of my own creed but catholic solicitors, helped me in my early struggle in my profession at the bar'. He is best known for his work and expertise in land law in Ireland. However, this was not an exclusive interest, and certainly could not have been one in his early years at the bar. In 1885 he was appointed as examiner in political economy for the Indian civil service, and in 1889 was appointed as the Reid professor of criminal and constitutional law in Trinity College (an office confined to members of the bar, held for a period of five years). Two sets of his lectures as Reid professor were published, one being lectures on the growth of criminal law in ancient communities, and the other being an outline of criminal law.[2]

In 1888 he published a book under the title, *The Irish land law and land purchase acts 1881, 1885 and 1887*, with a complete collection of rules and forms and notes of cases. This was described as being 'by Richard R. Cherry M.A., assisted by John Wakely', and the preface refers to 'the authors'. Such a publication plainly would have been of assistance in developing his practice at the bar and would also have furnished academic credentials when he was being considered for appointment as the Reid professor. The side binding of the first edition refers to 'Cherry and Wakely'. In 1893 a second edition was published, extended now to cover all the land law and land purchase acts from 1860 to 1891, and this was stated to be by Cherry 'assisted by Mr Wakely and Mr J.W. Brady Murray', with their names in rather smaller print than before and the preface signed by Cherry alone. There were many other competing publications on the subject, of which about half a dozen were published around the turn of the century, but Cherry's book was quickly accepted as the leading authority.[3]

In 1897 a royal commission was established to inquire into the workings of the land acts, and in particular questions about fair rents, the true value of a tenant's interest in a holding that a

2   The first was published in 1890, the second in 1892.
3   J.C.W. Wylie, *Irish land law* (1st ed., Dublin, 1975), para. 1.51.

landlord was acquiring by pre-emption and the general efficacy of the land purchase acts. The chairman was Sir Edward Fry, ex-lord justice of appeal in England, and as an indication of Cherry's acknowledged expertise on the subject (the *Irish Law Times and Solicitors' Journal* called him 'the well-known specialist'), he was appointed as the secretary. The commission held thirty-four public sittings between September and December 1897, in Dublin, Belfast, Cork and Galway and 183 witnesses gave evidence before it.[4] The report of the Commission influenced the drafting of the Irish Land Act of 1903.

The third edition of Cherry's book was published in 1903 (before the passing of the act). In the preface he remarked that 'the number of cases is now so great that the practitioner is apt to be confused rather than assisted by a multitude of references; it is to the leading cases decided by courts of highest authority that he needs to be referred'. Over 800 cases decided since 1894 were referred to, making a total of well over 2000. Supplements on subsequent acts were published by T.H. Maxwell, with Cherry's permission, in 1906 and 1910.

Cherry was called to the inner bar in 1895, fourteen years after he had first been called to the bar, a rather more rapid ascent in his profession than many of his contemporaries would have enjoyed. This progress in his career, and his political skills referred to below, throw doubt upon the validity of an unflattering account of Cherry's practice and demeanour that is contained in Maurice Healy's classic, *The old Munster circuit*, published in 1939:

Richard Cherry had not been a notable figure at the Bar. He was a conscientious plodder, with few forensic graces; but he had written a notable text-book upon the Irish Land Acts, and this had become as essential a part of the Irish barrister's equipment as the Annual Practice would be to an English lawyer. He did not enjoy a large court practice, and his mind was slow and philosophical rather than practical. His knowledge of his fellow-men was not extensive, and erred towards charity; a virtue in a saint, but not in a practising barrister.[5]

His practice at the bar was affected by his views on the Boer war (1899–1902), which he opposed. W.K. Tarpey, a colleague who had also been called to the bar in 1881, wrote to him upon his

4   *ILT & SJ*, xxxii (1898), 79.
5   M. Healy, *The old Munster circuit* (Dublin, 1939), p. 110.

appointment as attorney general in December 1905 that 'in the days when one was stigmatised as pro-Boer I know of no man on that side who was not playing, and did not know he was playing, a losing game for himself. To my wife and me it meant material loss; to Mrs Cherry and you I have no doubt it meant the same.'[6] His daughter, in her short biographical study of her father, said that the years of the Boer war were difficult for the family. Allegations of disloyalty, and of welcoming defeats of British troops in the war, were made against him in the course of the election campaigns he fought in Liverpool constituencies in the general elections of 1900 and 1906. Some details of these allegations are referred to below, and demonstrate how, as Cherry wrote in a public letter, 'in election time gross and scandalous charges are frequently made without adequate foundations'.

Cherry had no apparent connection with Liverpool before standing as the Liberal candidate for the Liverpool Kirkdale constituency in the general election in October 1900, the so-called 'khaki' election which was held during the course of the Boer war. He lost heavily, as did other Liberal candidates that year. Liverpool was a city with a vigorous and complicated political culture strongly connected with Ireland, in which around the turn of the century a number of candidates from Ireland or with Irish connections had stood for election. In addition to Cherry, other Irish lawyers who stood in Liverpool constituencies at this period were J. G.Gibson (Liverpool Walton in 1885 and 1886), C.H. Hemphill (Liverpool West Derby in 1886) and T.F. Molony (Liverpool West Toxteth in December 1910) – Gibson for the Conservatives and Hemphill and Molony for the Liberals. Hemphill was appointed solicitor general in the 1892–95 Liberal administration, and sat as Nationalist MP for North Tyrone between 1895 and 1905. Molony was appointed solicitor general in 1912, and after successive promotions was appointed lord chief justice in 1918.

John Redmond had stood in Kirkdale in the 1885 election. W.E.G. McCartney, Unionist MP for South Antrim 1885–1903, stood unsuccessfully against the Irish Nationalist T.P. O'Connor in the Liverpool Scotland division in the 1895 election. Captain O'Shea, whose Irish connections were less direct and who was

6 PRONI, Cherry papers, D.2166/2/2/1/17. Material from these papers is referred to by kind permission of the deputy keeper of the records of Northern Ireland, which is gratefully acknowledged.

subsequently imposed by Parnell as the Irish Parliamentary Party candidate in the Galway by-election in February 1886, was the Liberal candidate in the Exchange constituency in the 1885 general election.

Augustine Birrell, with whom Cherry was to work between 1907 and 1909 during the second half of his term as attorney general when Birrell held office as chief secretary for Ireland, had stood as a Liberal candidate in the Liverpool Walton constituency in 1885. He wrote in his memoirs: 'When I received a formal invitation and had limited my pecuniary contribution to £250, I accepted [the nomination] ... Liverpool as a whole was Tory, and was now dominated by the drink interest. My opponent was Mr J.G. Gibson, a brother of the Conservative Irish lord chancellor [Lord Ashbourne]. He wanted to get in, in order to get on.'[7] Birrell's comment about expenses indicates how a prospective member of parliament would ordinarily be expected at that time to contribute to campaign funds, altogether apart from the consideration that MPs received no official remuneration for their services, salary payments for MPs being introduced only in 1911.

The Liberal party in Liverpool for which Cherry became one of the two flag-bearers in the 1900 election was weak and declining. The local leader, also a national figure in the party organisation, was Edward Evans. He was a director of a family chemical manufacturing company who in 1886 became president of the Liverpool Liberal Federal Council and in 1894 was elected chairman of the National Liberal Federation.[8] He became a friend and sponsor of Cherry. However, a very strong and well-organised Conservative party machine dominated the city's politics,[9] and was led in tandem by the local magnate, the earl of Derby, and, a supreme professional local party manager, Archibald Salvidge.[10] Conservative politics in Liverpool were organised on an anti-Irish basis: 'The

---

7 Augustine Birrell, *Things past redress* (London, 1937), pp. 101–05. There is an interesting explanation by F.E. Smith of the financial aspect of his prospective candidacy for different Liverpool seats (he was elected in Liverpool Walton in the 1906 election) in S. Salvidge, *Salvidge of Liverpool* (London, 1934), p. 63.

8 W.T. Pike (ed.), *Liverpool and Birkenhead in the 20th century. Contemporary biographies* (Brighton, 1911), p. 105.

9 P.F. Clarke, *Lancashire and the New Liberalism* (Cambridge, 1971), p. 217.

10 D.J. Dutton, 'Lancashire and the new unionism: The Unionist Party and the growth of popular politics, 1906–1914' in *Transactions of the Historic Society of Lancashire and Cheshire*, 130 (1980), 133.

Conservative vote was ... organised not only in defence of the Union but also on a strident anti-Catholicism. The Liverpool Constitutional Association and the Conservative Working Men's Clubs in which Salvidge had made his name both banned Roman Catholics from membership.'[11]

Sectarian riots occurred in Liverpool of a nature that would have been familiar in Belfast: 'Protestant and Catholic violence was hardly unique to Liverpool in this period but conditions in Liverpool made it more bitter and chronic than anywhere else except Belfast.'[12] One of the leading cases on the power of magistrates to bind over a holder of public meetings to keep the peace and be of good behaviour, *Wise v. Dunning*,[13] arose from riots that took place in May 1901 in Liverpool after a militant protestant leader, George Wise, had held public meetings of a nature grossly offensive and provocative to catholics.

Conservative politics in Liverpool had a more democratic air than in other cities, Salvidge and his allies having led a protestant working men's revolt against more moderate local leadership in the early years of the century. However, each of Cherry's Conservative opponents, in 1900 and in 1906, represented the local commercial elite. David McIver (1900) was a steamship owner and a railway director. Charles McArthur (1906) was an average adjuster, president of the Liverpool chamber of commerce (1892–1896), a member of the lord chancellor's committee for codifying the marine insurance laws and a vigorous champion of protestant interests.[14] Both McIver and McArthur joined in an appeal for funds for Wise in 1905,[15] and F.E. Smith, then beginning his career in Liverpool politics, represented him in his appeal against the restraining order imposed in connection with the 1901 riots.

11 Randolph Churchill, *Lord Derby [1865–1948]: King of Lancashire* (London, 1959), p.133.
12 J. Bohstedt, 'More than one working class: Protestant and catholic riots in Edwardian Liverpool' in J. Belchem (ed.), *Popular politics, riot and labour: essays in Liverpool history, 1790–1940* (Liverpool, 1992), p. 174.
13 [1902] 1 KB 167.
14 *Who's who of British members of parliament: vol ii, 1886–1918*, ed. M. Stenton and S. Lees (Sussex, 1978), p. 227; Bohstedt, 'More than one working class', p. 170.
15 P.J. Waller, *Democracy and sectarianism: a political and social history of Liverpool, 1868–1939* (Liverpool, 1981), p. 227.

There was a significant Irish immigrant community in Liverpool and the Liverpool-Irish had a greater presence in city politics than their brethren elsewhere in Britain. Home rule city councillors began to be elected in the 1870s, and in the early years of the century the chief political opposition to the Tory protestants was the Irish Nationalist party, which had more than a dozen members on the city council.[16] A working arrangement with the nationalists was the core of local liberalism, and the Irish likewise saw advantage in co-operating with the Liberals: 'In Liverpool the Liberal candidates had the problem of conciliating the Irish without appearing to be their clients. This was most acute in the Exchange division where, so it was reckoned, four-fifths of the Liberal vote came from the Roman Catholics and the Nationalists.'[17] There were a number of divisive issues between the Liberals and local Nationalists, such as the Boer war itself, where the Liberals were divided between what was known as an imperialist wing, which was strong in Liverpool, and a pro-Boer group; education was also divisive, with the catholic Irish and the Conservatives having a common interest in supporting the principle of state funding of voluntary church schools, while members of the liberal non-conformist tradition held very strong contrary views.

In the general election of 1895 the Conservatives won eight out the nine Liverpool constituencies, the ninth being held by T.P. O'Connor. When the general election was called in September 1900 no Liberal candidates had been selected for any of the constituencies, and the chief whip, Herbert Gladstone (a son of W.E. Gladstone), suggested to the local organisation that if they would not fight they might at least give him money. P.F. Clarke has noted that 'Liverpool Liberals were reluctant to contest their own city – ten stood in other parts of the country in 1900 – and it was commensurately difficult to persuade outsiders to come in', and that after a visit by Evans to party headquarters in London, 'two carpet baggers were hustled into Kirkdale and Exchange where, of course, they were soundly beaten'.[18]

The candidate for Exchange was selected in London and dispatched to Liverpool for approval in the course of a single day, 25 September,[19] just nine days before the poll, and it seems

16 Bohstedt, 'More than one working class', p. 205.
17 Clarke, *Lancashire and the New Liberalism*, p. 254.
18 Ibid., p. 232.
19 Ibid., p. 238.

unlikely that Cherry would have had very much more time for the campaign in his constituency. How and when Cherry came into contact with the Liberal party headquarters is not known, but plainly he might have looked for some outlet in England as well as in Ireland for his interest in public affairs, although his home and legal career remained at all times in Ireland. Politics in Ireland at the turn of the century revolved around the home rule issue, and although Cherry supported home rule he 'was more of the type of English radical than of an Irish Home Ruler', according to his obituary in the *Irish Times* in 1923.

After his nomination in the 1900 election he campaigned enthusiastically. He was reported in a Liverpool newspaper as speaking at a meeting in Bankfield Street:

> ... in the open air some 300 working men had assembled ... Mr Cherry said he was in favour of better houses for the working classes, the taxation of land values and old age pensions. Those were questions the working man was interested in ... The Conservatives only pretend to sympathise with working men. So long as they can humbug them by waving the Union Jack, shouting Rule Britannia and talking about the grievances of millionaires seven thousand miles away they will do nothing for them and as long as this war fever continues Mr McIver [the Conservative candidate] can afford to treat any programme of social reform and any question as to the real interests of working men as 'rubbish' – the polite epithet which, as you are probably aware, he applied to my election address.

At the meeting the secretary of the firemen's union proposed that Mr Cherry was a fit and proper person to represent the constituency in parliament. At this point, according to the report, 'a working man took a stand upon an adjacent cab and addressed a number of working men about him in loud tones in the interests of Mr McIver. The resolution was put to Mr Cherry's meeting and carried amidst some disorder, the speaker from the cab meanwhile continuing his utterances.'

In 1900 Birrell had stood as a parliamentary candidate in the constituency of South East Manchester, and recalled that it was said that 'every vote cast for a Liberal was a vote for a Boer. Manchester was evidently anti-Boer, and my wife and I on the polling day, and a drizzling day it was, were followed through the mean streets by a mob, some of whom spat upon us whilst others pelted us with mud picked up from the filthy streets.'[20]

20 Birrell, *Things past redress*, p. 151.

THE LIVERPOOL ECHO, WEDNESDAY,

R. CHERRY ARRIVES AT THE JUNIOR REFORM CLUB AFTER THE POLL
LAST NIGHT.

'Mr Cherry arrives at the Junior Reform Club after the poll last night.'
Line drawing from the *Liverpool Echo*, 17 January 1906

THE RIGHT HONOURABLE

RICHARD R. CHERRY

THE LIBERAL AND FREE TRADE CANDIDATE.

Election hand-bill, *c.*1906.

Cherry's Conservative opponent, David McIver, in 1900 had accused him of sympathy for the Boers very shortly before election day, when there was plainly almost no opportunity to make an effective reply. Mr McIver wrote to a Liverpool newspaper during the 1906 election campaign to give his version of what had happened and, no doubt, to revive the allegation:

On the Monday immediately preceding the Liverpool election of the 4th October 1900, I was for the first time informed that Mr Cherry, who had recently made a holiday trip on Messrs Forwood's steamer Zwoena, had given much offence to his fellow passengers by the expression of pro-Boer sentiments of which they strongly disapproved. Matters seem to have culminated at Madeira, where they received news of the execution of Cordua (a prisoner who had broken his parole, and who was said to have been implicated in a plot to kidnap Lord Roberts and murder unarmed British officers while sitting at dinner). Mr Cherry, I was told, had not merely expressed strong sympathy with Cordua, but with the suggestion that the Boers should shoot British prisoners by way of reprisal.

I took the very first opportunity open to me, which happened to be a luncheon at the Junior Conservative Club the following day, of mentioning the matter publicly in the expectation that Mr Cherry would, with equal publicity, make what answer he could. I was not disappointed, as, speaking the same evening, Mr Cherry contradicted the story, whereupon I sent my informant's letter to the newspapers. It appears, I think, in your issue of 4th October 1900.

Cherry acknowledged in 1906 that 'I held, as all my friends know, very strong opinions in regard to the late Boer war. I expressed these opinions with a vehemence which I generally do when I am deeply moved. But I never acted or spoke disloyally.'[21]

Cherry's emphasis on social issues brought little success: 'His Unionist opponent, McIver, mentioned no domestic item except Protestantism but this, and a monotonous patriotism, brought him 4,333 votes against 1,738.'[22] The result gave McIver 71.4 per cent of the vote and Cherry 28.6 per cent, a 10 per cent swing to the Conservatives since the 1895 election, and the *Liverpool Daily Post* said that 'not even the most sanguine Conservative anticipated the alarming shrinkage of the Liberal total'[23] in the two contested constituencies. The Liberals did not put forward a candidate in the

21 PRONI, Cherry papers, D.2166 (album of newspaper cuttings), pp. 4 and 18.
22 Waller, *Democracy and sectarianism*, p. 180.
23 Clarke, *Lancashire and the New Liberalism*, p. 368.

Kirkdale constituency in the 1906 election, leaving the way open there for the new Labour Representation Committee, the seed of the Labour Party.

The obituary in the *Irish Times* on 12 February 1923, after making the 'English radical' remark, said of Cherry that 'even in his college days these views manifested themselves in the part that he took in the debates of the college historical society. He was a convinced Free Trader. His views were very much those of John Stuart Mill on economics and social science.' His inaugural address as auditor of the Hist in November 1882 had been entitled 'Democratic Progress'. He was a member of the Statistical and Social Inquiry Society of Ireland, of which he was president three times, and of the Anti-Vivisection Society. He spoke at the annual meeting of the Society for the Prevention of Cruelty to Animals in May 1914, after his appointment as lord chief justice.[24] He had a long interest in penal reform, which found more scope for expression after he had become a judge.

In 1910 he was made a freeman of the city of Waterford, and in an address on that occasion he said that he was anxious that judges would be in touch with the people:

… and that if in the discharge of their duties sometimes it becomes necessary to pass sentences of imprisonment and sentences of any kind this is done conscientiously by them for what they believe to be the good of the country. I must take the view – I took it as a law officer and I still take it as a judge – that the less imprisonment you can possible impose the better. Imprisonment is an evil in itself, and it is only when it is absolutely necessary for the security of the masses of the law abiding people that any sentence of any kind should be passed upon a person who is charged with a crime.[25]

In January 1911 he gave an address to the Statistical Society on juvenile crime and its prevention, a subject in which he had a particular interest. He said that he:

… had every hope, and by that he meant real expectation and belief not a mere conventional expression of desire, that by careful reformatory treatment of every case of juvenile crime, combined with proper means being adopted to secure honest employment for those who had gone through it, you could in time entirely get rid of the criminal class, as a class, in our large cities.

24 *Law Times*, 137 (9 May 1914), 46.
25 PRONI, Cherry papers, D.2166/1/1A (album of newspaper cuttings), p. 60.

This hope was encouraged by an examination of the effects of what had already been done to substitute a reformatory for a merely vindictive treatment of criminals, and especially of young criminals ... So far every step which had been taken to mitigate the severity of punishment and to substitute a reformatory for a vindictive treatment had resulted in a diminution in crime and a reduction in the number of prisoners.

He spoke about the formal establishment of the borstal system for the detention and reform of young offenders under the Prevention of Crime Act 1908, and said that the absence of purely punitive treatment, and the encouragement of self-respect, self-discipline and habits of industry among the inmates would have a most beneficial effect, and also supported the Discharged Prisoners' Aid Society. He remarked that the reformation of the prison system owed much to the interest that Asquith, then prime minister, had first shown in the subject as home secretary in 1894.

Standing in Kirkdale in the 1900 election gave Cherry good credit with Evans and the party machine generally, and he was then able to be considered for some other constituencies and eventually nominated as the candidate for the more promising Liverpool Exchange constituency at the next election. When he stood then, in January 1906, a Liberal tide swept him and more than two hundred other new members of the party into parliament,[26] in the course of an overwhelming election victory for the party, comparable to those of the Labour Party in the general elections of 1945 and 1997.

He had, in fact, made inquiries in the early years of the century about standing for parliament in various constituencies in England and in Ireland. In September 1903 Evans wrote to Cherry:

You were right not to go to Widnes. The fact is that so much depends upon the attitude of the government to the effect of Chamberlain's speech [see below] followed by others that the whole character of our Liverpool seats may be altered. Besides, there is [a] vast change of attitude as regards the [Boer] war since the report of the Commission. I know the party would like to have you in Liverpool again, ... and perhaps before you finally decide upon an Irish seat I will be able to place the real state of affairs before you.[27]

---

26 G.L. Bernstein, *Liberalism and liberal politics in Edwardian England* (Boston, 1986), p. 92.
27 PRONI, Cherry papers, D.2166/3/2/1.

In 1904 Cherry wrote to John Redmond, leader of the Irish Parliamentary Party, asking if he could stand in an Irish constituency as a Liberal without nationalist opposition. In February Redmond replied:

My friendship for you would naturally make me anxious to see you representing an Irish constituency, but only as a member of an Independent Party whose first and most essential pledge is to refuse to take office. I could not support your candidature on any other lines. I do not know yet whether we will feel bound to start a candidate of our own as a pledged member of our party. If we do not do so it will be open to you or anyone else who so chooses to come out on other lines, but I must frankly tell you that so far as I am personally concerned I will not publicly support any member of the Irish Bar unless on the understanding that he is not to look for [a] place [on the Bench].[28]

Upon the resignation of Arthur Balfour as prime minister in December 1905 the Liberals formed a government, under the leadership of Sir Henry Campbell-Bannerman, and Cherry was appointed attorney general for Ireland. This was one of the very few occasions on which a government resigned in advance of, and in anticipation of defeat at, a general election rather than after the election had been held and the results were known. In the general election that was immediately held, in January 1906, Cherry stood for and was elected as member of parliament for the Liverpool Exchange constituency. This was a marginal constituency and, as the name suggests, covered the central commercial district of the city. There had been seven contests in the Exchange division between 1885 and 1900, two of which were by-elections, and in which the seat had swung from side to side. In 1885 out of a total vote of about 6,000 the Conservatives had held the seat by 64 votes. In the 1886 election it had been won by the Gladstonian Liberals by 170, and they held the seat in a by-election in 1887 by a majority of 7. They held the seat again in 1892 with a majority of 66. The seat was won by the Liberal Unionists in 1895 by a majority of 254, was retained by them at a by-election in 1897 by a majority of 54 and in 1900 was held by them again with a majority of 1,297.

There are two or three contemporary descriptions of the Exchange constituency which are of interest. When Cherry

28 Ibid., D.2166/3/2/2.

resigned as member of parliament upon his appointment as a judge in December 1909, he thanked his supporters in a farewell public letter, saying it had been a very great honour to be 'the representative in parliament of the leading commercial constituency of the great city of Liverpool'.[29] Birrell wrote that 'Parnell himself in 1885 was [initially] a candidate for the Exchange Division, which contained, in addition to the big merchants, bankers, and cotton brokers of Liverpool, a rabble of Irish voters ... [but] he withdrew his nomination in favour of Captain O'Shea'.[30] T.P. O'Connor said in his memoirs that in 1885 he had stood for the Liverpool Scotland division, 'but Parnell, without any consultation with me or anybody else I know of, suddenly nominated two other Irishmen, Mr John Redmond for Kirkdale and O'Shea for the Exchange Division. Kirkdale for Redmond was quite hopeless, but there was a fair chance of winning Exchange Division, which had in its electorate a large number of English Liberals and an even larger number of Irish nationals.'[31] The Irish in Liverpool were regarded as particularly adept practitioners of personation, and 'the Conservative candidates in the Exchange division regularly took precautions against it by obtaining lists of dead voters and those at sea'.[32]

Cherry had been selected as prospective candidate for the Exchange division in January 1905, and at a meeting to adopt him formally in December 1905 he spoke about the importance of free trade: 'Protection in all its forms, whether called preferential trade, retaliation, reciprocity or fair trade or any other name was one and the same thing, it was economically, morally and politically unsound.' After that subject, he spoke very briefly about, but plainly did not emphasise, the importance of self-government for Ireland. With respect to education, he said that by compromise and concession the Liberal party would establish good government 'and in the same way they would settle the education question in a way that would remove grievance without imposing corresponding grievances on other people'. Various other speakers at the election meeting supported free trade, one (Mr A. Jacob) saying 'the wisdom of free trade received daily exemplification in the particular business in which he himself was interested – the biscuit trade'.

---

29 PRONI, Cherry papers, D.2166/1/1A (album of newspaper cuttings), p. 60.
30 Birrell, *Things past redress*, p. 106.
31 T.P. O'Connor, *Memoirs of an old parliamentarian* (London, 1929), ii, 6.
32 Clarke, *Lancashire and the New Liberalism*, p. 127.

At this time the Conservative party was deeply divided and demoralised over the issue of free trade or tariff reform. British industrial pre-eminence in the nineteenth century had been based upon the principle of free trade, but with the development of other industrial economies and the adoption of tariffs in other countries British manufacturers began to press for protective tariffs. The cry was taken up by Joseph Chamberlain and other leading unionists and in 1903 Chamberlain had resigned from the cabinet, calling for a change in the principle of free trade so as to give preference to the colonies, under the slogan of 'Empire free trade'. The Liberals were united on free trade, whereas the divisions among the Conservatives were particularly evident in mercantile cities such as Liverpool, where the manufacturing interest was comparatively less strong in comparison with the mercantile and trading interests than in other cities.

In the circumstances of 1906, Exchange was thus a relatively promising seat for Cherry. It was traditionally, as has been seen, a marginal constituency, and the large majority enjoyed by the Unionists in 1900 rested on Liberal abstentions.[33] David McArthur, the sitting MP, had been a member of the Free Trade League, but by 1906 was no longer a supporter of free trade, declaring it to be unsound.[34] Salvidge recognised that Liverpool business people were unhappy with this new approach, and 'McArthur endeared himself to neither Chamberlainites nor traditionalists'.[35]

The informal coalition of Liberals and the Irish voters was put under some strain by an apparent lack of enthusiasm for home rule among leading Liberals. R.B. Haldane in a speech to the Liverpool Reform Club in November 1905 had said that home rule was not a priority, and perhaps not desirable in the first place. The fact that Cherry was an Irishman and a supporter of home rule plainly bolstered the Irish vote for the Liberals, however, despite the fact that he was not a catholic. Indeed, the national Liberal coolness on home rule may have worked against the Conservative party, already split on free trade: 'The Liberals' want of commitment to home rule enfeebled the Unionist alliance … this liberalised the Unionist Free Traders, who deserted McArthur.'[36] Cherry himself expressed the view that:

33 Waller, *Democracy and sectarianism*, p. 186.
34 Clarke, *Lancashire and the New Liberalism*, p. 270.
35 Waller, *Democracy and sectarianism*, p. 222.
36 Ibid., p. 223.

The main plank of the Government platform was the maintenance of Free Trade. Secondly the government proposed to reduce the excessive national expenditure of the last 10 or 15 years. Thirdly there was to be a reduction of taxation especially the taxes on tea and sugar. Fourthly came social reform with, if possible, the old age pensions which the Tories had long promised without an effort to carry out the promise. [This was introduced in 1908, in what Roy Jenkins described as the most important piece of social legislation for several decades.[37]] Fifthly they sought to amend the antiquated poor laws according to the necessities of the times. Sixthly came better provision for workmen's dwellings. Seventh he placed legislation to encourage temperance. Eighth on his list was the reform of the laws as to trade disputes, so as to restore to working men the power of peaceful combination.

Finally they wanted to restore to the House of Commons its efficiency and that could only be effected by the taking away from the Imperial Parliament and the giving to local and national bodies [of] a considerable portion of the business now discharged at Westminster providing, as far as possible, that Irish local affairs should be managed by Irishmen in Ireland and not by Englishmen in England.

He spoke about the importance to Liverpool of the shipping industry. He said that the Liberals should be supported if voters wanted to 'make people temperate, give them good comfortable homes to live in, wholesome food and a life worth living'. And he continued: 'The Tory party was no real friend to the working men. If they wanted legislation in their interests, to protect themselves, their children's food, their right to work, right to combine, to raise their wages they must return the Liberal party to power.'[38]

In a vigorous open-air address in January 1906 he stressed free trade:

Mr Cherry, in an address, asked them were they going to fight for the cause of labour, for the cause of Ireland, and for the cause of cheap food for their children, or were they going to vote for Joseph Chamberlain ('No'). That was the question before them. They had a union here of three parties which would prove irresistible. The Labour Party were backing him up by every honourable means. The Irishmen of Liverpool would vote for him to a man, and the Liberals of Liverpool were putting him as an Irishman forward as their candidate. That showed the cordiality existing between all the forces of progress in this great city, and that union would win a tremendous victory for them at the poll. They wanted a free breakfast table. They want economy in the administration of the national finance, they wanted less money spent upon the Army and the Navy, they wanted a vigorous cutting down of their

---

37 Roy Jenkins, *Asquith* (London, 1964), ch. xii.
38 PRONI, Cherry papers, D.2166/1/1A (album of newspaper cuttings), p. 26.

expenditure, and their taxes reduced (applause). That was the policy, together with freedom of trade, free food, freedom for Ireland and the people of Liverpool, which he would advocate if returned to Parliament.

He also said that 'the policy of the Liberal party had always been cheap food for the people. They had no right to tax the poor in the back streets of Liverpool for the benefit of people living in Canada and Australia.'[39] His Conservative opponent responded by saying:

We have had a gentleman coming here from Ireland who has been adopted by the radical party and who has called himself an undisguised home ruler. The question before the electors, whether Liberal or Conservative, is whether or not they desire the Exchange Division to pass into the hands of the Nationalists. He has accepted the office of Attorney General for Ireland, and Ireland has provided him with an office and they might also be asked to provide him with a seat.[40]

After this vigorous campaign the result of the poll in the Exchange division on 16 January 1906 (held in 'evil weather'[41]) was that the Unionist majority of 1297 was turned into a small Liberal majority for Cherry of 121. What had been a 35/65 split in the vote became a 51/49 split, or a 16 per cent swing. The Liberals retained the seat at the general election in January 1910 after Cherry had stood down, but lost it in the second general election that year, in December, when Salvidge worked successfully to ensure that the commercial men were reminded that a vote for the Liberals was a vote for home rule and the Conservative voters had become more sanguine about tariff reform.[42]

Salvidge gave a commentary on the election results in Liverpool to Joseph Chamberlain in February 1906. Only two of the Conservative seats in Liverpool were lost in 1906, and five were retained, a much better result for the party than in Manchester and other parts of Lancashire and the north west in particular. Salvidge was critical of what he saw as a lack of public spirit among some of the Conservative supporters:

---

39 Ibid., p. 4.
40 Ibid., p. 14.
41 Lord Birkenhead, *F.E.: the life of F.E. Smith, first earl of Birkenhead* (London, 1965), p. 120.
42 Salvidge, *Salvidge of Liverpool*, p. 100.

In Liverpool we lost Exchange because of particular difficulties, the Irish vote going solidly to Cherry ... In Exchange and Abercromby it has to be admitted that there were abstentions on the part of some of the commercial community. No doubt in Liverpool there are various middle men of various kinds who find the free import systems suits them but whose private interests are not necessarily those of the country as a whole.[43]

Cherry's work as attorney general included advising on the drafting of important legislation at the time, including the Labourers (Ireland) Act 1906, and the Evicted Tenants (Ireland) Act 1907, in respect of both of which, when cases on their interpretation came before him subsequently as a judge, he was able to speak with authority about the legislative history and intent of certain provisions which were in dispute. The main legislation with which he will be associated, however, is the Irish Universities Act 1908, which established the National University of Ireland and Queen's University, Belfast as new independent institutions, and ended a protracted debate about whether Trinity College should be associated in some way with other institutions of higher learning.

Cherry valued his connection with Trinity College, and the provost of the College, Dr Anthony Traill, was pleased when he became attorney general in 1905 (and an MP soon afterwards), and thus would have a part in the drafting of the imminent universities legislation. Traill wrote to Cherry:

... to offer you my best congratulations – I don't forget that your first step upwards was a Professor here, – you certainly have won your way most creditably since. Please let us forget any little friction that occurred between us on the Fry Commission [of which Traill had been a member] – those are small matters which should not stand in the way of pleasant relations. As Head of this place, I am outside of all parties and politics, my sole object is to push this place forward and to extend its benefits to all, if they will only accept them – I trust a good deal to your co-operation in such a task, now that you are in power.[44]

Cherry's obituary in the *Irish Times* said that in the preparation of the legislation his advice 'undoubtedly had the effect of enabling Mr Birrell to avoid the pitfalls which surrounded the attempts of Lord Bryce [chief secretary between 1905 and 1907, when he was succeeded by Birrell] and others to settle the question of grouping other collegiate institutions with Trinity College'.

43 Ibid., p. 70.
44 PRONI, Cherry papers, D2166/2/2/1/21.

A controversial and embarrassing case in which Cherry was involved arose out of the appointment in 1908 of M. McDonnell Bodkin to be a county court judge. The story is told both in *The old Munster circuit*[45] and in Serjeant Sullivan's memoirs. Bodkin's appointment was open to question since he had only tenuous claims to having been a 'practising barrister', a necessary condition of appointment, and it was widely regarded as a political favour to the Irish parliamentary party. Cherry, with the solicitor general Redmond Barry, defended the appointment when a writ was taken out, at the instigation of Sullivan, querying the validity of a judgment given by Bodkin. Healy characteristically describes Cherry's presentation of the matter in court in a poor light, as being fussy and unprepared and having to be rescued by the solicitor general; 'like many men occupying a position beyond their average capacity, he suffered from what is now called an inferiority complex; and he determined that he was not going to allow his administration to be made into a laughing stock'. In the end, the objection to Bodkin was withdrawn when, as Sullivan wrote, Bodkin's friends 'had more sense than the lord chancellor and the attorney general ... They squared my client [the plaintiff], my retainer was withdrawn and the case ended.'[46]

Cherry was appointed lord justice of appeal in 1909 to succeed Lord Justice Fitzgibbon (who died on 14 October), although the actual appointment did not take place until the first week of December. This delay occurred since the government wished to retain Cherry's services in parliament for the final stages of the land bill of 1909, which greatly expanded the functions of the Congested Districts Board. On 20 October 1909, when Cherry was considering whether he would leave parliament and accept the office of lord justice of appeal, his wife wrote to him about his health:

I am afraid that these four years of political life have taken a lot out of you, the life is such a strain and of course to be in opposition would be worse than trying to work at your profession ... Do you think five years more of politics would be too much for you? I want you to think of your health first and then of your career. I am very anxious to know what view Asquith would take about you vacating the Exchange if you accepted the Judgeship.[47]

---

45 Healy, *The old Munster circuit*, pp. 187–90.
46 Serjeant Sullivan, *Old Ireland: reminiscences of an Irish KC* (London, 1927), p. 155.
47 PRONI, Cherry papers, D2166/1/1–6.

His work as attorney general and as a member of parliament would have been tiring, and it was accepted practice that an attorney general was entitled to any judicial vacancy that might arise, so the fact that he accepted judicial office in 1909 would not imply anything about his health at the time.

His daughter wrote that in 1913 he became conscious of the first symptoms of a creeping paralysis which 'was to make the rest of his life a constant struggle against increasing weakness'. As a young man there had been no sign of physical ill-health. He had been active in sport, and he was a bell-ringer for many years. His daughter said that as attorney general and judge he would take his place every Sunday among the men in the belfry to ring for services at St Patrick's cathedral in Dublin, to which he donated two bells. He and his family lived at 92 St Stephen's Green for almost thirty years until his death in 1923, within earshot of the bells.

After just over four years as a lord justice of appeal, Cherry was appointed lord chief justice of Ireland in February 1914, in succession to Lord O'Brien of Kilfenora, who had held the office for twenty five years. The appointment of a new lord chief justice had been awaited for quite some time. O'Brien had been unable owing to illness to take his seat in court since November 1912,[48] twelve months before he actually resigned. His continuing absence was commented on by the Dublin correspondent of the *Law Times* (London) at frequent intervals thereafter. In February 1913 it had been indicated officially that O'Brien would go abroad for health reasons for two months and resign at the opening of the Easter term if his health had not improved;[49] but although he did not then resume his duties neither did he retire. The *Law Times* reported that he had tendered his resignation at the end of October and been requested to withdraw this for a time, and had finally definitively resigned on 17 November.[50]

The lord chancellor of Ireland, Redmond Barry, retired owing to ill-health in March 1913. Ignatius O'Brien, then the attorney general, believed that Cherry would have been appointed as lord chancellor if he had so wished, but that he 'preferred either to remain as lord justice or to be appointed chief justice. He did not

48 *Law Times*, 134 (23 Nov. 1912), 90.
49 *Law Times*, 134 (8 Feb. 1913), 369.
50 *Law Times*, 135 (25 Oct. 1913), 580 and 136 (1 Nov. 1913), 18 and (22 Nov. 1913), 94.

feel his own health equal to what would be the more troublesome
job and which might at any time terminate on a change of
government.'[51] O'Brien himself was appointed lord chancellor to
succeed Barry, representing a successful conclusion to his own
decision to become associated with the Liberals as a means of
advancing his legal career, in which 'as a first adventure into some
form of political activity I helped the Attorney General Mr Cherry
in his contest for the Exchange division of Liverpool'.[52]

Initial speculation suggested that the appointment to succeed
Lord O'Brien as lord chief justice lay between Cherry and the
attorney general, J.F. Moriarty, who was considered the more
favoured candidate[53] and had been appointed successively solicitor
general and then attorney general in 1913. The *Law Times* remarked,
however, that Moriarty had never been elected to parliament nor
even contested a seat for his party whereas 'Lord Justice Cherry
had, before his elevation to the Court of Appeal, great political
service, and he has been a considerable success as a judge'.[54]

After Cherry's appointment as lord chief justice in early February
1914, Moriarty was eventually appointed to succeed him in the
court of appeal in June. The delay in filling the vacancy created by
Cherry's promotion, coming on top of the previous disruption
caused by the extended absence of O'Brien and the delay in
appointing his successor, gave rise to inconvenience to litigants
and frustration among the legal profession. Delays in appointments
were the responsibility of the government, even if it may not have
been open to the government to procure or expedite O'Brien's
retirement (although in rather different circumstances, set out below,
it endeavoured to procure Cherry's retirement within a couple of
years of his appointment). However, Cherry and the lord chancellor
were criticised by the *Law Times* for 'facilitating the tactics of delay
by resorting to artificial expedients to carry on business,' for instance
by Cherry agreeing to sit in the court of appeal during the Easter
sittings to enable that court to carry on its work.[55]

51 *The reminiscences of Lord Shandon* [Ignatius O'Brien], manuscript auto-
   biography in King's Inns library, p. 355, quoted by kind permission of the
   council of King's Inns.
52 Ibid., p. 342.
53 *Law Times*, 136 (22 Nov. 1913), 94, (6 Dec. 1913), 150 and (7 Feb. 1914),
   385.
54 *Law Times*, 136 (31 Jan. 1914), 355.
55 *Law Times*, 137 (23 May 1914), 95.

Cherry's main contribution to Irish law may well have been his scholarship in land law and the sharing of that expertise in his books on the subject. Many matters which might otherwise have resulted in litigation would have been resolved by lawyers being able to refer to his work and the exhaustive research and case law which he had assembled. In the court of appeal, he was able to refer a number of times very authoritatively to the provisions of the land acts:

The various provisions of the Irish Land Acts as to a landlord's right of resumption are to be found scattered through the Acts in a very perplexing manner.[56]

I do not see how any lawyer, familiar with the provisions of the Land Purchase Acts, could answer the questions submitted in this case in any other way than that in which Mr Justice Wylie has answered them.[57]

Mr Brown now contends that 'land' in Section 26 of the Land Act 1903 means the soil itself, the corporeal thing, as distinguished from any particular estate in the soil … There is no definition of the word 'land' in the Land Purchase Acts. A 'holding' is defined by Section 57 of the Act of 1881 as 'a parcel of land held by a tenant of a landlord'. In this definition, the word 'land' is evidently used as applying to the soil itself, as distinguished from any estate in the land, but I do not think it can be similarly restricted when the word is used in reference to sales under the Land Practice Acts generally, as Mr Brown contended in the present case. The land cannot, according to our law, be treated like a pound of butter or a sack of potatoes … To talk of a sale of land as distinct from a sale of some estate in the land is, to my mind, unmeaning.[58]

The clarity of his thought was exemplified in a couple of cases on the construction of wills, in which he suppressed any exasperation he may have felt at the confusion of thought which had led to the cases in the first place. In one case in 1910, *Conmy v. Cawley*,[59] a testator had bequeathed his farm to his widow, and then continued 'should my son John return from America sooner or later to give my wife, his mother, the sum of £60, also one half acre of land and one cow's grass, that if he be the owner or thinks well of it, and if not she is at liberty to sell to anyone she likes after

56 *Callwell v. Reilly* [1910] 1 IR 121, at p. 131.
57 *Re Borrowes' Estate* [1911] 1 IR 218, at p. 233.
58 *Latham v. Travers* [1912] 1 IR 306, at p. 322.
59 [1910] 2 IR 465, at p. 469.

tendering to be sent to John'. Cherry said that judgment should be based on:

> ... the principle that a clear gift in a will can only be cut down by words equally clear. If I was to hazard a conjecture as to what was in the testator's mind when he wrote the latter part of his will, I should say that he believed that his son John, if he returned home from America, would have some title to the land after his (the testator's) death and that in this event his own power of disposing of it by will would be in some way limited. But this is mere conjecture. Except the gift to his wife, which is clear and definitely expressed, everything else is confused and contradictory. If possibly we are not able to give effect to the whole of the testator's intentions, we can at least carry out as much of them as we can understand and interpret.

In a second case, in 1911, he said that 'the difficulty in this, and indeed in most of the cases on the construction of wills, is that the court is dealing with a state of facts which the testator did not contemplate at all. We are supposed to be ascertaining the testator's intention, but what we are really doing is rather speculating as to what his intention would have been if he had known beforehand what has actually occurred.'[60]

In a voter registration case in 1912 he made some remarks in his judgment about statutory confusion of thought:

> Let me say, in the first place, that I do not think any assistance can be obtained in these registration cases by appealing to principles of common sense, or to our old friend 'the man in the street'. The entire network of statutory provisions as to franchise and registration is so involved and so illogical that it is vain to look for any reason or common sense in these Acts, and 'the man in the street' treats them with the contempt and derision which they so richly deserve.[61]

In 1912 the court of appeal heard a case of malicious damage, where windows in a pub in Silvio Street in Belfast were broken on two successive days by the same person. The value of each window was less than, but the aggregate value of both windows exceeded, £5, which was the threshold for the local authority's liability for such damage. In his judgment Cherry agreed with the view of the lord chancellor that the breakages were a single event rather than discontinuous acts, and were therefore compensatable by the local authority:

---

60 *Reid v. Swan* [1911] 1 IR 405, at p. 416.
61 *O'Brien v. McCarthy* [1912] 2 IR 18, at p. 38.

The question of the unity of a number of individual acts so as to form one transaction, whether for the purpose of criminal or civil law is, to my mind, rather a question of fact than of law; or, perhaps it would be more correct to say, a question of mental intuition; one mind may unify a number of facts where another would refuse to do so, and the same mind may unify a set of facts for one purpose, and refuse to do so for another. If a burglar breaks into my house, and takes away silver spoons from the dining-room, books from the study, and a clock from the drawing-room, each of these acts is a separate act, and the wrongdoer could be indicted for larceny of any one of the articles stolen by him. Separate bills might be prepared for each of the larcenies, or all might be included in one indictment according as the pleader viewed them as separate acts, or as one transaction. In the same way, if a man wrongfully breaks several panes of glass, each breakage is a separate act, and may be regarded as such; but if he breaks the panes without any intermission of time, everyone would look upon the matter as one transaction. The question in each case is really a matter of degree, whether the acts ought to be regarded as one transaction or as several.[62]

Two cases heard by Cherry were of particular interest in Ulster. In the first of these, *The Irish Society v. Fleming*,[63] the 'Society of the Governor and Assistants, London, of the new Plantation in Ulster in the realm of Ireland' was entitled, under a charter of King Charles II, to a several fishery in Lough Foyle. The channels into the lough were fished by local people with driftnets in June and July each year. The Society (in an action by the attorney general, at the relation of the Society and the other lessees of the fishery) applied for an injunction to restrain driftnet fishing for salmon, and the defendants relied on their right as members of the public to capture as many salmon as they could by methods which were not illegal. The master of the rolls held, and the court of appeal affirmed, that the method of fishing adopted by the defendants and others was not a nuisance at common law, and that driftnets for the capture of salmon were not illegal in Ireland. The lord chancellor distinguished the law of Ireland from the law of Scotland and, although his usual practice was simply to concur, Cherry gave a fuller judgment than usual, in which he observed:

There is no substantial dispute as to the facts, and no very great conflict (allowing for a natural tendency to exaggerate) between the evidence of the witnesses for the plaintiffs and for the defendants ...

---

62 *O'Neill v. Belfast City Council* [1912] 2 IR 310, at p. 316.
63 [1911] 1 IR 323.

The evidence given by the plaintiffs as to the injury done to their fishery by the use of driftnets by the defendants and others was not very satisfactory. A great deal of evidence was given of the amount of salmon caught by driftnet fishermen, but it remains a matter of pure speculation how many of these salmon would have found their way to the plaintiff's waters if they had not been caught by the defendants. It is said that figures, properly manipulated, may be made to prove anything, but I do not think that the figures in the present case very much assist the plaintiffs.[64]

In the second case, *Hunter v. Coleman*,[65] heard by a divisional court of king's bench on which Cherry sat as lord chief justice, a challenge was made to the validity of a royal proclamation made on 4 December 1913, pursuant to section 43 of the Customs Consolidation Act 1876, which had prohibited the importation into Ireland of arms and ammunition and explosives for warlike purposes. Hunter & Co., a firm of gunsmiths in Royal Avenue, Belfast, had ordered cases of guns from Hamburg, which were shipped on 2 December. On arrival at Belfast on 18 December, they were seized by the customs. The plaintiff claimed damages for detention and conversion of the goods and also maintained that the proclamation was void and ultra vires. The case was heard in May 1914, with the judgment being delivered in June. The lawful importation of arms having been halted, the Ulster Volunteer Force had by this time taken the law into its own hands and organised a gun-running mission into Larne on 24 April.

Cherry, who with a majority upheld the validity of the proclamation, said that no proclamation had ever previously been issued under the section (or its predecessor act) and that he was not aware of any judicial decision bearing upon the question of the construction of the section. Was it open to the government to restrict the importation of any materials into a part only of the United Kingdom? Many ancient authorities, going back to *The Case of Proclamations* in 1610,[66] were cited. Cherry said that a general power to prohibit importation did not apply only to the United Kingdom as a whole; a power to prohibit in general terms would necessarily imply a power to define and regulate the scope of the prohibition.[67] He then continued:

---

64 Ibid., p. 385.
65 [1914] 2 IR 372.
66 (1610) 2 St Tr 723.
67 [1914] 2 IR 372, at p. 402.

I now come to the argument based upon the Act of Union, and strongly relied upon by the plaintiffs. The application of the proclamation prohibiting the importation of arms into Ireland only, apart from the rest of the United Kingdom, was said to be a violation of that Act. The 6th Article of the Union was particularly relied upon. It provided that 'His Majesty's subjects of Great Britain and Ireland shall from and after the first day of January 1801, be entitled to the same privileges and be on the same footing as to encouragements and bounties on the like articles, being the growth, produce or manufacture of either country respectively, and generally in respect of trade and navigation in all ports and places in the UK and its dependencies'. The argument based upon this article was only pressed to the extent that the court ought to adopt a construction of the Customs Acts which would not conflict with it, if the construction of these Acts was at all doubtful, for it was not denied that an Act of Parliament might alter or amend the Act of Union in the same way as any other Act of Parliament.

I do not think that this argument goes any further than the general argument against a power of discrimination being conferred upon the Crown, with which I have already dealt. Such powers may of course be abused, but we are not bound to assume that they will be abused. The proclamation in the present case does not really interfere with the trade of Ireland in any way, or does not confer any trading privileges on His Majesty's subjects of Great Britain which are not possessed by his Irish subjects. Legislation of a similar restraining character as regards the importation into, and the carrying of arms in, Ireland has frequently been passed by Parliament without applying to England or Scotland.[68]

A number of cases involved the interpretation of statutes which had been introduced by the Liberal government after it had taken office in 1905. Thus, in 1911 a case was heard as to whether it was open to the government to suspend and reclaim payment of an old age pension (introduced by the Old Age Pensions Act 1908), where it transpired that the pensioner had not reached the pensionable age of seventy years. In particular, were the findings of a local old age pension committee upon entitlement 'final and conclusive' and not subject to any review or appeal? The court held that decisions of such committees could be reviewed.[69]

A case in 1914 raised the question whether the Trade Disputes Act 1906 applied to the stevedores at the Dublin docks. A conspiracy was alleged between the Transport Union and a number of the stevedores to damage the business of the plaintiff, and the issue was whether these were acts done 'in contemplation or

---

68 Ibid., p. 407.
69 *Murphy v. The King* [1911] 2 IR 88, at p. 104.

furtherance of a trade dispute'. The jury found that there was no dispute between the plaintiff and the dock labourers, but there was a dispute between the plaintiff and the Stevedores Association, which was assisted by Larkin, Hopkins and Redmond. The act defined a 'trade dispute' as 'any dispute between employers and workmen or between workmen and workmen', and 'workmen' were 'all persons employed in trade or industry'. But were the stevedores 'workmen'? Cherry held that although stevedores were in one sense 'employed in trade or industry' they were not 'employed' in the sense of meaning 'hired under a contract of service'.[70]

A divisional court in 1916 was asked to consider whether 'the respondent, who is the Recorder of the City of Belfast, and County Court Judge of County Antrim, is liable to pay contributions under the National Insurance Acts, 1911 to 1913, as employer of the crier of his court'. Cherry was 'clearly of opinion that the crier is not employed under any contract of service with the Recorder. Whether or not he is 'employed under' the County Council or the Corporation we cannot now decide, as the proper parties are not before the court.'[71]

Cherry's work as lord justice of appeal was not confined to the court of appeal and before his appointment as lord chief justice, which of course gave rise to him presiding over jury trials in the king's bench division, he occasionally sat as a high court judge on circuit. In 1913 he 'passed severe comments upon the action of Belfast juries'. Not a single person had been found guilty in connection with disturbances in the shipyards in July 1912 as a result of which over eighty people had been treated in hospital for injuries. The jury in all but two cases had acquitted the persons charged with assault and in those two cases the jury disagreed. 'The Lord Justice said that in every case religious prejudice had been introduced.'[72]

After the outbreak of war in 1914 Cherry, in common with other judges, encouraged recruitment, and was reported as chairing a recruitment meeting at Skerries in September 1915.[73]

Although Cherry's period of office as lord chief justice, of just less than three years, was not very long, it would have been very

---

70 *Long v. Larkin* [1914] 2 IR 285, at p. 354.
71 *Irish Insurance Commissioners v. Craig* [1916] 2 IR 59, at p. 69.
72 *Law Times*, 134 (5 Apr. 1913), 550.
73 *Law Times*, 139 (4 Sept. 1915), 393.

much shorter if he had succumbed to the political pressure that was brought to bear on him within about fifteen months of his appointment and at intervals thereafter to step down and create a vacancy that could be filled by the promotion of James Henry Mussen Campbell KC, MP. Campbell was a leading unionist politician who represented Dublin University in parliament and had been the solicitor general for Ireland from 1901 to 1905, and attorney general for a few months in 1905. He was subsequently raised to the peerage as Lord Glenavy. In May 1915, a coalition government was formed in place of the Liberal government, and a bitter struggle for office took place, at many levels. R.F.V. Heuston referred to this period in the first volume of his *Lives of the lord chancellors* and also in the first of the annual discourses given to this Society in 1988.[74] A crisis arose over an offer to Campbell of the position of lord chancellor of Ireland and the subsequent withdrawal by the prime minister, Asquith, of that offer after very strenuous objections had been raised by the Nationalist party. It became necessary to placate Campbell and his political colleagues in the Unionist party by seeking an alternative high office to which he could be appointed, and Campbell's frustration was compounded when further unanticipated difficulties prevented implementation of the first of these alternatives, a proposal for his appointment as an additional lord of appeal in ordinary.

In these circumstances Asquith and Birrell, who was still the chief secretary for Ireland, thought of the possibility of creating a vacancy in the office of lord chief justice. It is not apparent whether at this time they communicated this to Campbell or had obtained his acceptance of the position in the event of a vacancy arising. Campbell appears to have had little interest in displacing Cherry and in holding the office of lord chief justice, as such, regarding it and indeed any other of a number of other positions in Ireland or England that were spoken of as potentially suitable for him as simply a staging post prior to the appointment he expected to receive as lord chancellor or as a lord of appeal. At all events, soon after the formation of the coalition government,

---

74 *Lives of the lord chancellors 1885–1940* (Oxford, 1964), pp. 270–74 and 'Legal history and the author; some practical problems of authorship' in W.N. Osborough (ed.), *The Irish Legal History Society: inaugural addresses* (Dublin, 1989), pp. 28–30.

Birrell wrote to Cherry gently inviting him to resign. According to Heuston, 'it is not often a judge has to sustain pressure from the executive comparable to that resisted by Cherry during the next few months'.[75] On 23 June 1915 Asquith wrote to Cherry:

You will already have heard from Birrell. I want to add one or two lines on my own account. I am very sorry to hear that the state of your health is not altogether satisfactory. But if – as is possible – you should think this a possible moment for resignation, you will put me under a great debt of gratitude (for reasons which Birrell has indicated), and I should be glad to recommend (in addition to your pension) that you should receive a mark of royal favour.[76]

Cherry declined the suggestion.

In November 1915 a meeting took place between Asquith and Campbell, one of a series of exchanges on the latter's prospects of promotion, in which an arrangement was made that if Cherry resigned Campbell would succeed him.[77] This did not give rise immediately to any new invitation to Cherry to retire, but that came in February 1916 when Asquith, acting on information from Birrell that Cherry's 'health is in a bad way and [he] is in a mood to resign' and in the light of new pressures to find a suitable judicial office for Campbell, wrote again to Cherry:

I was very sorry to hear from Birrell, with whom I have been talking this morning, that the hopes which you expressed to me some months ago of improvement in your health have not been realised. We (you and I) are old friends and colleagues, and I have the most agreeable and grateful memories of our association in the work of government and parliament.

If, as I gather from Birrell, you have come to the conclusion that it would be right for you to retire, there will, of course, be no difficulty in the matter of pension. And I should be delighted if there is any honorific mark of recognition which would be grateful to you, to do my best to secure it.[78]

---

75 Heuston, *Lives of the lord chancellors*, p. 270.
76 Ibid., p. 271.
77 Campbell to Bonar Law, 5 Nov. 1915 (Bonar Law papers, HL Record Office, BLP/51/5/11) [hereafter cited as *Bonar Law papers*]. Permission for the use of citations from the Bonar Law papers has kindly been granted by the clerk of the records of the house of lords acting on behalf of the Beaverbrook Foundation Trust.
78 Heuston, *Lives of the lord chancellors*, p. 273.

The confidence of Asquith and Birrell that Cherry would retire at this time seems to have been quite high. Campbell told Sir Edward Carson, who in turn informed the Unionist leader, Bonar Law, in December 1916, when the final arrangements for him to succeed Cherry were being made, that in February that year Asquith had written asking him to take Cherry's place pending the office of lord chancellor becoming available.[79] In June 1916 when James O'Connor, the solicitor general, was writing to Asquith about a judicial vacancy then existing, he remarked that he had been informed by Birrell a few months previously that the arrangements for Campbell to become chief justice were practically complete.[80] In the event Cherry again declined to retire and Heuston records that he produced a medical certificate that his health was satisfactory. Campbell was appointed attorney general in April 1916, shortly before the Easter rising.

Cherry's resignation was not finally arranged until the autumn of 1916. Asquith wrote to Campbell offering him the position in definite terms, which he accepted by letter dated 7 November, but then followed with a request that the appointment would not be made for a few weeks.[81] Cherry continued to hold office until the end of the law term, although rumours of his retirement surfaced in the press at the end of November.[82] One reason for Campbell's request for a delay in the appointment may have been the death in action of his third son on 13 November. A further level of complication arose from the government crisis in the early part of December which led to Lloyd George replacing Asquith as prime minister. This in turn created uncertainty and anxiety on Campbell's part, eventually overcome, as to whether he would wish to accept the office of lord chief justice unless it was clear that Lloyd George would be prepared to acknowledge the understanding that Campbell believed he had made with Asquith that acceptance of it would not prejudice his claim to the office of lord chancellor of Ireland or to appointment as a lord of appeal.

79 Campbell to Sir Edward Carson, 12 Dec. 1916 (*Bonar Law papers*, BLP/81/1/56).
80 O'Connor to Asquith, 9 June 1916 (Asquith Papers, Bodleian Library, Oxford, 45:3).
81 Campbell to Bonar Law, 7 Dec. 1916 (*Bonar Law papers*, BLP/81/1/12).
82 *ILT & SJ*, 50 (2 Dec. 1916), 317.

The last reported case in which Cherry sat as a judge was heard on 14 December 1916, and he retired on 22 December. The coincidence of his retirement with the change of prime minister might suggest that he had resigned out of a sense that, having regard to his health, he should facilitate the new coalition government under Lloyd George as prime minister in making whatever judicial or legal promotions it might wish. However the fact that at the start of November Asquith was clearly in a position to offer the position to Campbell and the definite nature of Campbell's acceptance of the offer suggests that it was the state of his health, rather than any fresh pressure from Asquith at that time, that was the deciding factor in the timing of his eventual retirement, and that this timing had been settled before there could have been any connection with the change of government.

After Cherry had resigned his office he 'lived in retirement, although his life was in no sense that of an invalid', in the words of his daughter. He devoted time to church affairs. Summers were spent at Killincarrig House at Greystones, Co. Wicklow. He died on 10 February 1923, at the age of sixty-three, at his home in St Stephen's Green, Dublin.

The Irish lords of appeal in ordinary

LORD LOWRY[*]

WHEN I STARTED TO COMPOSE this talk, I had intended to devote it to the four lords of appeal in ordinary who were promoted from the Irish bar, one directly and three via the judicial bench. It then struck me that there were three very notable Irishmen whom it would be a pity to leave out. Curiously enough, none of these had served as a judge before being appointed to his high office. Had I adopted an even wider criterion, my list would have been long; but, even as it was, things were already out of hand and I now realise, and I would like my audience to know, that all I can hope to do is to give you only the most superficial account of seven men whom I have found fascinating for both their attainments and their personal qualities. Some of you, however, may feel the impulse, and find the time, to dig a little deeper and perhaps to take the investigation further in relation to particular individuals.

For the background to my chosen subjects I owe much to the *Dictionary of national biography*; not so much, it must be said, in respect of Lord MacDermott, because I wrote his entry myself. I am also very grateful to the librarians of the house of lords and King's Inns and the secretary for academic affairs of University College Galway for their help so willingly given.

FITZGERALD

To begin with, appeals to the house of lords were heard by peers who held or had held high judicial office; but the Appellate Jurisdiction Act 1876 authorised the appointment of lords of appeal in ordinary, on whom a life peerage was to be conferred. In 1882 John David Fitzgerald became the first Irish lawyer to hold that office, in which he served until his death in 1889. Born in

---

* An address delivered at the premises of the Royal Irish Academy, Dawson Street, Dublin on 4 October 1996.

Dublin on 1 May 1816 and educated at Mr Mundy's school in Williamstown, he entered King's Inns and Gray's Inn in 1834 and was called to the Irish bar in 1838. He joined the Munster circuit and his progress was said to be 'unexampled for rapidity'. Starting in chancery, he turned to the courts of common law and was soon reputed the best pleader in Ireland. His industry was immense and, according to the *DNB*, he attributed his success to 'giving up to work the spare half hours that other men wasted'. History does not relate how he escaped the insidious habit of drinking coffee and gossiping, which in the library I always found so much more attractive than work.

Taking silk in 1847, Fitzgerald acquired an enormous practice. He also became a Liberal MP for Ennis in 1852, solicitor general for Ireland in 1855 and attorney general in 1856. In that year he had an unusual and distressing experience. While the Tipperary Bank was being wound up, James Sadleir, a director and an MP for Tipperary, absconded. Cusack-Smith MR in court accused Fitzgerald of conniving at Sadleir's escape from justice. This amazing charge caused the attorney general to make a parliamentary statement[1] in which he showed that Sadleir's swift flight had been caused by the injudicious and irregular observations of the master of the rolls himself and turned the tables on his accuser. According to *The Times*,[2] he sat down, having concluded his statement 'amid loud and general cheering'.

With a short break in 1858, when the Liberals were out of office, Fitzgerald continued as attorney general until in 1860 he was appointed a judge of the court of queen's bench. During the next twenty-two years he presided over a number of important trials, including the trial of Alexander Martin Sullivan and Richard Pigott in 1868 for seditious libel and (with Barry J) the trial at bar of Charles Stewart Parnell and thirteen others for criminal conspiracy to discourage and prevent tenant farmers from paying their rent. Fitzgerald's charge to the jury in that trial,[3] which resulted in a disagreement, on the ingredients of criminal conspiracy has been held up as a model of clear and authoritative exposition. You may, incidentally, think that the 'two senior' controversy of recent years is quite put in the shade by the

1 See *Hansard's Parl. Deb.*, 3rd ser., vol. 143, cols. 866–95 (15 July 1856).
2 16 July 1856.
3 14 Cox CC 508.

strength of the representation for the crown: the attorney general, the solicitor general, Serjeant Heron, James Murphy QC, Porter QC, Naish QC and two juniors.

Fitzgerald's judgments in the house of lords, like those which he delivered before going there, were undemonstrative but are notable for their clarity and their relevance to the main point in the case. Their author also had the happy knack of being right. His deep learning ranged widely and his statutory interpretation is impossible to fault. In short, he was a very good judge.

He also took part in debates, especially on Irish subjects, and commanded attention by virtue of his knowledge and his moderation. He was a commissioner of national education from 1863 until his death, a visitor of the Queen's Colleges and a governor of the Royal Hibernian Military School. In 1885, when Sir Edward Sullivan died, he was offered, but after reflection declined, the lord chancellorship of Ireland. Fitzgerald was survived by his thirteen children and his three eldest sons became queen's counsel, two in Ireland and one in England.

MORRIS

Michael Morris was appointed a lord of appeal on 25 November 1889 and served in that office until his retirement in 1900, when he accepted the hereditary peerage of Killanin and was known thereafter as Lord Morris and Killanin. He died on 8 September 1901.

Michael Morris was born on 14 November 1826 at Spiddal, Co. Galway, the elder son of Martin Morris JP, who was high sheriff of Co. Galway in 1841, the first catholic to hold that office since 1690. His was an ancient catholic family which formed one of the fourteen tribes of Galway. He attended the Erasmus Smith school, Galway and entered Trinity College, Dublin with an exhibition in 1842. His religion disqualified him from becoming a scholar of the house, but in 1846 he graduated as first senior moderator in ethics and logic with a gold medal. His sporting activity at Trinity was racquets, of which he remained a skilful exponent. He was called to the Irish bar in 1849 and made rapid progress, which his biographer in the *DNB* attributes to 'his abounding commonsense, his wit and his strong Galway brogue'. He was high sheriff of Galway for 1849–1850 and from 1857 to 1863 he was recorder of Galway. He took silk in 1863 and became a member of parliament for Galway in 1865. The *DNB* tells us about his election that 'he issued no address and identified himself with no party, yet 90 per cent of the electorate voted for him owing to the local popularity of himself and his family'.

He at once made his mark in the house of commons, where he sat with the Conservative party and, although of independent temperament and impatient of party ties, he was distrustful of democracy, devoted to the Union and hostile to home rule. In 1866 he was made solicitor general for Ireland, the first catholic to hold that office under a Conservative government, and in the same year attorney general, and in 1867 he was appointed a judge of the court of common pleas. He became chief justice of that court in 1876, a year before the Judicature Act reorganised the superior courts, and lord chief justice of Ireland in 1887. It is said that on the bench his outstanding qualities were good humour and practical wisdom, combined with an uncanny ability to get a jury to do what he wanted.

After his elevation to the house of lords Morris, it is further said, distinguished himself by his good-humoured contempt for legal subtleties and by his witty shrewdness. He frequently dissented but, while doing so, appears to me to have at least held his own in argument with his brethren. In *McLeod v. St. Aubyn*,[4] a privy council appeal which is concerned with contempt of court by scandalising a court of justice, in a characteristically robust judgment he pronounced committals for this kind of contempt 'obsolete in this country' because, as he put it, 'courts are satisfied to leave to public opinion attacks or comments derogatory or scandalous to them'. He continued: 'But it must be considered that in small colonies [the appeal came from St. Vincent], consisting principally of coloured populations, the enforcement in proper cases of committal for contempt of court for attacks on the court may be absolutely necessary to preserve in such a community the dignity of and respect for the court.'

I should like to recall and then to comment on the *DNB*'s assessment of Morris' judicial decisions: '[They] were vigorously phrased and were marked by greater regard for the spirit than for the letter of the law. He made no pretence to legal erudition and boldly scorned precedent. Yet his insight into human nature compensated for most of his defects of legal learning.' I do not

4 [1899] AC 549, at p. 561.

quarrel with this except for the reference to 'defects of legal learning'. Morris was an intellectual, as his academic record confirms. He was also a man of superior intelligence, which is not always the same thing. I am confident that he had quite as much legal learning as any judge requires; but I suspect that he had concluded that the law was at times a bit of an ass and I believe that, in contrast to some judges, he was quite prepared to say so.

Without attempting a close analysis, I would refer to three cases in the last year of his tenure of judicial office, 1900. *Seaton v. Burnand* [5] shows Morris giving practical advice on the questions to be left to a civil jury; in *Cartwright v. Sculcoates Union*,[6] a rating case, we see an impressively sound judgment on another practical point, the hypothetical rent of a hereditament, and in *Powell v. Main Colliery Co. Ltd.*[7] there is a convincing dissent concerning the statutory time-limit for making a claim under the Workmen's Compensation acts.

Going back to 1894, I would draw your attention to the famous case of *Nordenfelt v. Maxim Nordenfelt Guns & Ammunition Co. Ltd.*,[8] which was concerned with a worldwide restraint of trade for twenty-five years. The old common law rule had strictly confined the territorial scope of such restraints; but the house of lords adapted the common law to modern needs by upholding the restraint. Morris spoke last and in a one-page judgment expressed this illuminating thought: '[W]e have now reached a period when it may be said that science and invention have almost annihilated both time and space.'[9] The decision was unanimous. There were two other Irishmen sitting on that case, Ashbourne and Macnaghten. It is interesting to note that the plaintiff sued as a pauper.

Like Lord Fitzgerald, Morris was deeply interested in Irish education and he was involved for many years in several ways. He was a commissioner of national education from 1868 and became a senator of the Royal University in 1880 and vice-chancellor in 1899. He was also a visitor of Trinity College Dublin, which conferred on him an honorary LLD in 1887, as it had done on Lord Fitzgerald in 1870.

5 [1900] AC 135, at p. 143.
6 [1900] AC 150, at p. 154.
7 [1900] AC 366, at p. 374.
8 [1894] AC 535.
9 Ibid., p. 575.

In 1860 Morris married Anna, daughter of Baron Hughes. She survived him, with seven of their ten children.

ATKINSON

Five years after Lord Morris' retirement, John Atkinson was appointed a lord of appeal, taking the title of Baron Atkinson of Glenwilliam in the county of Limerick, and he served in that office until his retirement in 1928. He was born in Drogheda, the elder son of Dr Edward Atkinson of Glenwilliam Castle, Co. Limerick, and Skea House, Enniskillen, and his wife, Rosetta, daughter of John Shaw McCulloch. He enjoyed the advantage of attending the Royal Belfast Academical Institution, after which he entered Queen's College, Galway, in 1858. There he had a most distinguished career, with scholarships in every undergraduate and postgraduate year and first class honours in his BA (1861), Diploma in Elementary Law (1864) and LLB (1865). He entered King's Inns and the Inner Temple in 1862 and was called to the Irish bar in Hilary term 1865. There is a puzzle about his age. *Who's who, DNB* and his obituaries give his date of birth as 13 December 1844, which would mean his entering Queen's College, Galway, at 13, a possibility in those days, I have been told, and being called at 20. But the Queen's College records show him as entering at 16 and his signed memorial for call to the bar in January 1865 states that he attained 23 on 13 December 1864. This date is confirmed by the *King's Inns admission papers*, published by the Irish Manuscripts Commission in 1982, which give Atkinson's date of birth as 13 December 1841. The school records for the period have perished and the Irish registers of births do not pre-date 1864. The most likely explanation of the discrepancy may be that '1844' in *Who's who* is a misprint which was never corrected.

There is no trace of Atkinson's having taken the bar final at King's Inns. The lectures there started in 1850 and the bar examination in 1864. Up to 1872 the lectures and the exam were alternative ways of qualifying for the bar, but thereafter both were compulsory.

Atkinson joined the Munster circuit, his practice grew and he took silk in 1880. He became solicitor general in 1889 and attorney general in 1892. Salisbury's government then fell; but in 1895 Atkinson was again attorney general and also the Conservative and Unionist member of parliament for North Londonderry.

Having remained in office for the next ten years, he became in 1905 the first member of the Irish bar (although not the first Irishman) to be appointed a lord of appeal directly from the bar. His appointment, to succeed Lord Lindley, was criticised as political; but his judicial performance for the next twenty-three years lacked nothing, in my opinion, in competence and impartiality. On his death, tributes were paid by Lord Dunedin, sitting in the house of lords, and by the second Lord Russell of Killowen in the privy council, to his industry, sound judgment, patience and courtesy. *The Times*, having described his appointment as political, which no doubt it was, said that he proved a great addition to the judicial strength of both tribunals and added:

He was attentive and industrious and a remarkable memory enabled him to assimilate legal precedents and principles with many of which at the start of his judicial career he must have been unfamiliar. [A little dig there.] Above all, his instinctive sense of justice led him through the subleties that might cloud the vision of some of his more intellectual colleagues [mark that!] to the real merits of a case and so to what the conclusion should be.[10]

Then a surprise:

His weakness lay in a deficiency in the sense of style, which rendered his judgments diffuse and sometimes obscure.

The graph goes up again:

Apart from their style, however, it must be said that his judgments had much to recommend them. They showed great industry and independence of mind; he was never merely acquiescent or disposed to concur in the opinion of a colleague whom he might think more learned than himself and he had a very strong sense of doing justice and a fund of shrewd good sense assisted him to this end.

The Times' assessment of Atkinson's judicial qualities concluded thus:

His high sense of duty, proclaimed in deeds but never in words, combined with his other great qualities to make him, during his long term of office, one of the most useful elements in the two appellate tribunals.

10 *The Times*, 15 March 1932.

The most unflattering picture of Atkinson is painted by the contributor ('R.B.S.'[11]) to Simpson's *Biographical dictionary of the common law*.[12] The note starts by describing him as 'an ardent Irish protestant', a label which, unless the subject is an evangelist, is not usually held to be a compliment. The writer continues: 'He was not a distinguished judge; not only was he not a first-rate lawyer but he showed little interest in the appellate process. Insofar as he had a judicial style, it was a formalistic one. Yet, under the guise of restating the law, he was able to inject his own extremely conservative brand of politics.' To support his views the biographer cited five cases which, having regard to the nature of his comments, I have had the curiosity to read with some care. The report of my conclusions must be brief; but you do not need to be a rabid Instonian to agree that the criticisms of Atkinson's impartiality and judicial competence are hard to sustain on the evidence provided.

In Kerr v. Ayr Steam Shipping Co. Ltd.,[13] which supposedly illustrates Atkinson's bias against workmen, a ship's steward fell overboard and was drowned. The occurrence was unexplained and, the question being whether there was evidence on which the sheriff-substitute could reasonably find it proved that the death was caused by an accident arising out of and in the course of employment, the house by a majority of three to two reversed the majority decision of the inner house of the court of session and restored his award. Lord Atkinson's speech, agreeing with the majority in the court below, is temperately phrased and closely reasoned and Lord Dunedin strongly agreed with him.

Coming to the next case, the biographical note continues: 'Occasionally he was unable to restrain judicial attacks on "dangerous liberal tendencies". The best known of these attacks was in *Roberts v. Hopwood*.[14] There Atkinson attacked "the eccentric principles of socialist philanthropy" and "the vanity of appearing as model employers" shown by Poplar Borough Council, which wished to operate a policy of equal pay for men and women.' I

---

11 R.B. Stevens, president of Haverford College, Pennsylvania and since 1993 master of Pembroke College, Oxford.
12 *A biographical dictionary of the common law*, ed. A.W.B. Simpson (London, 1984).
13 [1915] AC 217, at p. 224.
14 [1925] AC 578, at p. 590.

think this is Professor Stevens' best case, if only by reference to the language employed; but I also have regard to the facts. The district auditor surcharged the council, which had fixed a minimum *weekly* wage of £4 for men and women, on the ground that they had authorised unlawful expenditure by fixing wages so excessive as to pass the reasonable limits of discretion in a representative body, an example of what we would now call *Wednesbury*[15] unreasonableness. The divisional court upheld the surcharge; the court of appeal by two to one removed it, and the house of lords unanimously restored it, only Lord Carson saying that he had at first leant towards the court of appeal's view but had been eventually driven to hold otherwise.

The assault resumes: 'Atkinson also expressed himself unclear as to why it was necessary for the judiciary to make any special effort to protect civil liberties.' The case cited is *R. v. Halliday, ex parte Zadig*,[16] which dealt with the home secretary's power to intern under regulation 14B of the Defence of the Realm regulations. The house (Finlay, Dunedin, Atkinson and Wrenbury, Shaw dissenting) held in his favour and I would submit that their decision was as clearly right as the majority decision under the new regulation 18B was wrong in *Liversidge v. Anderson*.[17]

Finally, and again I quote: 'The one exception was his willingness to go out of his way [please note that emotive phrase] to protect the wealthy taxpayer from the depredations of the graduated income tax, for example, in *Attorney General v. Duke of Richmond and Gordon*[18] and *Attorney General v. Milne*.'[19] Well, the house in the first case unanimously affirmed the court of appeal and in the second, admittedly by three (Loreburn, Macnaghten and Atkinson) to two (Collins and Shaw), affirmed Bray J and the court of appeal. So, you may think, perhaps his lordship did not have to go so very far out of his way to help the taxpayer.

While reading these decisions, to which Lord Atkinson made a full contribution, I had the opportunity to admire his clarity of reasoning, grasp of principle and felicity of language. There is scarcely the need, and certainly not the time, for further argument. I

15 See *Associated Provincial Picture Houses Ltd. v. Wednesbury Corporation* [1948] 1 KB 223.
16 [1917] AC 260, at p. 271.
17 [1942] AC 206.
18 [1909] AC 466, at p. 475.
19 [1914] AC 765, at p. 771.

shall be content, taking a few cases from [1906] Appeal Cases, to point out that in *Williams v. North's Navigation Collieries (1889) Ltd.*[20] Atkinson vigorously upheld the principle of the truck acts, saying that even judgment debts could not be set off against wages due, and that in *Johnson v. Marshall Sons and Co. Ltd.*[21] he held in favour of a workman that his accident was not caused by his 'serious and wilful misconduct'. The decision in *Cavalier v. Pope*,[22] strongly influenced by the law of contract, was pro-landlord if you like; but that case held the field until its glory was dimmed by *Donoghue v. Stevenson.*[23]

This biographical note on Atkinson concludes: 'Atkinson was not well-loved. In 1915 the first coalition government sought to ease him out of office to provide a job for Campbell. He was eventually encouraged to resign in 1928 after a campaign in the Quebec press to reduce the number of "old fogeys" in the Privy Council.' I think the first sentence here must be regarded as special pleading, since it would be surprising if the proposed removal had been inspired by either dislike of Atkinson or deep affection for James Campbell. That something did happen in 1915 is clear. *The Times*' obituary refers to a plan to create a vacancy among the lords of appeal to 'adjust the spoils of office between the parties' and says that pressure was brought on Atkinson to resign, which he regarded as shabby treatment after his many years of political and judicial service. It is reported that he said to a friend on his way to Downing Street: 'They want to throw me on the dust-heap but they won't succeed'. He served for a further thirteen years.

Atkinson married in 1873 Rowena Jane, daughter of Richard Chute MD, of Tralee. They had four sons, only one of whom survived his father. Atkinson died in London on 13 March 1932.

Having come thus far, I digress momentarily to say that I am always sorry when, in crediting a judge with common sense, the writer implies an absence of legal learning, as if to say that the possession of both by the same person is incompatible.

Before coming to Lord MacDermott, who was of a later generation, I wish now to mention my three other Irishmen, Lord Macnaghten, the first Lord Russell of Killowen and Lord Carson.

20 [1906] AC 136, at p. 144.
21 [1906] AC 409, at p. 414.
22 [1906] AC 428, at p. 431.
23 [1932] AC 532, as Lord MacDermott was to recognise in 1961 – see further below.

MACNAGHTEN

Lord Macnaghten belonged to a family settled in Co. Antrim from 1580. He was born in London on 3 February 1830, the son of a former receiver of the court of chancery in Calcutta. His early years were spent at Roe Park, Limavady. He attended Dr Cowan's school, The Grange, in Sunderland, whence he proceeded to Trinity College, Dublin, in 1847 and then to Trinity College, Cambridge, as a scholar in 1850. There he won the Davis university scholarship in 1851 and was bracketed senior classic in 1852. He was a noted oarsman, winning the Colquhoun Sculls at Cambridge in 1851 and the Diamond Sculls at Henley in 1852, and rowed twice for Cambridge in the boat race. He became a fellow of Trinity in 1853 and was called to the bar by Lincoln's Inn in 1857. Having been an equity junior for twenty-three years, he became in 1880 a member of parliament for Co. Antrim and in the same year was given silk by Earl Cairns LC. During the next six years, Macnaghten made a deep impression both in the chancery courts and in the house of commons. It is said that he refused a judgeship twice and the home secretaryship in 1886. The next year he went straight from the bar to succeed Lord Blackburne as a lord of appeal in ordinary, an unprecedented promotion. Until 1903 he took part in debates, speaking mainly on legal and Irish topics. He never ceased to be interested in public affairs. Indeed, notwithstanding his public office, he signed the Ulster Covenant against home rule in 1912.

Macnaghten was a justice of the peace for Co. Antrim and, when visiting the family home near Bushmills, he would sit on the magistrates' bench. The case of *R. (Giant's Causeway Tramway Co.) v. Justices of Co. Antrim*[24] provides for ordinary mortals a comforting illustration of Homer nodding. The case also casts an interesting light on Macnaghten himself. A pauper mendicant had been fined half-a-crown for trespassing on the Portrush-Giant's Causeway tramline and was again prosecuted, this time in his absence, for committing the same offence at a different place on the line. Lord Macnaghten was presiding at petty sessions that day and, although about to leave the bench, he was asked, rather unwisely I fear, by Dr Traill, the distinguished provost of Trinity (whose well-known north Antrim family owned the line), to stay

24 [1895] 2 IR 603.

and help try the case. He did so and, having displayed some impatience at the idea of prosecuting the defendant a second time, at the end of the prosecutor's evidence asked the tramway company's solicitor: 'Is there not a public right of way here?' There was no reply and, with only the resident magistrate dissenting, the bench dismissed the case on the merits. The indignant prosecutors sought a writ of certiorari in the high court to quash the dismiss. Acrimonious letters were exhibited in lengthy affidavits and the legal representation was more than worthy of the occasion, with Ronan QC, Campbell QC (a future lord chancellor) and Traill for the applicants and Atkinson QC, Ross QC (also a future lord chancellor) and Harrison for the magistrates. Some time before the prosecution for trespass, Lord Macnaghten had walked upon the line in order to assert the existence of a public right of way and the company relied in court on his alleged bias as a ground for quashing the magistrates' decision.

Before the hearing Dr Traill had tried to conciliate Lord Macnaghten by offering to let him and his family, but *not* his servants, walk on the line, except during the busy season. He received a rather frosty answer:

Dear Dr Traill – Your brother, Mr. W.A. Traill, is, I will not say unreasonable, but rather fickle perhaps and inconstant. When he comes to town he is kind enough, without even the formality of a previous intimation or the ceremony of a subsequent acknowledgment, to refer house agents and tradespeople to me, as if I were a most intimate friend, and a person of at least outward respectability. In the country he writes to me as if I and mine were given over to malicious outrages, and warns us off the tramway accordingly. These alternations of sunshine and cloud are, as you may imagine, sadly trying to an old man like myself. I am not sorry that the correspondence which he began, if it has to be continued, has passed into other hands. I am therefore much obliged for your note. But I should be unwilling to avail myself of any favour, however slight and trivial, when offered in terms which seem to me to be grudging and unneighbourly.

> Yours truly,
> Macnaghten.

This was not the only stricture which the distinguished provost of Trinity was forced to endure. The high court refused the tramway company's application on the main ground that certiorari of a dismiss on the merits would be unheard of, and in his judgment Sir Peter O'Brien CJ said:

Dr Traill, when the *bona fides* of the Company was impugned, unhappily forsook that calm – that philosophic calm – which is characteristic of those academic precincts of which he is an ornament, and suffered himself – I say it regretfully – to be betrayed into making grave and unwarrantable imputations. Dr Traill tells us himself that he asked Mr Boyle, one of the magistrates who had taken part in the decision, how he came to assist Lord Macnaghten in getting what was practically a decision in his own favour on a point in dispute between him and the Company. The imputation conveyed by this question, whether made in a frivolous spirit or a serious spirit, is, in the opinion of each member of the Court, wholly unwarrantable and unfounded, and, in my opinion, wholly unworthy of Dr Traill, of his vigorous intellect and his better self.[25]

You might think that the bias was not confined to Bushmills petty sessions.

This mischievous story must not be allowed to detract from Macnaghten's deserved pre-eminence. As an appellate judge he is unsurpassed and unforgettable. I have made brief extracts from Lord Sumner's note in the *DNB*: 'He possessed in a happy combination the gifts of listening with patience and deciding without doubt …' and 'It was remarkable that both Bench and Bar fell into the way of citing a sentence or two of an opinion of Macnaghten and of accepting it without discussion as an authoritative statement of the law.'

One example of Macnaghten's powers is found in his speech in *Pemsel's case*,[26] which to most students of every degree is best known for his enunciation of the four heads of charity. Of course, those four heads are already found in the well-known Irish text-book, *Hamilton on Charities*,[27] and were no doubt derived from the argument of Romilly, as counsel for the next-of-kin before Lord Eldon LC in *Morice v. Bishop of Durham*.[28] It is not on this commonplace, as Macnaghten would have called it, but on his remarks about the special commissioners that I wish to focus. They, abandoning their longstanding practice, had suddenly decided to treat the words 'charity' and 'charitable' in the Income Tax Act 1842 as being used in their popular meaning of the relief

---

25 Ibid., p. 640. The letter to Dr Traill is quoted at p. 609.

26 *Commissioners for Special Purposes of the Income Tax v. Pemsel* [1891] AC 531, at p. 574.

27 F.A.P. Hamilton, *The law relating to charities in Ireland* (Dublin, 1881).

28 (1805) 10 Ves Jun 522, at p. 532; 32 Eng Rep 947, at p. 951 (on appeal from the judgment of Grant MR (1804) 9 Ves Jun 399; 32 Eng Rep 656).

of poverty. Their innovation prospered at first in Scotland,[29] but Mr Pemsel, the treasurer of the Moravian church, sought a writ of mandamus to compel the commissioners to grant an allowance of £73. 8s. 3d. in favour of a religious trust, namely a trust to maintain missions to the heathen. The procedure was, in modern parlance, by way of judicial review of the commissioners' decision. In the divisional court of two judges, Lord Coleridge CJ was for the revenue and Grantham J for the taxpayer, so the conditional order was discharged; the court of appeal (Lord Esher MR and Fry and Lopes LJJ) held for the taxpayer, and their decision, though not all of their reasoning, was affirmed by four to two in the house of lords, Lord Halsbury LC and Lord Bramwell dissenting.

When you recall that Macnaghten was about to disapprove of the decision of the inner house in Scotland, condemn the reasoning of the court of appeal and disagree with the lord chancellor, you will, I am sure, admire the assured confidence of his opening remark: 'The question itself is important, but it does not, I think, involve serious difficulty.' To appreciate the clarity and cogency of the reasoning one must read the entire eighteen pages of this speech. I shall mention only two passages. First, having referred to the long continued exemption from tax:

At length ... the Board of Inland Revenue discovered that the meaning of the legislature was not to be ascertained from the legal definition of the expressions actually found in the statute, but to be gathered from the popular use of the word 'charity'.

Then, referring again to that exemption, he commented sharply:

With the policy of taxing charities I have nothing to do. It may be right, or it may be wrong; but, speaking for myself, I am not sorry to be compelled to give my voice for the respondent. To my mind it is rather startling to find the established practice of so many years suddenly set aside by an administrative department of their own motion, and after something like an assurance given to Parliament that no change would be made without the interposition of the legislature.

From 1895 until his death Macnaghten was chairman of the council of legal education and he has been called the founder of the new system of professional training which was developed during his chairmanship.

---

29 See *Baird's Trustees v. Lord Advocate* (1888) 15 R 682.

Engraved portrait of Lord Fitzgerald. Artist and date unknown

Photograph of Lord Morris, by Chancellor, Dublin, 1887

Portrait of Lord Atkinson, by John St Helier Lander

Portrait of Lord Macnaghten, by Hugh de Glazebrook

Portrait of Lord Carson, by Sir John Lavery (1922)

Portrait of Lord Russell of Killowen (detail), by John Singer Sargent, 1900

Portrait of Lord MacDermott

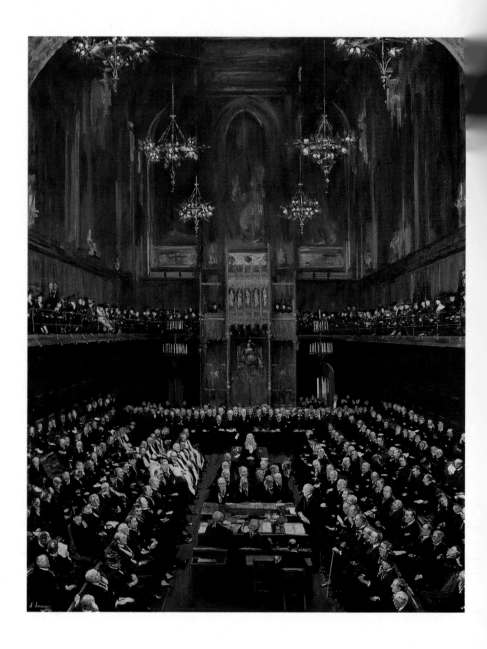

Sir John Lavery's painting of Earl Morley, for the government, proposing the Irish Treaty in the House of Lords in December 1921. The Treaty led to the partition of Ireland. Lord Carson, by now a law lord, can be seen sitting not on the cross benches but on the government benches.

He married in 1858 Frances Arabella, only child of Sir Samuel Martin, a baron of the exchequer. They had five sons and six daughters. She died in 1903 and he on 17 February 1913.

RUSSELL

Charles Russell, the first Lord Russell of Killowen, was one of the very greatest advocates that Ireland has produced and also one of the most distinguished lord chief justices of England for the last hundred years and more. If I do him less than justice here, it is in the confidence that the high points of his career are well known and in the knowledge that he is the subject of a sympathetic and copiously detailed biography.[30] He was born on 10 November 1832 on the Co. Armagh side of Newry, the elder son of Arthur and Margaret Russell, and, while he was still a child, his family moved to Killowen, near Rostrevor in Co. Down. His father died in 1845 and thereafter his uncle, Dr Charles William Russell, later to be president of St Patrick's college, Maynooth, took a close interest in his welfare and upbringing. After leaving Castleknock college, he was at the age of seventeen apprenticed to Cornelius Denvir, a Newry solicitor. When Denvir died in 1852, Russell's articles were transferred to Alexander O'Rorke, a Belfast solicitor. He was admitted a solicitor in 1854 and practised on his own account in counties Antrim and Down. His forensic talents were so marked that many friends, including at least two in the church, persuaded him to go to the bar.

In 1856 Russell entered Lincoln's Inn and, having been called to the English bar in 1859, he practised largely in commercial cases in the Liverpool court of passage and took silk in 1872. In 1880, although opposed by Irish home rulers, he was elected to parliament (after two previous unsuccessful attempts) as an independent Liberal member for Dundalk, but changed to the London constituency of South Hackney in 1885. He became attorney general in the Liberal government of 1886, having by then become a strong advocate of home rule. Despite the claims of a vast and lucrative practice, he would assiduously address public meetings all over England. The Liberals were soon out of power after the defeat of the first home rule bill, and in 1888

---

30 R. Barry O'Brien, *The life of Lord Russell of Killowen* (London, 1901).

Russell represented Parnell at the special commission which had been set up to examine allegations in a series of articles in *The Times* on 'Parnellism and crime'. There he almost literally destroyed Richard Pigott, the forger, by his cross-examination. Extracts are quoted in E.W. Fordham's interesting anthology, entitled *Notable cross-examinations*,[31] and derisively renamed 'Notable material for cross examination' by an old friend of mine. But it is the use which counsel makes of the material in the Russell-Pigott confrontation that must arouse the reader's admiration, most of all, I think, by reason of the timing and arrangement of the questions.

In 1892 Russell was again attorney general and on 7 May 1894 he was appointed a lord of appeal. He held that office for only fifty-seven days, because on 3 July 1894 he was appointed lord chief justice of England on the death of Lord Coleridge. His tenure of that great office was brilliant but too brief, for six years later, after being taken ill on circuit, he died on 10 August 1900. His having been appointed as a lord of appeal meant that his status was that of a life peer, and therefore his son and grandson (with the latter of whom I had the privilege and pleasure of sitting) owed their peerages (in relation to which they took the same title as the first Charles Russell – Lord Russell of Killowen) not to heredity but to their own appointments as lords of appeal, a most illustrious family record.

Of Russell's judicial work as a lord of appeal there is naturally little to say; but as lord chief justice he delivered judgments which demonstrate his talent for clear exposition, his sense of relevance, his mastery of the law in every field and his ability, just as when at the bar, to concentrate on the vital point. The celebrated case of *Kruse v. Johnston*,[32] which was concerned with the validity of bye-laws, is a good example. The most notable criminal trial over which Russell presided, in 1896, arose out of the 'Jameson raid', an armed incursion into the South African Republic, the object of which was to overturn the Boer government. The leaders, including Dr Jameson, who had been encouraged by Cecil Rhodes to undertake their unlawful enterprise, were captured and handed over to the British authorities and tried in London for their crime, which involved a violation of the Foreign Enlistment Act 1870. Public opinion was on the side of the defendants; but Russell

31 Published in London in 1951.
32 [1898] 2 QB 91.

secured their conviction by putting a number of specific questions to the reluctant jury instead of merely accepting a general verdict.

No doubt influenced by his own great experience of commercial litigation, Russell was a strong advocate of a commercial court, the institution of which had been for so long opposed by his predecessor, Lord Coleridge. Another object to which he devoted himself was the improvement of formal legal education, the lack of which, as his opponents were pleased to point out, did not appear to have disadvantaged Russell himself. It is said that his advocacy of a more practical approach to legal training fell on deaf ears; but, having regard to Lord Macnaghten's assumption in 1895 of the chairmanship of the council of legal education, I would like to think that on this important subject an effective alliance had been forged between these two brilliant and formidable Irishmen of such different outlook and origin.

In 1858 Russell married Ellen, eldest daughter of Joseph Mulholland MD of Belfast. She, together with their four sons and five daughters, survived him.[33]

CARSON

Edward Henry Carson was born in Dublin on 9 February 1854, the second son of Edward Henry Carson, a civil engineer, and his wife, Isabella, daughter of Captain Peter Lambert of Athenry, Co. Galway. He was educated at Portarlington School and Trinity College, Dublin, and was called to the Irish bar in 1877. He acquired a successful practice in Dublin and on the Leinster circuit. In 1887 he was appointed junior counsel to the attorney general by John Gibson, and on Gibson's elevation to the bench in 1888, was re-appointed by Peter O'Brien, later lord chief justice of Ireland. Having prosecuted in several important trials, Carson took silk in 1889 and, at the instance, it is said, of A.J. Balfour, who had formed a high opinion of him when chief secretary for Ireland, he was appointed solicitor general for Ireland in June

---

33 [*Editorial note*: Mr Robert Marshall has drawn our attention to the following item in *ILT & SJ*, 36 (1902), 20 relating to Lord Russell's grave in Epsom cemetery: 'The cross now set in its place is reproduced from drawings Lady Russell had made after an ancient pattern still to be seen in the cemetery of the ruined Abbey of Clonmacnoise [and] the little wall of inclosure round the tomb is made of granite brought into Surrey from the late Lord Chief Justice's own Newry mountain.']

1892, shortly before the end of Lord Salisbury's administration. In July 1892 he was elected a member of parliament for Dublin University, and so remained for twenty-six years, until becoming the member for the Belfast constituency of Duncairn in 1918. He was called to the English bar by the Middle Temple in 1893, took silk the following year, became a bencher in 1900 and was treasurer of the inn in 1922.

Carson enjoyed an outstandingly successful career at the English bar, mainly at nisi prius. He refused office under the Conservatives in 1895, but was solicitor general from 1900 to 1905. In 1910 he succeeded W.H. Long as leader of the Irish unionists in the house of commons. The next year he refused to let his name be considered for the leadership of the Conservative opposition, preferring to devote his political energies to the cause of Irish unionism. In 1911–1912 it was *Ulster* unionism which began to take over the unionist field and partition of the country was on the cards for the first time as a political alternative; but it should be remembered that Carson, a Dublin protestant, had always himself been an *Irish* unionist. As he said years later: 'From the day I first entered Parliament up to the present, devotion to the Union has been the guiding star of my political life.' I need not for present purposes recount the history of what followed in Ireland, including the organisation of the Ulster Volunteer Force and the signing of the Ulster Covenant on 28 September 1912. At all events, the outbreak of the great war in August 1914 imposed a delay on further efforts to find a solution of the Irish question.

Carson filled three wartime government posts and we may infer that his proximity to the heart of government under two Liberal prime ministers was not divorced from the government's Irish problems. That said, it appears that Carson did not spare himself in office and was a most dedicated and hard-working minister. In Asquith's coalition of 1915, Carson was appointed attorney general; but he resigned in 1916, concerned with aspects of the conduct of the war and also anxious about Irish affairs. In the same year he became first lord of the admiralty under Lloyd George and then a member of the war cabinet in 1917. But in January 1918 he again resigned from the government, believing that Lloyd George was about to introduce a new home rule bill which would apply to the whole of Ireland. Later he supported the bill which became the Government of Ireland Act 1920, since the alternative was the coming into force of the Government of

Ireland Act 1914. The 1920 act provided for separate devolved government in the six counties of 'Northern Ireland' and the twenty-six counties of 'Southern Ireland'; but this act, which became law on 22 November 1920, was overtaken by events in the shape of the war of independence and the Irish Free State (Consequential Provisions) Act 1922, and in the end applied only to Northern Ireland.

Carson resigned the unionist leadership on 4 February 1921 and finally left the house of commons on being appointed a lord of appeal on 24 May 1921. He discharged the duties of that office until his resignation in October 1929. After being appointed Carson said to a friend: 'I died on the day I left the House of Commons and the Bar.' This, to be sure, is a strange note on which to begin a judicial career, and must arouse our curiosity as to how Carson was to discharge his duties as a law lord. I have nothing unusual to report. He often was content to deliver either a very short speech or a formal concurrence; but sometimes he spoke at greater length and on several occasions delivered the judgment of the privy council on behalf of the board. When Carson did speak, he appears to have spoken with judgment and with a conscientious regard for the need to reach a clear and correct conclusion. But his energy, genius and commitment had already been poured out and well-nigh exhausted in the realms of advocacy and politics.

Carson married first, in 1879, Sarah Annette Foster, who died in 1913, and was the adopted daughter of Henry Persse Kirwan of Triston Lodge, Co. Galway. They had two sons and two daughters, of whom the elder son and younger daughter predeceased their father. He married secondly, in 1914, Ruby, elder daughter of Lieutenant Colonel Stephen Frewen. They had one son. Carson died in 1935.

MacDermott

John Clarke MacDermott was born in Belfast on 12 April 1896, the third surviving son and sixth of seven children of the Rev Dr John MacDermott, minister of Belmont church and a moderator of the general assembly. He went to school at Campbell College and in 1914 was awarded a scholarship at Queen's University, Belfast. Four years were to pass before he could take up the scholarship, because he joined the machine gun corps, saw much active service in France and won the military cross. Resuming his studies, he graduated LLB with first class honours and the Dunbar Barton Prize, and at King's Inns he was Victoria Prizeman and an exhibitioner. With first class honours in the bar final, he was called to the bar in Dublin and then also in Belfast.

Endowed with ability, learning and industry, his progress was sure. His sense of relevance, courteous but firm approach, pleasant and clear voice and impressive appearance constituted a formidable armoury. He lectured in jurisprudence at Queen's University from 1931 until 1935, four of his busiest years, thereby foreshadowing the close links with the university and the interest in legal education that were to become part of his life. Taking silk in 1936, he was immediately busy, as thorough and careful as ever and strong and formidable as well. I heard him as counsel only once, when at Co. Down assizes he prosecuted a man defended by my father and Desmond Chambers for a motor manslaughter, a notoriously difficult charge on which to get a conviction. Mr MacDermott, as a schoolboy of eighteen respectfully called him, greatly impressed me, and no less the jury, and with cold and clinical efficiency secured a conviction which, despite filial loyalty, seemed to me both just and inevitable.

In 1938 MacDermott entered the Northern Ireland parliament as a Unionist member for Queen's University; but, when war broke out, he again joined the army and was commissioned as a major in the royal artillery. After Dunkirk he was released at the government's request to be minister for public security, in which post he showed an organising genius typical of the man but unusual in our profession. Appointed attorney general in 1941, he further distinguished himself by his learning, integrity, firmness and now legendary industry.

When raised to the high court bench in 1944, he showed himself to be ideally suited for the role of a judge which, if one includes his valuable work after retirement, was to be his portion for the next thirty-five years. As a judge MacDermott was inspired above all by a deep sense of right and wrong which was informed by Christian standards of morality and conduct. He was a splendid lawyer and knew every branch of the law, but he was the master of his law and not just its humble and obedient servant. His keen eye for the merits and his sense of what a just result ought to be, while not causing him to spurn the law (which he loved and respected), often enabled him to find a path to the goal by way of the law and not in spite of it.

When the defence of common employment, which had already disappeared in England, was fighting a rearguard action in Northern Ireland, he put it to flight; the only mourner was the solicitor for the Great Northern Railway. A prejudiced counsel for the revenue or the commissioner of valuation might have considered his interpretation of the word 'charitable' to be adventurous, notably in *Londonderry Presbyterian Church House Trustees v. Commissioners of Inland Revenue*[34] – until suddenly realising that his lordship had seen a little further round the next corner than anyone else and until reflecting how right he was (this time perforce on the touchline, as a governor of his old school) in the famous *Campbell College* valuation appeal,[35] in which the house of lords exposed a fallacy of high authority and fifty years' standing.[36]

The quality of MacDermott's judicial work was such that two and a half years after becoming a puisne judge he was appointed a lord of appeal in April 1947. He held that office for four years and one could fill a book with the beautifully written and closely-reasoned judgments which he composed during that period. He sometimes found himself in the minority, but many of his dissenting speeches are particularly valuable for the quality of their legal thinking.

I can make only a brief reference to the judgments given by him in the house of lords and in the judicial committee of the privy council. In *Glasgow Corporation v. Neilson*,[37] where the cause of action arose while common employment was still a defence, he kept up his work so well begun and disposed of the obnoxious doctrine on the facts. *Hill v. William Hill (Park Lane) Ltd.*[38] saw what must have been Lord MacDermott's closest contact with a bookmaker, when by four to three, with Lord MacDermott in the majority and on the side of the punters, the house ruled that the money which the bookmaker sought to recover was a gaming debt and overruled the reasoning of *Hyams v. Stuart King*.[39] In *Paris v.*

---

34 [1946] NI 178. The court of appeal reversed MacDermott J's decision, which is not reported.
35 *Campbell College, Belfast (Governors) v. Commissioner of Valuation for Northern Ireland* [1964] NI 107, at p. 169.
36 *Council of Alexandra College v. Commissioner of Valuation* [1914] 2 IR 447.
37 [1948] AC 79, at p. 85.
38 [1949] AC 530, at p. 570.
39 [1908] 2 KB 696.

Stepney Borough Council[40] MacDermott helped, in a three to two decision concerning the special duty of care to a one-eyed workman, to extirpate what I would (with all respect) call the *Morton v. Dixon*[41] fallacy. I later attended the funeral in *Cavanagh v. Ulster Weaving Co. Ltd.*[42] Probably, if the same case arose today, everyone would agree that there was a duty in the circumstances to provide goggles for all workmen, and not just for those with one eye. And in *Oppenheim v. Tobacco Securities Trust Co. Ltd.*,[43] Lord MacDermott found himself alone in holding charitable a trust for the employees of a company which his brethren considered was not of a sufficiently public nature to qualify. His was a bold but, in my respectful view, doomed venture, which was opposed by modern authority as well as older precedent. He said, however: 'It is a long cry to the age of Elizabeth, and I think what is needed is a fresh start from a new statute.'[44] That was another way of saying: 'I know I can't win, but it is time the law was changed.'

An important case in which MacDermott's view exercised in the end a decisive influence was *London Graving Dock Co. Ltd. v. Horton*,[45] in which the house held by a majority that a subcontractor's workman on a ship under repair could not as an invitee complain of an unusual danger of which he was aware, although he could not take effective steps to avoid that danger if he was to get on with his work. His speech, with which Lord Reid agreed, is a perfect exposition of the true principles and was no doubt an important factor leading to the introduction of the Occupiers' Liability Act 1957, which reversed the effect of *Horton's* case.

Although he greatly enjoyed his work in London and the life of Gray's Inn and had made many new friends, MacDermott always regarded as home the big comfortable house in Belfast where he and Lady MacDermott had brought up their family of two sons and two daughters. Therefore, in 1951 on the death of Sir James Andrews, he readily accepted the appointment of lord chief justice of Northern Ireland, which he held for twenty years and in which he was given further opportunities to deploy his genius for

---

40 [1951] AC 367, at p. 387.
41 1909 SC 807.
42 [1960] AC 148.
43 [1951] AC 297, at p. 313.
44 Ibid., p. 319.
45 [1951] AC 737, at p. 758.

administration and reform. Not only did he continue to produce judgments of the highest quality, not least in the criminal field, but he taught us all to think and kept every member of the bar on his toes. He held legal authorities in respect, but not in awe, and, after the first shock, it was salutary to have one's best ball swept imperiously to the boundary with the observation: 'That's only the Court of Appeal; how do we know it's right?' And what could not be disregarded was, if necessary, distinguished.

I have said all too little on this occasion by way of personal tribute; that is something which I tried to do in court shortly after Lord MacDermott's death. But I am conscious that it is not possible for me to pay tributes of that kind to the other subjects of my dissertation. No judicial appreciation would, however, be complete without a reference to MacDermott's interest in people. That involved another quality which went to make him such a good judge, especially in the field of wardship, of which he was a master and which calls for penetrating insight into the human heart. It was in character that, when asked in 1957 to deliver the Hamlyn Lectures, he chose for his subject 'Protection from power'. In those brilliant lectures he merged two themes to which he had always been dedicated, the importance of the rule of law and the rights and personality of the individual.

With many of MacDermott's cases as lord chief justice to choose from, I shall mention only one, *Gallagher v. N. McDowell Ltd.*[46] It was just a small case, but it provides a good example of conclusive argument and definitive analysis. The wife of a housing trust tenant sustained injury, as alleged, through catching the heel of her shoe in a hole in the floor of a new house and sued the builder for negligence. At the trial, supported by some reasonably strong authority, the defendants succeeded in getting the case withdrawn from the jury on the ground of no duty owed. In the court of appeal, the lord chief justice took up the ball and spreadeagled our defences.[47] It reminded me of Jack Kyle's try at Ravenhill against the French. Our full back was *Cavalier v. Pope*;[48] but to the cry of *Donoghue v. Stevenson*[49] the Chief swerved effortlessly past. When a new trial had been ordered, I turned to

46 [1961] NI 26.
47 Ibid., p. 27.
48 [1906] AC 428.
49 [1932] AC 532.

the defendants' experienced and enterprising solicitor, saying: 'Harry, that could mean the House of Lords'. He replied: 'I'm not so sure. It all sounded horribly right to me.' We settled with the plaintiff and *Gallagher v. McDowell* has been confidently cited many times since then.

In conclusion, what do we discern as the common factors which link these seven men of such diverse natures, backgrounds and talents? They are, I believe, professional success, the respect of those who knew them, a strong, fearless and independent character and an unswerving devotion to the cause of justice. Of each one of them the poet could truly have written:

> *Iustum et tenacem propositi virum*
> *Non civium ardor prava iubentium,*
> *Non vultus instantis tyranni*
> *Mente quatit solida.*[50]

---

50 Horace, *Odes*, III. iii. 1. ['The just man having a firm grasp of his intentions, neither the heated passions of his fellow men ordaining something awful, nor a tyrant staring him in the face, will shake his convictions' – ed.]

Mysteries and solutions: experiencing Irish legal history

W.N. OSBOROUGH[*]

THE WRITER CATHERINE COOKSON died in June this year. I caught the news of her death from the BBC on my car radio. Straightaway, as is the apparent norm these days, the BBC broadcast an extract from an interview Dame Catherine had given some years before. In her inimitable accent, Dame Catherine related something of her rags to riches story – no inappropriate description since, as is generally known, she entered the world as the child of a single mother and was raised in a workhouse. In the interview, she told of her determination to become an author and how, from an early age, she came to discern that the passage to the success she craved was best assured by frequent visits to the local public library, and avid reading. I recall two sentences uttered by Dame Catherine in the course of the interview: 'I'd been nowhere' and 'I knew nothing'.

In 1897 Henry James and Joseph Conrad met for the first time. Conrad had sent James a copy of one of his books. Thus commenced a relationship which, despite goodwill on both sides, never quite managed to fructify. Conrad regarded James as 'the master'. The compliment was not to be returned. This fraught relationship did, however, prompt an increasing frankness in the exchanges between the two men, and on no occasion was this so pronounced as when James wrote to Conrad in November 1906, expressing his appreciation of Conrad's latest book, *The mirror of the sea*. 'No one has *known* – for intellectual use', James wrote, 'the things you know, and you have, as the artist of the whole matter, an authority that no one has approached'.[1] There is a perplexing

---

* The edited version of an address delivered in The Queen's University of Belfast on 24 October 1998.
1 Henry James to Joseph Conrad, 1 Nov. 1906, quoted Z. Najder, *Joseph Conrad: a chronicle* (Cambridge, 1983), pp. 324–25.

217

dimension to Conrad's tales of adventure and Conrad invariably resented being typecast. His reported response on this occasion was neither unappreciative nor dismissive, but it might certainly have baffled James. Conrad, in his reply, chose rather to declare: 'I know nothing, nothing.'[2]

Working at legal history and, if you will, Irish legal history, is a constant struggle to plug the many gaps in the contemporary understanding of our legal past. Is it the case that if, like Catherine Cookson, we commit ourselves to a punishing diet of reading and research, all in time will be revealed, and we only have to be patient? Or is it the case that, like Joseph Conrad, we may be forced to admit, however paradoxical this indubitably sounds, that the more we learn, the less in fact we truly understand?

The magnitude of the challenge facing those who would seek to penetrate the arcana of legal history and propound solutions, is a commonplace in the writings of legal historians. F.W. Maitland lit on an attractive metaphor by way of emphasising the point with regard to Anglo-Saxon legal material. 'Many an investigator', he remarked, 'will leave his bones to bleach in that desert before it is accurately mapped.'[3] In a valedictory commentary on his own distinguished contribution to the study of early Irish law – the law to be found, in the main, in the law tracts – the late D.A. Binchy frankly acknowledged that Maitland's remark was 'in our day, equally relevant to the native Irish legal sources'.[4] The tone became progressively personal in Binchy's peroration: 'At one time I had hoped to provide future explorers with a rough sketch-map, but *deis aliter visum*. As things are, all I can do is offer them a ticket of admission to the desert and wish them God-speed.'[5]

The furnishing of maps, navigational accessories and tickets is a boon that it is far from me to decry. But what if Conrad is right, and the effort we put into our learning has the unintended consequence of postponing more and more into the future the sort of illuminating knowledge we are eager to acquire? As it happens, I am certain that there are some mysteries that do admit of a solution – and here, naturally, Catherine Cookson's recipe for

2 See N. Sherry, *Conrad and his world* (London, 1972), p. 5.
3 *The collected papers of Frederick William Maitland*, ed. H.A.L. Fisher (3 vols., Cambridge, 1911), iii, 506.
4 D.A. Binchy, 'Irish history and Irish law – II' in *Stud. Hib.*, xvi (1976), 7 at p. 45.
5 Ibid.

success makes sound sense. But, equally, I am convinced that there remain others that, on investigation, will be found not to constitute a single mystery but to be comprised of several, making the attainment of the knowledge and broad comprehension we aspire to, very difficult indeed. Lastly, too, though I have not mentioned this hitherto, there are plenty of mysteries where I suspect neither this generation of explorers nor any future one will manage to find any solution at all, because the evidence that might enable this to be done, simply no longer exists – if, in certain instances, it ever did.[6]

A foundation document circulated over a decade ago, before this Society was inaugurated, listed one hundred projects that the proposed society might conceivably undertake. At the rate of one resultant volume a year, a century of putative publications was thus envisaged – an ambitious plan which, by my reckoning, would take us down to the year 2088, a long way away indeed. None of the suggested volumes has as yet appeared; but of the seven in the Society's annual series that have, I think it can justly be claimed they have helped to dispel a number of mysteries or helped to clarify the obscure: each one has surely added in some fashion to our understanding of Ireland's legal past. An appreciation of the position occupied by lawyers in Irish society down the centuries has perhaps benefited most.[7] One collection of essays, the Society's very first venture into publishing, *Brehons, serjeants and attorneys*,[8] was thus exclusively devoted to the profession; as were two books by Colum Kenny, one of which focused on the earlier history of King's Inns and the other on reforms of legal education in the nineteenth century.[9] A second collection of

---

6 In the middle ages and down to the early 1600s, the administration of law in Gaelic and Gaelicised Ireland was not accompanied by any system of maintaining records. For insight into problems linked to understanding legal developments in a society firmly wedded to oral tradition, see N. Patterson, 'Brehon law in late medieval Ireland: "antiquarian and obsolete" or "traditional and functional"' in *Cambridge Medieval Celtic Studies*, xvii (1989), 43.

7 This development was anticipated perhaps by Daire Hogan's *The legal profession in Ireland, 1789–1922* (Dublin, 1986).

8 D. Hogan and W.N. Osborough (ed.), *Brehons, serjeants and attorneys: studies in the history of the Irish legal profession* (Dublin, 1990).

9 C. Kenny, *King's Inns and the kingdom of Ireland: the Irish 'inn of court', 1541–1800* (Dublin, 1992); *Tristram Kennedy and the revival of Irish legal training, 1835–1885* (Dublin, 1996).

essays – *Explorations in law and history*[10] – was something of a
mixed bag, but here again the emphasis on different facets of the
history of the profession was pronounced. Other books – to
continue this inventory – have concentrated on the work of the
Irish privy council in the sixteenth century,[11] and on the story of
policing in Belfast in the first two-thirds of the nineteenth century.[12]
My own book on lawsuits linked to the growth of Dublin in the
modern era[13] adopted a somewhat unusual perspective – one that
was designed, however, to impress upon the local historian the
message that the legal dimension to local historical study was
ignored at his or her peril. Today's cognoscenti will be familiar
with legal problems linked to the removal of whelks, winkles and
lugworms from the foreshore of Strangford Lough in Co. Down;[14]
but who in Belfast, I wonder, remains aware of the litigation in
which Robinson & Cleaver were instantly embroiled – over the
damage that the excavations for its foundations did to adjoining
premises, when it opened for business at the junction of Donegall
Place and Donegall Square in 1888?[15]

Apart altogether from works published under the aegis of the
Society, many other books and articles have appeared in recent
years whose no less significant contribution to the dispelling of
ignorance on matters of Irish legal history deserves to be placed
on record.[16] There are now four volumes in the Early Irish Law
series brought out by the Dublin Institute for Advanced Studies.
Texts on the legal aspects of bee-keeping – *Bechbretha*[17] – and on

---

10 W.N. Osborough (ed.), *Explorations in law and history: Irish Legal History
    Society discourses, 1988–1994* (Dublin, 1995).
11 J. G. Crawford, *Anglicizing the government of Ireland: the Irish privy council and
    the expansion of Tudor rule, 1556–1578* (Dublin, 1993).
12 B. Griffin, *The Bulkies: police and crime in Belfast, 1800–1865* (Dublin, 1997).
13 *Law and the emergence of modern Dublin: a litigation topography for a capital city*
    (Dublin, 1996).
14 *Adair v. National Trust* [1998] NI 33.
15 See *James McLees (Crozier & Co.)* v. *Robinson & Cleaver*, Co. Antrim assizes,
    July 1888, as reported in *Irish Builder*, xxx (1888), 195.
16 The listing that follows does not claim to be comprehensive. No attempt has
    been made to list articles. There are also chapters devoted to legal matters in
    books which lack a general legal focus that it would be folly otherwise to
    overlook – see, for example, S.G. Ellis, *Reform and revival: English government
    in Ireland 1470–1534* (Woodbridge, Suffolk, 1986), chs. 4 and 5, and T.C.
    Barnard, *Cromwellian Ireland: English government and reform in Ireland,
    1649–1660* (Oxford, 1975), ch. 9.
17 *Bechbretha: an Old Irish law-tract on bee-keeping*, ed. T. Charles-Edwards and
    F. Kelly (Dublin, 1983).

the status of poets – *Uraicecht na ríar*[18] – have been edited. And two major books have come from the pen of Fergus Kelly – *A guide to early Irish law* (something approaching the sketch-map D.A. Binchy himself was planning), and now, more recently, *Early Irish farming*,[19] with its heavy reliance on the law tracts. Staying with early Irish law there is Neil McLeod's book on contract[20] and Robin Chapman Stacey's *Road to judgment*.[21] Paul Brand's collected essays on the medieval common law[22] bring together his key articles on the early history of the common law in Ireland, all of which represent an important addition to the earlier achievements of G.J. Hand and of the late H.G. Richardson and the late G.O. Sayles. Another Armagh register has been edited, the fourteenth-century register of Archbishop Sweteman,[23] thus constituting an excellent companion for the register of Archbishop Mey.[24] Publication here was under the auspices of the Irish Manuscripts Commission, and both in the Commission's journal, *Analecta Hibernica*, and in other books produced by it, legal material is very far from being ignored. Mention here can appropriately be made of J.C. Appleby's calendar of relevant admiralty material concerning Ireland from the reign of Henry VIII down to that of Charles I.[25]

For the seventeenth century, there has been a single major addition since Hans Pawlisch brought out his book on Sir John Davies[26] – Dr L.J. Arnold's important account of the Restoration land settlement.[27] It is also right to draw attention to an important

18 *Uraicecht na ríar: the poetic grades in early Irish law*, ed. L. Breatnach (Dublin, 1987).
19 F. Kelly, *A guide to early Irish law* (Dublin, 1988); idem, *Early Irish farming: a study based mainly on the law-texts of the 7th and 8th centuries AD* (Dublin, 1998).
20 N. McLeod, *Early Irish contract law* (Sydney, 1996).
21 R.C. Stacey, *The road to judgment: from custom to court in medieval Ireland and Wales* (Philadelphia, 1994).
22 P. Brand, *The making of the common law* (London and Rio Grande, 1992).
23 *The register of Milo Sweteman, archbishop of Armagh, 1361–1380*, ed. B. Smith (Dublin, 1996).
24 *Registrum Johannis Mey: the register of John Mey, archbishop of Armagh, 1443–1456*, ed. W.G.H. Quigley and E.F.D. Roberts (Belfast, 1972). See, too, *The register of John Swayne, archbishop of Armagh and primate of Ireland, 1418–1439*, ed. D.A. Chart (Belfast, 1935).
25 J.C. Appleby, *A calendar of material relating to Ireland from the High Court of Admiralty examinations, 1536–1641* (Dublin, 1992).
26 H.S. Pawlisch, *Sir John Davies and the conquest of Ireland: a study in legal imperialism* (Cambridge, 1985).
27 L.J. Arnold, *The Restoration land settlement in County Dublin, 1660–1688*

initiative undertaken by the University of Caen in France: the translation into French of William Molyneux's celebrated tract on Irish legislative independence, first published in Dublin in 1697.[28] A point worth noting in the case of this initiative is the decision of the translation team to render into French passages in the original which Molyneux gives in Latin.

For the eighteenth century, we have Neal Garnham's distinguished survey of the criminal law and its administration.[29] It is yet another book that manages to demonstrate the wealth of material that exists and that only awaits the assiduous researcher to winkle out. Brian Henry's *Dublin hanged* serves as a companion volume.[30] Turning to the penal laws, the posthumously published collected essays of Maureen Wall on the subject[31] contain a great deal of invaluable information, and are strongly recommended. Somewhat different in style, Ann Kavanaugh's account of the life of John Fitzgibbon, earl of Clare, fills a very obvious biographical lacuna.[32] One United Irishman trial, that of William Drennan in 1794 for seditious libel, is the subject of modern critical analysis.[33]

By the time we reach the nineteenth century, there is a veritable flood of new literature – for example, on the landlord and tenant

---

(Dublin, 1993). Arnold's achievement puts one in mind of another classic work that facilitated understanding of a later land settlement – J.G. Simms, *The Williamite confiscation in Ireland, 1690–1703* (London, 1956; repr. Westport, Conn., 1976).

28 *Discours sur la sujétion de l'Irlande aux lois du parlement d'Angleterre*, trans. under direction of J. Genet and E. Hellegouarc'h and with intro. by P. Gouhier (Caen, 1993). See, too, J.G. Simms, *William Molyneux of Dublin 1655–1698*, ed. P.H. Kelly (Dublin, 1982).

29 N. Garnham, *The courts, crime and the criminal law in Ireland, 1692–1760* (Dublin, 1996). Mention also deserves to be made of J. Kelly, '*That damn'd thing called honour*': duelling in Ireland, 1570–1860 (Cork, 1995), which contains a number of useful insights.

30 B. Henry, *Dublin hanged: crime, law enforcement and punishment in late eighteenth-century Dublin* (Dublin, 1994).

31 *Catholic Ireland in the eighteenth century: collected essays of Maureen Wall*, ed. G. O'Brien (Dublin, 1989). And note, too, T.P. Power and K. Whelan (ed.), *Endurance and emergence: Catholics in Ireland in the eighteenth century* (Dublin, 1990).

32 A.C. Kavanaugh, *John Fitzgibbon, earl of Clare: a study in personality and politics* (Dublin, 1997). For earlier in the century we now also have *The letters of Lord Chief Baron Edward Willes to the earl of Warwick, 1757–1762: an account of Ireland in the mid-eighteenth century*, ed. J. Kelly (Aberystwyth, 1990).

33 *The trial of William Drennan on a trial for sedition, in the year 1794 and his intended defence*, ed. J.F. Larkin (Dublin, 1991).

relationship,[34] the resident magistracy,[35] and the police.[36] A collection of essays brought out by Queen's University law school to mark the sesquicentennial of Queen's itself includes many helpful pieces on key nineteenth-century themes.[37] A further volume containing another collection of essays marked the bicentenary of the Four Courts in Dublin,[38] a most welcome initiative certainly. An earlier collection of essays – a third – edited by John McEldowney and Paul O'Higgins, and entitled *The common law tradition*,[39] covers a somewhat broader chronological spectrum than the other two.

Two twentieth-century legal history volumes also merit inclusion in this inventory: Colm Campbell's *Emergency law in Ireland, 1918–1925*[40] and Mary Kotsonouris' account of the revolutionary Dáil courts.[41]

Finally, three important works of reference should be mentioned. The first two of these are Paul O'Higgins' matchless *Bibliography of Irish trials*[42] and Donovan and Edwards' guide to British sources for Irish history from the Tudors down to 1641.[43] The utility of both volumes is easily on a par with the *King's Inns admission papers, 1607–1867*,[44] brought out in 1982.

The huge amount of new knowledge being generated by this profusion of books, and of articles too, is not always easy to digest or to assimilate. Even so, it could lead the sceptic to ask: 'What

---

34 W.E. Vaughan, *Landlords and tenants in mid-Victorian Ireland* (Oxford, 1994).

35 P. Bonsall, *The Irish RMs: the resident magistrates in the British administration of Ireland* (Dublin, n.d.[1997]).

36 J. Herlihy, *The Royal Irish Constabulary: a short history and genealogical guide, etc.* (Dublin, 1997); J.D. Brewer, *The Royal Irish Constabulary: an oral history* (Belfast, 1990).

37 N. Dawson, D. Greer and P. Ingram (ed.), *One hundred and fifty years of Irish law: 1845–1995* (Belfast and Dublin, 1996).

38 C. Costello (ed.), *The Four Courts: 200 years* (Dublin, 1996).

39 J. McEldowney and P. O'Higgins (ed.), *The common law tradition: essays in Irish legal history* (Dublin, 1990).

40 C. Campbell, *Emergency law in Ireland, 1918–1925* (Oxford, 1994).

41 M. Kotsonouris, *Retreat from revolution: the Dáil courts, 1920–24* (Dublin, 1994).

42 P. O'Higgins, *A bibliography of Irish trials and other legal proceedings* (Abingdon, Oxon., 1986).

43 B.C. Donovan and D. Edwards, *British sources for Irish history, 1485–1641* (Dublin, 1997).

44 E. Phair, P.B. Phair and T. Sadleir (ed.), *King's Inns admission papers, 1607–1867* (Dublin, 1982).

remains to be found out?' The short answer to that is: 'a considerable amount'.

If we examine the lists of new books and articles carefully and
painstakingly, one notes a number of things. First of all, there are
certain historical periods that remain relatively unexplored: whatever
the reason, periods persist in Irish history that have held little
attraction for the would-be legal historian. More significantly even,
from the standpoint of the needs of legal history itself – and to
help relate it to the modern world – with but few exceptions, little
effort has been expended on coming to grips with a species of
problem that the lawyer *qua* lawyer knows in his or her heart it is
folly, possibly even dangerous, to ignore: how, in the case of law in
Ireland, doctrines with which he or she is, hopefully, thoroughly
familiar came to evolve the way they did, and to be shaped the way
they were. Both 'how' and 'why', it will be recalled, served in
Kipling's platoon of 'six honest serving-men' that taught *him* all he
knew.

The complete understanding of doctrine – the reasons underlying
it, the exact ramifications entailed by it – has furnished a challenge
to members of the legal profession from the earliest times. The
challenge was assuredly present in the Ireland of the medieval and
early modern periods and, from the example I am about to supply,
not exclusively in a common law context either. I refer to the
custom of tracts or tracks, recognised in Gaelic and Gaelicised
regions and other areas besides, harbingers of which Stephen as
well as Pollock and Maitland were later to discover in Anglo-
Saxon legal sources.[45] The custom was designed as a means of
discouraging and of combating theft, and especially theft of cattle.
It worked as follows. When cattle were stolen, the occupier of the
land where the trail left by the cattle terminated was made legally
answerable for the loss. A crude solution, doubtless, but one for a
while at least that was apparently effective and clearly tolerated.[46]

The custom was observed even in English Ireland down to
around 1640; but, intriguingly, we know most about 'the exact
ramifications' from an early fourteenth-century handbook of

---

45 J.F. Stephen, *A history of the criminal law of England* (3 vols., London, 1883),
    i, 66; F. Pollock and F.W. Maitland, *The history of English law before the time of
    Edward I*, 2nd ed. of 1898 repr. with new intro. by S.F.C. Milsom (2 vols.,
    Cambridge, 1968), ii, 157.
46 See W.N. Osborough, 'The Irish custom of tracts' in *Ir Jur*, xxxii (1997), 439.

contemporary Irish law and practice ascribed to Giolla na Naomh mac Duinnshléibhe Mac Aodhagáin (d. 1309).[47] Giolla na Naomh – let me call him that for short – in an unusually detailed discussion of the custom, maintained that four factual situations existed where liability was not imposed on the occupier of land:

- where the trail petered out prematurely on account of the hardness of ground (as would occur during a period of prolonged drought, such as happened in 773, 1129 or 1638);
- where the trail led into, and coalesced with, a common cattle trail (making it impossible to follow the trail of specific cattle);
- where there was evidence that the cattle had been brought on to the land of the occupier entirely against the will of the latter (recognition of the defence of *force majeure*); and
- where there was unmistakeable circumstantial evidence that, although the trail may have petered out in Whiteacre, the cattle were subsequently present in Blackacre – evidence that would be supplied by indications that the cattle had been slaughtered and consumed by the thieves on their home territory (perhaps – let me interject – at some gargantuan barbecue where, hopefully, the facilities of efficient *fulachta fiadh* had been available).

Fully to comprehend the doctrine that underpinned this particular custom requires answers to a baffling array of questions. How, for example, was the list of exemptions – or defences – arrived at? Then, too, we would certainly like to know the extent to which Giolla na Naomh's approach was observed in later centuries, not least in that part of English Ireland where the custom appears to have lasted longest – the province of Ulster.

The provenance of this Irish custom is unclear; but that kind of problem – tracing the origins of legal doctrine – is by no means uncommon. Let me furnish another illustration through introducing you to what is best described as the incident at Diskin's Crossing. In September 1989, in the Republic, a train taking pilgrims to Knock was derailed at an accommodation crossing,

---

47 See G. Mac Niocaill, 'Aspects of Irish law in the late thirteenth century' in *Historical Studies: X*, ed. G.A. Hayes-McCoy (Indreabhán, Co. na Gaillimhe, 1976), pp. 25ff. [Giolla na Naomh is also the subject of the first paper in this collection, by Fergus Kelly – see above, p. 1 – ed.]

known as Diskin's Crossing, on the line between Ballyhaunis and
Claremorris in Co. Mayo. The derailment took place as a result of
cattle trespassing on the line. Many passengers on board were
injured and apparently no less than 250 writs were later served.
The judge presiding at the hearing of the first negligence claim –
plainly something of a test case – held that both the owner of the
cattle, a Mr Patrick Diskin, and Iarnród Éireann (Irish Rail) were at
fault. He fixed the proportions at 70 per cent in the case of Mr
Diskin and 30 per cent in that of Iarnród Éireann. When it became
clear that Mr Diskin would be unable to satisfy any part of the
£16,000 award of damages in favour of the plaintiff, a Mr Giovanni
Gasperi, and that Mr Gasperi insisted, as he was entitled to do, on
his full legal rights, the trial judge entered judgment against Iarnród
Éireann for the total amount of the damages – the £16,000.

Iarnród Éireann, faced with, potentially, a very high legal bill in
dealing with all the remaining claims – a bill calculated by it to
approach £4 million – launched high court proceedings to have
struck down as unconstitutional those provisions in the Civil
Liability Act 1961[48] which, in the circumstances that had arisen,
gave authority to the trial judge to award judgment against Iarnród
Éireann for the full amount of the damages. In an instructive
judgment on this unprecedented constitutional action, Keane J
rejected Iarnród Éireann's claim,[49] and that judgment was to be
upheld by the supreme court,[50] with O'Flaherty J writing for the
latter tribunal that the relevant rule obliging the less negligent or
less blameworthy tortfeasor to bear the total cost of the accident,
was 'in harmony with the core principles underlying civil liability'.[51]
So doubtless it was, and is; but it remains legitimate to ask 'why?'
or 'how so?' In his lengthy judgment in the high court, Keane J
embarks on some historical detective work into the salient rule –
long upheld within the tradition of the common law – but does
not, I think, manage to cast very much light on why it ever evolved
or why it continued to be tolerated. The solution to these two
riddles, of course, lies preeminently within the domain of
England's legal history, whence all modern Irish law on joint and
several tortfeasors was to be derived.

---

48 1961, no. 41.
49 *Iarnród Éireann v. Ireland* [1996] 3 IR 321.
50 Ibid., p. 370.
51 Ibid., p. 377.

The sway that the common law of England was fated to hold over Ireland – both north and south – means that many, arguably most, of the problems linked to the origins of doctrines in force today have their roots in English soil. This is no reason at all for would-be Irish researchers not to try and track them down there. Should they choose to do so, they would be following the splendid lead given many years ago by the late F.H. Newark.[52]

I would have to admit, however, that special interest attaches in Ireland to doctrinal developments that occurred here entirely independently. One of these developments – a striking variation in Irish law – has engaged my attention for a number of years: where and when in Ireland did the judicially-inspired suspended sentence come into vogue?[53] That provision existed for the judicial bench to impose suspended prison sentences, albeit without statutory authority, long before the two separate Irish jurisdictions came into existence in the 1920s, the Northern Ireland court of criminal appeal in *Wightman's* case in 1950 concluded was quite evident.[54]

A report on what I personally have managed to establish, following that first piece of detective work, may not here be reckoned entirely out of place.

It became clear at an early stage that this particular legal initiative went back into the nineteenth century. But whatever about surviving court records, there was a deafening silence in all the books on Irish criminal practice that I consulted – a strange omission indeed. Then, by accident, I came across what appeared to be a reference to the practice of suspending sentences in evidence given by an assistant barrister (our later county court judge) to a parliamentary inquiry on criminal and destitute children in Ireland held in the early 1850s.[55] Walter Berwick, the assistant barrister in question, then based in Cork, indicated in one of his answers to the parliamentary inquiry that at that date he and a number of his colleagues were prepared to suspend prison

---

52 Newark's seminal articles on historical aspects of the law of torts are conveniently reproduced in *Elegantia juris: selected writings of F.H. Newark*, ed. F.J. McIvor (Belfast, 1973).

53 W.N. Osborough, 'The suspended sentence in Northern Ireland' in *Ir Jur*, ii (1967), 30; idem, 'A Damocles' sword guaranteed Irish: the suspended sentence in the Republic of Ireland' in *Ir Jur*, xvii (1982), 221.

54 *R v. Wightman* [1950] NI 124.

55 *Report from the select committee on criminal and destitute children; together with the minutes of evidence*, p. 342, H.C. 1852–53 (674), xxiii, 366.

sentences on juveniles convicted of offences. The context shows that Berwick and the others may have deliberately embarked on this course of action when governmental procrastination and indecision had brought about the postponement in Ireland of the inauguration of special custodial institutions for the young offender. Questions of finance and difficulties over choice of sites understandably contributed to the delay, but another factor seems to have been involved – the continuing controversy over the risk of proselytisation of inmates in all closed Irish institutions. The row over the Richmond penitentiary in Dublin, a row linked to these fears, was not long distant in the past.[56] And another row over religion in closed Irish institutions, albeit, on the surface, of a very different calibre, beckoned, and was destined to run for a considerable number of years – the refusal of the resident medical superintendents at the Belfast and Armagh lunatic asylums to sanction the appointment of any chaplains to their respective asylums.[57] Berwick's disclosure in 1852 is meagre evidence on which to construct a totally convincing explanation for the emergence of the judicially-inspired Irish suspended sentence. But the explanation itself is certainly plausible. This, of course, scarcely helps to tell us how the practice of suspending sentences spread geographically or even vertically – from quarter sessions and recorders' courts up to assizes and city commissions. The more we learn, perhaps, indeed, the less proportionally we truly know.

Furnishing dates for the recognition in Ireland of rules of the common law remains one of the more intractable problems of Irish legal history. Not until the early nineteenth century, when Irish law reporting gets into its stride, does evidence become generally available that enables such conundrums to be pursued with reasonable prospects of success. Before then, the researcher must be prepared to follow any clue his or her work of detection has brought to light, however slender that clue appears.

One such clue is afforded by an entry that Richard Boyle, the great earl of Cork, made in his diary for 12 February 1635: 'This

---

56 H. Heaney, 'Ireland's penitentiary, 1820–1831: an experiment that failed' in *Stud. Hib.* xiv (1974), 28.

57 See *R v. Belfast Lunatic Asylum* (1858) 5 ICLR 375. The impasse resulting from this decision to the effect that the two RMs were acting within their rights was finally removed by legislation in 1867: see the District Lunatic Asylums Officers (Ire.) Act (30 & 31 Vict, c. 118).

morning about 5 of the clock my perfidious servant and farmer Richard Blacknoll departed this life in Mr Burdale's house beyond the bridge in Dublin.' Boyle's entry continues: 'God forgive him [Blacknoll] his sins and particularly the high deceits and unexpressable wrongs he did to myself in my reputation and estate.'[58] Boyle, a key figure in the commercial as well as the political world of early seventeenth-century Ireland,[59] became involved in innumerable lawsuits, and probably none of them more protracted and complex than that involving Blacknoll, his erstwhile employee. Claims and counterclaims proliferated once the relationship had soured and terminated. One of the claims against Boyle came on for hearing before what I think was the board of the Irish privy council presided over by Lord Deputy Wentworth on 5 June 1635, just under four months after Blacknoll's death. Blacknoll's widow used the occasion to argue that, as her husband's executrix, she was entitled to have the particular claim adjudicated upon. Counsel for Boyle, however, was to demur, protesting that, in essence, the widow's claim sounded in trespass and had ceased to be justiciable on Blacknoll's death: *actio personalis moritur cum persona*. At this, according to the entry in Boyle's diary, uproar erupted on the council board. Loftus, the lord chancellor and no friend of Boyle's, urged Wentworth to accept that the suit still merited to be heard since a bill of revival had been filed. Dispute over both the facts and the law then ensued. Boyle himself entered the fray, and tempers rose when Boyle assailed Loftus for his assertion of opinion, whereupon Loftus, apparently, turned on Boyle and expressed little confidence in the latter's legal views, adding, doubtless to rub salt into the wounds, that he, Loftus, cared 'not a rush' for Boyle. Wentworth finally re-established decorum, but not, one suspects, without great difficulty.[60]

What is instructive about this extraordinary episode is the identity of the rule of law that was set to spark off the quarrel, the rule called in aid by Boyle's counsel, the future Serjeant Sambach

58 *Lismore papers*, ed. A.B. Grosart (two series, 10 vols., London, 1886–88), 1st series, iv, p. 71.

59 N. Canny, *The upstart earl: a study of the social and mental world of Richard Boyle, first earl of Cork, 1566–1643* (Cambridge, 1982); D. Townshend, *The life and letters of the great earl of Cork* (London, 1904); T. Ranger, 'Richard Boyle and the making of an Irish fortune, 1588–1614' in *IHS*, x (1956–57), 257.

60 *Lismore papers*, 1st series, iv, pp. 80 and 109–10.

– *actio personalis moritur cum persona* – the rule that in England the Law Reform (Miscellaneous Provisions) Act was only to set aside in 1934.[61]

If we wish to reconstruct the story of the final triumph of the common law in seventeenth-century Ireland, no option is available other than to go through all the extant material and start listing all the recorded instances of doctrinal borrowings and doctrinal elaborations. Davies's law reports are there at the start of the century;[62] but these deal, as is well known, with a mere eleven cases. Perforce, the researcher must turn elsewhere for the enlightenment that is so conspicuously lacking.

The diaries and correspondence of Richard Boyle, even in their printed form, in the *Lismore papers*, are a good place to start. As I have already indicated, Boyle was involved in plenty of lawsuits other than that which saw him ranged against Blacknoll. The dislocation of commercial activity between 1641 and well into the 1650s produced a crop of lawsuits which promises further rich pickings. Then there is the century's most celebrated Irish lawsuit (more celebrated even, I believe, than the *Bishop of Derry's* case) – *Giffard v. Loftus* – which begins in 1636 and is only brought to a final conclusion some forty-odd years later. We are indebted to the Historical Manuscripts Commission for printing material that enables the progress of this remarkable lawsuit to be followed down the years.[63]

Another group of proceedings, started late in the seventeenth century and which continued into the eighteenth, is likely to prove equally fruitful. Here the beneficiary is the student of canon or ecclesiastical law for, at the core of these proceedings set in train in 1694 by a Church of Ireland archdeacon, one Lemuel Mathews, was a range of problems linked to the maintenance of clerical discipline – the entitlement of a commission of three bishops to investigate Mathews and to deprive him of ecclesiastical office, and the failure of the post–Reformation legal authorities to permit Mathews to appeal against his sentence and deprivation. The Mathews affair is described by Stokes in his *Some worthies of the*

---

61 24 & 25 Geo V, c. 41.
62 Sir John Davies, *Le primer report des cases & maters en ley resolues & adiudges en les courts del roy en Ireland* (Dublin, 1615); H.S. Pawlisch, *Sir John Davies and the conquest of Ireland: a study in legal imperialism* (Cambridge, 1985).
63 HMC, *9th rept., pt. 2, app.*, pp. 293–330 (Drogheda MS).

Irish church;[64] but Stokes lay no claim to covering, in anything approaching comprehensive fashion, the legal dimension to Mathews's protracted battle to clear his name. Helpfully, however, Stokes lists in his account the large number of contemporary printed documents which the Mathews affair generated and which Mathews may well have commissioned himself.

The Mathews business illuminates much that is of importance in the spheres of doctrine and procedure, but I accept that there are other aspects to it that might command greater attention. It deserves to be asked, by way of example, why Mathews and his co-defendants (including Bishop Thomas Hacket) were tried by a commission of bishops and not by their metropolitan, the archbishop of Armagh, Michael Boyle. Contemporaries knew the answer: Boyle was elderly, perhaps senile, and could not have served in person. As it happens, it was to be left to a nineteenth-century archbishop of Canterbury, E.W. Benson, to explain in a contemporary English case involving another supposedly delinquent bishop, Edward King of Lincoln, the remarkable circumstances that had led in the Ireland of the 1690s to the employment of a commission made up of a trio of bishops. Boyle, Benson wrote in the judgment he delivered as archbishop of Canterbury in *Read v. Bishop of Lincoln*,[65] had long been incapacitated from the performance of public functions. He had taken no part for ten years past even in consecrating bishops for his own province, though six consecrations took place between 1683, when he officiated for the last time,[66] and 1702, when he died at the age of ninety-three, 'his memory gone, deaf and almost blind, a mere wreck of the past'.[67]

A further aspect of the affair is the inordinate number of attempts, invariably abortive, made by Mathews to secure review of his case. What, one is tempted to ask, was going on behind the

---

64 G.T. Stokes, *Some worthies of the Irish church* (London, 1900), pp. 234–40. There is a short synopsis of the affair in J.A. Froude, *The English in Ireland in the eighteenth century* (3 vols., London, 1872–74), i, 243–45.

65 (1889) 14 PD 88. For the background to these proceedings, see O. Chadwick, *The Victorian church: II* (2nd ed., London, 1972), pp. 353–54. Chadwick was to write: 'The spectacle of an archbishop in the library of Lambeth Palace deciding amid wigs and legal paraphernalia which side of the holy table one of his bishops should be standing was not edifying.'

66 See 'Records of consecrations of Irish bishops', supplement to *Irish Ecclesiastical Gazette*, 1866.

67 (1889) 14 PD 88, at p. 124. See also C.J. Abbey, *The English Church and its bishops, 1700–1800* (London, 1887), ii, 315.

scenes? The short answer appears to be: 'a very great deal'. Most pieces of the jigsaw puzzle are missing, but one has come to light in the Ellis papers in the Public Record Office of Northern Ireland, and has recently been publicised by the Irish Manuscripts Commission.[68] This is a letter written by one of the bishops who sat on the original commission warning his contact in London (the Irish secretary, Sir Robert Southwell) against a traveller about to arrive in the English capital who had taken up cudgels on Mathews' behalf and would, unless stopped, arouse needless consternation. The bishop, William King of Derry, was later to be translated to Dublin as archbishop there. The traveller, whose character King thus sought to traduce, was no less a personage than Richard Pine, at the time chief justice of the Irish king's bench. 'Archdeacon Mathews, the worst of the whole lot', King wrote, 'the chief justice espouseth and encourages and gives him such countenance that it is very much apprehended that he will do mischief to the church by it, and truly I am apt to believe he so designs it, for this chief judge is singular in this as almost in everything else.'[69] According to King, by the autumn of 1696 when he wrote this letter to Southwell, it had cost the administration over £40,000 in legal fees – a huge sum at the time – to defend the sentence of the 1694 commission against Mathews's 'litigious attempts to get a prohibition or overthrow it'.[70]

Undoubtedly, such additional insights make it that much more pleasurable to pursue the more mundane activity of meticulously recording early allusions to the use made in Ireland of mainstream legal principles.

The identical approach has equally to be followed where it is sought to furnish a comprehensive account of the institutional framework within which in Ireland the common law came to operate. There is, I believe, no other way. Each reference, whether in print or in manuscript, has to be carefully jotted down before anything approaching a rounded portrait can be offered. The system for regulating the hearing of appeals is one obvious candidate for the recommended treatment. If the broad picture is generally clear, there is an alarming number of hitherto disregarded

---

68 T.W. Moody and J.G. Simms (ed.), *The bishopric of Derry and the Irish Society of London, 1602–1705, vol.2: 1670–1705* (Dublin, 1983), pp. 170–71.

69 King to Southwell, 5 Oct. 1696: loc.cit.

70 Ibid.

problems which demand an answer. Following confirmation by the Sixth of George the First[71] of the exclusive jurisdiction of the British house of lords to entertain Irish appeals, how many supposedly final decrees of the Irish house of lords, if any at all, were subject to further review?[72] Again, when exactly did the Irish judiciary begin to hear criminal cases reserved for their opinion by the returning judges of assize – the arrangement eventually formalised with the establishment on a statutory basis of the court for crown cases reserved in 1848?[73] (The answer seems to be late in the eighteenth century, but I am unaware of our ability to be more specific.) The Irish court of exchequer chamber also invites examination. A domestic court of this name existed to handle appeals from the court of exchequer from at least the reign of Charles I.[74] Later, in 1800, a complete restructuring of the court turned it into a general court of appeal, interposed between the Irish courts and what was to become the new United Kingdom house of lords.[75] What is certainly less well known is that in 1727 statutory reform had also given the then court of exchequer chamber what could also be described as a new lease of life. That this fact is so little appreciated may be due to the circumstance that the change itself is concealed in section 3 of an act of the Irish parliament which is described as one 'for continuing several temporary statutes made in this kingdom, now near expiring'.[76]

To turn to areas of public law, one is forced to conclude, perhaps surprisingly, that not all the idiosyncrasies of Irish constitutional practice have been as thoroughly ventilated as one might have wished. The problems here vary in magnitude: the employment by the Irish privy council of acts of state, effectively legislative decrees, which represent one of the hallmarks of Irish governmental practice under the Tudors and Stuarts, raises issues of major constitutional importance.[77] The procedure for resigning one's seat in the house of commons of the pre-Union Irish parliament is altogether of lesser significance, though, clearly, as

71 6 Geo I, c. 65 (GB).
72 See note 95 below.
73 11 & 12 Vict, c. 78.
74 15 Chas I, c. 5.
75 40 Geo III, c. 39.
76 1 Geo II, c. 17.
77 For a brief discussion, see W.N. Osborough, 'The Irish custom of tracts' in *Ir Jur*, xxxii (1997), 439 at pp. 444–45.

Marquis Cornwallis makes plain in his correspondence, that was not the view he took of the question as he struggled, along with Castlereagh, to secure a majority for the adoption of the Act of Union.[78]

Let me, however, focus on certain difficulties thrown up by observance of Poynings' law of 1495.[79] Down to 1782, it will be recalled, no Irish parliament could be summoned until the Irish council had certified to the English privy council 'the causes' for summoning it, in other words, the details of the legislative programme it was intended to enact. As is well known, Irish parliamentarians were to manifest growing impatience with what in essence amounted to an English constitutional veto. What is less well known is the attitude of Irish chief governors and members of the Irish privy council to the arrangements they were obliged to administer. That omission deserves to be rectified.

Consider this. In 1662 Ormond, as lord lieutenant, in accordance with the provisions of Poynings' law, forwarded a group of proposed legislative bills to London. He was soon informed that some of these measures were acceptable and could therefore be introduced as 'official bills' in the Irish parliament. Others were turned down on the scarcely illuminating ground that they were displeasing to his majesty; they contained, so it was put, clauses 'derogatory to the crown'.[80] Ormond, doubtless supported by his colleagues on the Irish council, thought that this was not good enough, and wrote to Secretary Bennet, the future Lord Arlington, in London to inquire in what particular respect the rejected bills had failed to give satisfaction, so that, as Ormond himself phrased it, 'my inadvertency or ignorance for the time to come may not involve me in mistakes so contrary to my purposes and principles'.[81] Bennet took a little time to reply. When he did, it is sad indeed

---

78 See the letters of Marquis Cornwallis to the duke of Portland in May 1799: *Correspondence of Charles, first Marquis Cornwallis*, ed. C. Ross, 2nd ed. (3 vols., London, 1859), iii, 97–100; and Portland to Cornwallis, 25 May 1799, *Memoirs and correspondence of Viscount Castlereagh*, ed. Charles Vane, marquess of Londonderry (4 vols., London, 1848), ii, 320.

79 10 Henry VII, c. 4.

80 Secretary Bennet to Ormond, 10 Nov. [1662], *Cal. S.P. Ire.*, *1663–65*, p. 279. This letter would appear to have been misdated to 1663.

81 Ormond to Bennet, 21 Nov [1662], *Cal. S.P. Ire.*, *1663–65*, p. 297 (also misdated to 1663). See, too, Ormond and council to Bennet, 17 Dec. 1662, *Cal. S.P. Ire.*, *1660–62*, pp. 661–62.

that we do not know how Ormond reacted, for the tenor of the reply was most certainly not designed to flatter Ormond or, for that matter, to win friends and influence people. What Bennet wrote was this: 'The Council here neither by reason of state nor directed by any precedent do hold themselves obliged to give account of the reasons which may move their lordships to alter or suspend the sending back any bills sent hither.'[82] On this it is right to remark that in 1640 the earl of Strafford, the former Wentworth, over similar problems then, had not been treated to such a conspicuous display of arrogant constitutional insensitivity.[83]

Divisions within the Irish council over the choice of legislative measures to be recommended to London are also worth charting. Hard evidence confirming the existence of such divisions is not easy to come by. But there is such evidence from the autumn of 1695, when Lord Capel was lord deputy. In the parliamentary session that commenced in August, the Irish house of commons moved the heads of a habeas corpus bill. These heads were brought before the Irish council and, after what sounds an argumentative session, were transformed into a council–endorsed draft bill which was then forwarded to London. The English privy council, with the king, William III, in attendance, considered this specific proposal at a meeting held at Kensington on 13 November. The duke of Shrewsbury, as secretary of state, introduced this item on the agenda, adding that, though the draft bill had received the blessing of the Irish council, Capel, the lord deputy, had been against it. Sir William Trumbull, the other secretary of state, kept a minute of the meeting. That note reads: 'On hearing Shrewsbury's revelation regarding Capel's attitude, the king intervened'. If that was Capel's attitude, why had he been party to sending over the measure at all?[84] To complete the story, it is worth recalling that there was to be no Irish Habeas Corpus Act until nearly ninety years later, in 1782.[85] (Scotland's equivalent legislation, the Act anent wrongous imprisonment, was passed in 1701.)

---

82 Bennet to Ormond, 1 Dec. 1662: *Cal. S.P. Ire., 1669–70, with addenda 1625–70*, p. 478.

83 '*De commissione speciali Thome comiti Strafford*, 25 March 1640: report on bills transmitted – why certain measures authorised for enactment but with provisoes': *Liber mun. pub. Hib.*, i, pt. 4, p.142.

84 BL, Trumbull MS, formerly in the Berkshire Record Office. I am grateful to Mr John Bergin for this reference.

85 21 & 22 Geo III, c. 11.

An abundance of mysteries and a relative paucity of solutions. If we are honest, this is not exactly an edifying state of affairs. For part of the explanation at least, it is inevitable that we should highlight the lack of allure manifested by the discipline of legal history itself. Professor L.M. Friedman in his *History of American law* has addressed the self-same theme. Whilst Friedman has the United States primarily in mind, his conclusions would seem to apply equally this side of the Atlantic:

> The dominant ideology of the law schools was such that these were not centers of legal research. They taught legal method, legal reasoning, analytical skills, how to take cases apart, and how to put them back together again. Legal scholars and lawyers were interested in precedents, but not in history; they twisted and used the past, but rarely treated it with the rigor that history demands. Historians, for their part, were not aware of the richness and importance of legal history; the lawyers, jealous of their area, showed them only a dreary battlefield of concepts; historians were unwelcome there: the landscape was technical and strewn with corpses and mines.[86]

That diagnosis was penned in 1973 and, despite some optimistic signs in more recent years, would seem to be still generally applicable. The precise remedy to be prescribed – if we are rash enough to seek one – is not altogether easy to identify. Changes of attitude productive of a deepening of interest are called for at different levels, and in a variety of contexts. Let me confine myself to advancing but one consideration. We lose sight of something valuable in education if we fail to convey the sense of excitement that inevitably and necessarily accompanies the making of any kind of intellectual discovery. As I have attempted to show, there is no shortage of intellectual discoveries to be made by the would-be researcher into Irish legal history. It is a form of self-indulgence, I suppose, to talk about the pleasure – the sense of personal fulfilment – that comes from finding out something novel by oneself. But is this something for which the world obliges us to apologise?

Literary comment pronounced on law and lawyers as both pass by in the cavalcade of history can be included in discoveries that promise a *frisson* of excitement. Jonathan Swift's tirade directed at

---

86 L.M. Friedman, *A history of American law* (New York, 1973), pp. 9–10.

the pre-Union Irish parliament over the resolution on agistment tithe of March 1736[87] – his bitter denunciation of the Legion Club[88] – is the sort of thing I have in mind. Unconstitutional that resolution almost certainly was. No less remarkable is Cornwallis's recital of another piece of Swiftian doggerel in conveying to a confidant, Major-general Ross, his personal distaste at involvement in the system of bribery and corruption resorted to as a means of securing a majority in the Irish parliament for the Act of Union of 1800.[89] These were the lines from the penultimate stanza of 'A libel on the Reverend Dr. Delaney and His Excellency John, Lord Carteret':

> So, to effect his monarch's ends,
> From hell a Viceroy devil ascends,
> His budget with corruptions crammed
> The contributions of the damned;
> Which with unsparing hand, he strews
> Through courts and senates as he goes;
> And then at Beelzebub's Black Hall
> Complains his budget was too small.[90]

Southey's lines, lines by no means over-endowed with uncritical republican sentiment, on Emmet's speech from the dock in 1803,[91] and Byron's obsequious celebration of the reversal of the attainder of Lord Edward Fitzgerald in 1819,[92] are apt additions to this somewhat idiosyncratic inventory.

Naturally, even greater excitement must attend the unearthing and the identification of unique source material. The destruction of Irish legal records has taken place on so vast a scale that it is sometimes difficult to remember that, even so, against all the odds, a very great deal indeed managed to survive. And this is there waiting patiently in the wings, waiting only to be discovered

---

87 *Commons' jn. Ire.*, iv, pt. 1, 219 and iv, pt. 2, lxv–lxx.
88 'A Character, Panegyric and Description of the Legion Club': *Jonathan Swift: the collected poems*, ed. P. Rogers (London, 1983), p. 550.
89 *Correspondence of Charles, first Marquis Cornwallis*, iii, 102.
90 *Jonathan Swift: the collected poems*, at p. 409.
91 'Written immediately after reading the speech of Robert Emmet on his trial and conviction for high treason, Sept. 1803': *The poetical works of Robert Southey* (London, 1859), pp.140–41.
92 'To the Prince Regent – on the repeal of the bill of attainder against Ld. E. Fitzgerald July 1819': Lord Byron, *The complete poetical works*, ed. J.J. McGann (7 vols., Oxford, 1980–93), iv, 242.

or rediscovered or have its value and significance explained. Discoveries and rediscoveries notched up in the past that, perhaps, merit special mention would embrace the important collection of Irish law tracts acquired by Edward Lhuyd from Eoin O Gnimh in Larne in 1699, and which eventually found its way into the library of Trinity College in Dublin, thanks to Edmund Burke and members of the Sebright family,[93] and the journals of the Irish house of commons from 1641 to 1647 that went missing around 1690, but which later came to light again in 1764 when one Michael Dugan offered them for sale.[94] Most of the discoveries that remain to be made are probably buried deep in surviving collections of manuscript material. Here as little as a paragraph or a sentence in some unprepossessing extant letter can yield considerable enlightenment,[95] so the reader must be prepared to go slowly – counsel, alas, that it is not always easy to follow when the writing itself, as unfortunately all too often is the case, is not Vere Foster copybook. But, as regards exercises of this calibre, it would be folly to ignore the multitude of printed books and the possibility that some unique insight could be embedded there. The patent, bearing the date of May 1609, appointing John Franckton to the office of king's printer in Ireland was finally tracked down in the most improbable of volumes: an Edinburgh imprint of 1826, the author of which was a John Lee. And the title? *Additional memorial on printing and importing Bibles!*[96]

This has been a year of many anniversaries, as Betsy Gray, were she alive, would also be able to remind us. Vasco de Gama landed in India, having earlier rounded the Cape of Good Hope – the exploit celebrated by Camoens in his *The Lusiads* – five hundred years ago, in 1498. The same year Savonarola was burnt at the stake in the centre of Florence – the dreadful culmination of his

93 A. and W. O'Sullivan, 'Edward Lhuyd's collection of Irish manuscripts' in *Transactions of the Honourable Society of Cymmrodorion*, 1962, 57.

94 *Commons' jn., Ire.*, i, 290; vii, 345–46 (4 May 1764) and 356 (10 May 1764).

95 An interesting example is a short reference in a letter of Edward Southwell, jn., Irish secretary, in the 1730s to the question of whether the British house of lords would subsequently alter judgments handed down by the Irish house of lords prior to the latter losing their appellate jurisdiction under the Sixth of George I: see Southwell to Marmaduke Coghill, 10 Jan. 1735/36 (NLI, MS 875).

96 See M. Pollard, 'Control of the press in Ireland through the king's printer's patent, 1600–1800' in *Irish Booklore*, iv, no. 2 (1980), 79.

remarkable career from which the courageous Romola of George Eliot's novel of the same name chose to avert her gaze. A hundred years nearer us, the year 1598 saw the promulgation by King Henri IV of France of the edict of Nantes, a key document in the history of religious toleration in Europe, though, if we accept the opinion of Mousnier, it was the murder of the king twelve years later and the manner of its accomplishment that had greater impact for France in the longer term.[97] It is, however, another French anniversary to which I should like to refer, in full knowledge at the same time that it is an anniversary of which little notice has been taken elsewhere: 1998 marks the one hundred and fiftieth anniversary of the abolition of slavery in all French colonies and possessions (*l'abolition de l'esclavage dans toutes les colonies et les possessions françaises*).[98]

The exact date when abolition was decreed was 27 April 1848, and it might therefore have been anticipated that the French prime minister, M. Jospin, would have been present in Paris on 27 April 1998 at some appropriate ceremony to mark the occasion. Such anticipation would have been misplaced, for on the critical date the prime minister and his entourage had chosen to mark the anniversary at the village of Champagney, near Mulhouse in eastern France, in the department of Haute-Saône. The choice was deliberate and no accident: the people of that village, in completing their *cahier de doléances*, requested from throughout France by King Louis XVI on the eve of the Revolution, were the only ones to include a demand for the abolition of slavery. That demand was no. 29 in the list returned by the sixty villagers of Champagney on 19 March 1789.

That Champagney had included this prescient demand only became public knowledge in 1971 when announcement of the discovery – or rediscovery – was made by Jean-René Simonin, a retired lawyer. The celebrations in Champagney in April this year, some twenty-seven years later, doubtless partook of the nature of a political jamboree. The rewards of hard unremitting toil at the coal-face of legal history – I have taken the liberty of transporting us all there from Maitland and Binchy's desert – are unlikely, in

---

97 R. Mousnier, *The assassination of Henry IV: the tyrannicide problem and the consolidation of the French absolute monarchy in the early seventeenth century* (London, 1973).
98 For what follows, see *Le Monde*, 24 April 1998.

most other countries, to be reflected in any comparable governmental response or gesture. But there is surely a moral to be
drawn from this contemporary continental fable. Those of us who
care, if not passionately, at least intelligently, about the past rightly
dread the onset of an ignorance that must militate against our
understanding it and – certainly no less important – militate
against our ability to learn from it.

The richness of the tapestry that writers on legal history are in
a position to weave is no less significant a consideration that
hopefully will continue to propel forward the work of this Society.
My concern has been to raise an awareness of the difficulties and
the hazards, and by no means whatever to underplay the quintes-
sentially human qualities that will continue to be demanded –
skill, dedication, imagination and perseverance.

Index

The Irish Legal History Society

Established in 1988 to encourage the study and advance the knowledge of the history of Irish law, especially by the publication of original documents and of works relating to the history of Irish law, including its institutions, doctrines and personalities, and the reprinting or editing of works of sufficient rarity or importance.

PATRONS

The Hon. Mr Justice Keane
Chief Justice of Ireland

Rt. Hon. Sir Robert Carswell
Lord Chief Justice
of Northern Ireland

COUNCIL, 1999–2000

PRESIDENT
Professor D.S. Greer

VICE-PRESIDENTS

J.F. Larkin, esq., BL

J.I. McGuire, esq.

HONORARY SECRETARIES

Professor W.N. Osborough

Professor N.M. Dawson

HONORARY TREASURERS

J.L. Leckey, esq.

R.D. Marshall, esq.

COUNCIL MEMBERS

The Hon. Mr Justice Geoghegan
J. Gordon, esq.
R. O'Hanlon, esq., BL

Professor G.J. Hand
Daire Hogan, esq.
His Honour Judge Hart, Q.C.

* Volumes 1–7 are published by Irish Academic Press.